KING'S COLLEGE LONDON

MEDIEVAL STUDIES

III

KING'S COLLEGE LONDON MEDIEVAL STUDIES

CULTURES IN CONTACT IN MEDIEVAL SPAIN:

Historical and Literary Essays Presented to L.P. Harvey

Edited by

DAVID HOOK

and

BARRY TAYLOR

King's College London

Medieval Studies

1990

ISSN 0953-217X

ISBN 0 9513085 2 1

British Library Cataloguing in Publication Data

Cultures in Contact in medieval Spain: historical and literary essays
presented to L.P. Harvey. – (King's College London Medieval
Studies; 0953-217X; 3)
1. Spanish literature, to 1516 – Critical studies 2. Spain, 711-1516
I. Hook, David II. Taylor, Barry
860.9'001

ISBN 0-9513085-2-1

Printed on

Acid-free long life paper

by

Short Run Press

Exeter

1990

LIST OF CONTENTS

ACKNOWLEDGEMENTS

The Editors wish to record their gratitude to Claire Isoz, who read the book on behalf of the Editorial Board of King's College London Medieval Studies. They are also grateful to Harold Short, Roy Wisbey, and David Yeandle for technical assistance and facilities. Their particular thanks are due to Martin Jones for his invaluable advice and expertise in the final stages of producing camera-ready copy, and to June Harvey.

INTRODUCTION

Since its foundation in 1831, the Department of Spanish at King's College London has, with the exception of brief periods of hiatus between the appointments of staff during the nineteenth century, been continuously engaged in teaching and publication on Spanish themes. The Cervantes Chair of Spanish, the establishment of which in 1916 speaks for a commitment to scholarship undaunted by the turmoil of contemporary events, has been held by a succession of distinguished Hispanists: James Fitzmaurice-Kelly, Antonio Pastor, Edward M. Wilson, Alexander A. Parker, R.O. Jones, and L.P. Harvey, who succeeded Roy Jones in 1973 and retired as Cervantes Professor and Head of Department in 1983, a date of which the significance will be all too apparent to observers of the contemporary British academic world. As will be seen from our list of L.P. Harvey's publications, the years since 1983 (during which he has continued to serve both the Department and Hispanism, first in a part-time capacity, then as Emeritus Professor) have witnessed an increase in scholarly productivity fostered by freedom from the burdensome administration which has fallen so heavily upon senior academic staff in the last decade. It is, moreover, our confident expectation that works in press and in prospect will rapidly render our list of publications an historical statement rather than a complete catalogue; we have already been delighted to have to update it during production of this volume, and, like Pat Harvey's *curriculum vitae*, it is open-ended. It is, however, exhaustive to 1990, with the exception of book reviews. The purpose of this collection of essays at this point in Pat Harvey's career is not principally to commemorate his retirement, therefore, but rather to honour the continuing work of someone whose breadth and depth of learning and exacting scholarly standards are as much a feature of the man as are his humanity, generosity and *mesura*.

Because of practical constraints, the contents of this volume are but a partial reflection of Pat Harvey's professional interests. Hispano-Arabic studies are represented by the papers of Charles Burnett and T.J. Gorton, and the relations between Islamic and Christian Spain in the fields of literature, culture, and history by those of Samuel G. Armistead, Roger Boase, Brenda Fish, Richard Hitchcock and Francisco Marcos Marín; contacts between east and west also underlie the textual transmission studied by Barry Taylor, and Arabic loan-words in Spanish, though not the principal subject of Ralph Penny's paper (itself a reminder of Pat Harvey's interests in historical linguistics), abound in his lists of examples. The other minority of medieval Iberia in which Pat has been interested, Spanish Jewry, forms the cultural backdrop to John Edwards's examination of the problems encountered by a fifteenth-century bishop. A wide range, in theme and period, is thus spanned in essays exploring various aspects of the contact between the three principal cultural and religious communities in the Peninsula, and some clearly successful contacts are discussed in addition to the failures, though the latter bulk larger in the historical record. We are inevitably reminded of Pat Harvey's observation that 'Cultures can come into contact . . . but only with the utmost difficulty can they communicate' (*JRAS*, 1977, p. 117).

The insights which a comparative approach opens up are a feature of Pat's work on the Old Spanish epic, beginning with his important article of 1963 on the *Poema de Mio Cid* and Yugoslav heroic songs. In the present volume, Alan Deyermond's paper on the influence of biblical modes of thought upon traditional epic legend reveals one aspect of the interplay of different levels within a single Christian culture; points of contact between Spain and two other areas of Western European culture are also represented in our collection, with David Hook's examination of the debt of Spanish epic to French epic phraseology, and the suggestion by Roger Walker and Milija Pavlović that the influence of Germanic legal concepts helps to explain an obscure statement in the *Poema de Mio Cid*.

It is a matter of regret to the editors that more contributors could not be invited to participate, but the volume does represent in this way, albeit summarily, the major fields in which Pat Harvey has worked. It is particularly pleasing, moreover, that, in addition to the London colleagues and the former students of Pat's who form a large part of our team, we have received the enthusiastic collaboration of scholars from other universities in Britain, Spain, and the United States. That Arab scholarship is not represented among our contributors is due entirely to the limitations of the editors' professional range; Pat Harvey, of course, is equally at home in Europe and in the Islamic world, and it would be perfectly possible for his Islamicist colleagues to produce a volume in his honour which did not overlap in content with this one, and still did not exhaust the range of themes on which Pat has written, edited, spoken, or chaired conferences and colloquia: for even such a volume would be unlikely to embrace both textual criticism and Canadian placenames.

King's College London
The British Library

David Hook
Barry Taylor

CURRICULUM VITAE OF L.P. HARVEY

Born 29 February 1929

Education

Alleyn's School, Dulwich, 1940-1947
(National Service, 1947-1949)
Magdalen College, Oxford, 1949-1958
    William Doncaster Scholar in Modern Languages, 1949-1952
    B.A. (First Class), Modern Languages, 1952
    B.A. (Second Class), Oriental Studies, 1954
    M.A., 1956
    D.Phil., 1958 (*Thesis title:* 'The Literary Culture of the Moriscos, 1492-1608.
    A study based on the extant manuscripts in Arabic and Aljamía', 2 vols)

Academic Appointments

Lecturer, University of Oxford, 1957-1958
Lecturer, University of Southampton, 1958-1960
Lecturer, Queen Mary College, London, 1960-1963
Reader in Spanish and Head of Department, Queen Mary College, 1963-1967
Visiting Professor, University of Victoria, British Columbia, 1966-1967
Professor of Spanish, Queen Mary College, 1967-1973
Dean of the Faculty of Arts, Queen Mary College, 1970-1973
Cervantes Professor, King's College London, 1973-1983
Dean of the Faculty of Arts, King's College London, 1979-1981
Member of the University Grants Committee, 1979-1983
Chairman, Education Committee, Hispanic and Luso-Brazilian Council, 1984-1987
Emeritus Professor, King's College London, from 1984

Current Academic Address
Department of Spanish and Spanish-American Studies
King's College London
Strand
London WC2R 2LS
United Kingdom

PUBLICATIONS OF L.P. HARVEY

'Yūse Banegas: un moro noble en Granada bajo los Reyes Católicos', *Al-And*, XXI (1956), 297-302.

'Un manuscrito aljamiado en la Biblioteca de la Universidad de Cambridge', *Al-And*, XXIII (1958), 49-74.

'The Morisco who was Muley Zaidan's Spanish Interpreter', *Miscelánea de estudios árabes y hebraicos de la Universidad de Granada*, VIII (1959), 67-97.

'The People of the Peacock Angel', *Natural History*, LXVIII (1959), 566-75.

'*Amaho, dešamaho, maho, amahar . . .:* a family of words common to the Spanish speech of the Jews and of the Moriscos', *BHS*, XXXVII (1960), 69-74.

'A Morisco Manuscript in the Godolphin Collection at Wadham College, Oxford', *Al-And*, XXVII (1962), 461-65.

'The Metrical Irregularity of the *Cantar de Mio Cid*', *BHS*, XL (1963), 137-43.

'A Morisco Reader of Jean Lemaire de Belges?', *Al-And*, XXVIII (1963), 231-36.

'Crypto-Islam in sixteenth-century Spain', in *Actas del primer congreso de estudios árabes e islámicos* (Madrid: Comité Permanente del CEAI, 1964), 163-78.

'A Morisco Prayer-book in the British Museum', *Al-And*, XXIX (1964), 373-76.

(with R.O. Jones and Keith Whinnom) 'Lingua Franca in a villancico by Encina', *RLC*, XLI (1967), 572-79.

'Castilian *mancebo* as a calque of Arabic '*abd*, or how El Mancebo de Arévalo got his name', *MP*, LXV (1967-68), 130-32.

'Nugeymath Turquia: *Primera Crónica General*, chapter 956', *JSemS*, XIII (1968), 232-40.

'Una nota sobre las "formas descompuestas en el español antiguo", *RFE*, 1963, XLVI, pp. 31-48', *RFE*, LI (1968 [1970]), 239-42.

(with Brian Dutton and R.M. Walker), *Cassell's Compact Spanish-English, English-Spanish Dictionary* (London: Cassell, 1969), xv + 444 pp.

'Samuel Miklos Stern', *BHS*, XLVII (1970), 57-59.

'The Arabic Dialect of Valencia in 1595', *Al-And*, XXXVI (1971), 81-115.

'Textes de littérature religieuse des moriscos tunisiens', in *Études sur les Moriscos andalous en Tunisie*, edited by M. de Epalza and R. Petit (Madrid: Instituto Hispano-Árabe de Cultura, 1973), pp. 199-204.

'The *alfaquí* in *La dança general de la muerte*', *HR*, XLI (1973), 498-510.

'The Discoverer of the Juan de Fuca Strait between Vancouver Island and the State of Washington', in *Actes du XIe Congrès International des Sciences Onomastiques (Sofia, 28.VI.-4.VII.1972)* (Sofia: Academie Bulgare des Sciences, Centre de Linguistique et Littérature, 1974), I, 375-87.

(editor) S.M. Stern, *Hispano-Arabic Strophic Poetry* (Oxford: Clarendon, 1974), xvi + 252 pp.

'Oral Composition and the Performance of Novels of Chivalry in Spain', *FMLS*, X (1974), 270-86; reprinted in *Oral Literature: Seven Essays*, edited by Joseph J. Duggan (Edinburgh: Scottish Academic Press, 1975), pp. 84-100.

The Moriscos and Don Quixote, inaugural lecture in the Chair of Spanish delivered at University of London King's College, 11 November 1974 (London: King's College, 1975), 18 pp.

'Fernán González's Horse', in *Medieval Hispanic Studies Presented to Rita Hamilton*, edited by A.D. Deyermond (London: Tamesis, 1976), pp. 77-86.

'Sobre *Al-Andalus*, XXXIX, pp. 273-81', *Al-And*, XLI (1976), 235-37.

'Aljamiado Literature', *The Year's Work in Modern Language Studies*, XXXVII (1975 [1976]), 247-48.

'The Alfonsine School of Translators: translations from Arabic into Castilian produced under the patronage of Alfonso the Wise of Castile (1221-1252-1284)', *JRAS*, 1977, no. 1, 109-17.

'An Observation on "Two Notes on Dunbar" (*FMLS* XII, 1976, pp. 367-9)', *FMLS*, XIII (1977), 190.

'The Survival of Arabic Culture in Spain after 1492', *Actes du 8me Congrès de l'Union Européenne des Islamisants* (Aix-en-Provence: Edisud, 1978), pp. 85-88.

'El Mancebo de Arévalo y la literatura aljamiada', *Actas del coloquio internacional sobre literatura aljamiada y morisca (Departamento de Filología Románica de la Facultad de Filosofía y Letras de la Universidad de Oviedo, 10 al 16 de Julio de 1972)*, Colección de Literatura Española Aljamiado-morisca, III (Madrid: Gredos, 1978), 21-47.

'Medieval Spanish', in *Traditions of Heroic and Epic Poetry*, edited by A.T. Hatto, I: *The Traditions*, Publications of the MHRA, 9 (London: MHRA, 1980), 134-64.

'"The Thirteen Articles of the Faith" and "The Twelve Degrees in which the World is Governed": two passages in a sixteenth-century Morisco manuscript and their antecedents', in *Medieval and Renaissance Studies on Spain and Portugal in Honour of P.E. Russell*, edited by F.W. Hodcroft, D.G. Pattison, R.D.F. Pring-Mill and R.W. Truman (Oxford: Society for the Study of Mediaeval Languages and Literature, 1981), pp. 15-29.

(with D. Hook) 'The Affair of the Horse and the Hawk in the *Poema de Fernán González*', *MLR*, LXXVII (1982), 840-47.

'Leyenda morisca de Ibrahim', *NRFH*, XXX (1981 (1983)), 1-20.

'ABC in the *Lapidario* of Alfonso X = *al-ḥurūf al-abjadiyya*', *La Corónica*, XIII (1984-85), 137-41.

'A New Sacromonte Text? Critical Notes', *Revue de l'Histoire des Religions*, CCI (1984), 421-25.

'"Alfaqueque": a mistaken etymology in the *Siete Partidas* of Alfonso the Wise', in *Homenaje a Álvaro Galmés de Fuentes*, I (Oviedo: Universidad; Madrid: Gredos, 1985), 635-37.

'"(A)guisado" in the *Poema de Mio Cid*: the ghost of a pun in Arabic?', *BHS*, LXII (1985), 1-6.

'The Terminology of Two Hitherto Unpublished Morisco Calendar Texts', in *Les Actes de la première table ronde du Comité International d'Études Morisques sur "La littérature aljamiado-morisque: hybridisme linguistique et univers discursif"*, edited by Abdeljelil Temimi, Publications du Centre de Recherche en Bibliothéconomie et Sciences de l'Information, XIII (Tunis: CRBSI, 1986), 65-83 (Arabic text, 85-106).

'*Aljamia portuguesa* Revisited', *Portuguese Studies*, II (1986), 1-14.

'Pan-Arab Sentiment in a Late (A.D. 1595) Granadan Text: British Library MS Harley 3507', *Revista del Instituto Egipcio de Estudios Islámicos en Madrid*, XXIII (1985-86 [1987]), 223-33.

'The Moriscos and the Hajj', *Bulletin of the British Society for Middle Eastern Studies*, XIV (1988), 11-24.

'First International Colloquium on the *kharjas*', *La Corónica*, XVII (1988-89), 116-18.

'Los moriscos y los cinco pilares del Islam', in *Las prácticas musulmanas de los moriscos andaluces (1492-1609). Actas del III Simposio Internacional de Estudios Moriscos*, edited by Abdeljelil Temimi, Publications du Centre d'Études et de Recherches Ottomanes, Morisques de Documentation et d'Information (Zaghouan: CEROMDI, 1989), pp. 93-97.

'In Granada under the Catholic Monarchs: a call from a doctor and another from a *curandera*', in *The Age of the Catholic Monarchs, 1474-1516. Literary Studies in Memory of Keith Whinnom, BHS*, special issue, edited by Alan Deyermond and Ian Macpherson (Liverpool: University Press, 1989), 71-75.

'Límites de los intercambios culturales', in *Actas de las I Jornadas de Cultura Islámica (Toledo, 1987): Al-Andalus, ocho siglos de historia* (Madrid: Instituto Occidental de Cultura Islámica, 1989), pp. 89-94.

'A Second Morisco Manuscript at Wadham College, Oxford: A 18.15', *Al-Qantara*, X (1989), 257-72.

'A Morisco Collection of Apocryphal Ḥadīṯhs on the Virtues of Al-Andalus', *Al-Masāq: Studia Arabo-Islamica Mediterranea*, II (1989), 25-39.

Islamic Spain, 1250 to 1500 (Chicago: University Press, 1990), 400 pp.

LIST OF ABBREVIATIONS

AEM	*Anuario de Estudios Medievales*
AHDE	*Anuario de Historia del Derecho Español*
AHDLMA	*Archives d'Histoire Doctrinale et Littéraire du Moyen Age*
Al-An	*Al-Andalus*
BAE	Biblioteca de Autores Españoles
BH	*Bulletin Hispanique*
BHS	*Bulletin of Hispanic Studies*
BL	British Library
BNM	Biblioteca Nacional, Madrid
BRABL	*Boletín de la Real Academia de Buenas Letras*
CFMA	Classiques français du Moyen Age
CHE	*Cuadernos de Historia de España*
CSIC	Consejo Superior de Investigaciones Científicas
DCECH	Joan Corominas & José A. Pascual, *Diccionario crítico etimológico castellano e hispánico* (Madrid: Gredos, 1980-)
DCELC	Joan Corominas, *Diccionario crítico etimológico de la lengua castellana*, 4 vols (Bern: Francke, 1954)
EUC	*Estudis Universitaris Catalans*
FMLS	*Forum for Modern Language Studies*
His	*Hispania* (USA)
HR	*Hispanic Review*
HSMS	Hispanic Seminary of Medieval Studies
JArabL	*Journal of Arabic Literature*
JAOS	*Journal of the American Oriental Society*
JRAS	*Journal of the Royal Asiatic Society*
JSemS	*Journal of Semitic Studies*
LNL	*Les Langues Neo-latines*
MAe	*Medium Aevum*
MHRA	Modern Humanities Research Association
MLR	*Modern Language Review*
MP	*Modern Philology*
NQ	*Notes & Queries*
NRFH	*Nueva Revista de Filología Hispánica*
P&P	*Past & Present*

PL	*Patrologiae cursus completus (Series Latina)*, edited by J.-P. Migne.
PMLA	*Publications of the Modern Language Association of America*
PQ	*Philological Quarterly*
RCEH	*Revista Canadiense de Estudios Hispánicos*
RF	*Romanische Forschungen*
RFE	*Revista de Filología Española*
RLC	*Revue de Littérature Comparée*
Ro	*Romania*
SATF	Société des Anciens Textes Français
Sp	*Speculum*
TLF	Textes Littéraires Français

AN ANECDOTE OF KING JAUME I AND ITS ARABIC CONGENER

Samuel G. Armistead

The *Crònica* or *Libre dels feyts* of Jaume I, el Conqueridor – narrated in the royal first person *nós* – includes a brief, but remarkable episode.[1] Campaigning against the Muslim kingdom of Valencia, King Jaume had set up camp, probably at El Puig, and was about to march toward Burriana, but, because a swallow had made its nest near the top of the tent pole, the King ordered his tent to be left standing until such time as the bird and its chicks had been able to fly away:

> E fom a Borriana, e, quan venc que en volguem llevar la host, una oreneta havia feit niu prop de l'escudella en lo tendal, e manam que no en llevassen la tenda tro que ella se'n fos anada ab sos fills, pus en nostra fe era venguda.[2]

This delightful vignette has quite justifiably attracted the attention of Hispano-medievalists. Martí de Riquer, stressing the intimacy characteristic of certain passages of the *Libre*, observes:

> Precisament el fet que el rei volgués deixar constància d'aquest fet minúscul ens deixa veure un altre aspecte de la seva personalitat, que no tot és conquerir regnes dels sarraïns, guanyar batalles i vessar coratge, sinó també tendresa envers les bestioles que s'acullen 'a la fe' del monarca, com si també fossin vassalls seus.[3]

Ferran Soldevila also alludes to 'aquest delicat episodi, que mostra la tendresa d'ànima del Conqueridor',[4] and Menéndez Pidal, comparing King Jaume's story to a late and distantly similar incident attributed to the Cid, alludes to the 'delicado sentimentalismo de un rey venturoso'.[5] In suggesting an exquisite concern for the fate of small and defenceless animals, King Jaume's deference to the nesting swallow does indeed sound an attractive note of personal intimacy and kingly compassion. And it is quite possible, perhaps, that a swallow may in fact have built its nest atop the King's tent pole and, so, have placed itself under his royal protection. But the incident, I believe, originally had other implications, which can only be fully understood within an Islamic context.

The first two parts of the *Libre dels feyts* (through Chapter 327) were probably composed around 1244.[6] The great Arab geographer, Yāqūt ibn ᶜAbdallāh al-Rūmī, assembled his vast dictionary, *Muᶜjam al-buldān* ('Dictionary of Towns'), between 1212 and his death in 1229.[7] With reference to the conquest of Egypt by the famous general, ᶜAmr ibn al-ᶜĀṣ (or al-ᶜAṣī), Yāqūt relates an intriguing story. Having conquered the

1

Roman fortress of Babylon – located in what is now al-Fusṭāṭ (Old Cairo) – ᶜAmr broke camp to march northward against Alexandria:

فلما جاز عمرو ومن معه ما كان في الحصن، أجمع على المسير الى الاسكندرية، فسار اليها في ربيع الاول سنة ٢٠، وامر عمرو بفسطاطه ان يُقَوَّضَ، فاذا بيَمَامة قد باضت في اعلاه، فقال: "لقد تَحَرَّمَتْ بجِوَارِنا؛ أقِرُّوا الفسطاط حتى تَنْقُفَ وتطيّر فراخَها"، فأقِرَّ فسطاطُه، ووكَّل به من يحفظه ان لا تُهاج، ومضى الى الاسكندرية، واقام عليها ستة اشهُر حتى فتحها الله عليه.

And when ᶜAmr [ibn al-ᶜĀṣī] and those who were with him had passed through what was in the fortress, he decided to travel to Alexandria, so he journeyed toward it in [the month of] Rabīᶜ I of the year A.H. 20 [= A.D. 640]. ᶜAmr ordered his tent (*fusṭāṭ*) to be struck, but a dove (*yamāma*) had laid her eggs on top of it, whereupon he said: 'She is inviolable in our proximity (*jiwāri-nā*). Let the tent remain standing until she hatches her chicks and makes them fly away.' So his tent was left to stand, and he put in charge over it one to guard it from being disturbed, and proceeded to Alexandria, where he remained for six months until God opened it up to his conquest.[8]

In King Jaume's solicitude for the swallow, Western scholarship has perceived only a delicate sentimentality. From an Islamic point of view, however, Yāqūt's essentially identical story acquires a very specific meaning, rooted in ancient Arabian and even earlier Semitic tradition. ᶜAmr's treatment of the dove fulfills an almost sacred obligation: in taking refuge in his tent, the bird, like any other traveller, has placed itself under ᶜAmr's protection. The Arabic text reads: '*taḥarramat bi-jiwārinā*', 'she is *ḥarām* (inviolable, forbidden, sacred) in our proximity (or neighbourhood)'; implying that the bird has become a *jār*, here not merely a 'neighbour', but a 'client' and, hence, she is fully protected by tribal law. ᶜAmr, by strictest custom, is thus honour bound to afford the dove his complete protection.[9] In giving sanctuary to the dove, ᶜAmr, as a leader of Muslims fighting and in peril in a foreign land, is making an important cultural statement: he is reaffirming the Arab tradition.

The agreement between the key phrases of the Catalan and Arabic stories is striking: 'pus en nostra fe era venguda'/'She is inviolable in our proximity' (which could equally well be translated, as in Butler: 'She has taken refuge under our protection'). But while Jaume's concern for the swallow appears to be merely a charming anecdote,

2

an indication of the chronicle's 'intimitat' and possibly of one aspect of the King's personality, ᶜAmr's protection of the dove is charged with meaning for his community of desert warriors; it evokes a whole system of values which are crucial to the episode's cultural context. One story is personal and incidental; the other is fully and richly functional. Such characteristics would seem to qualify the Arabic story – some version of it, but doubtless not Yāqūt's – as the probable genetic antecedent of its Catalan analogue.

The current individualist-traditionalist debate has generally tended to overlook the possibility of an Arabic contribution to the origins or to the later development of the Romance epic.[10] The considerable scholarly attention recently focused on parallels between Arabic and Romance – and, specifically, Spanish – heroic narratives has been neglected by 'conventional' Hispano-medievalism.[11] Furthermore, a recent book on the modern popular Arabic epic, which has lived in unbroken oral tradition since the Middle Ages and continues to be cultivated today, both in long epic forms (*sīra*) and in short ballads (*mawwāl*), now places the entire problem in a different and even more complex perspective.[12] The Arabic and Catalan stories discussed here cannot be characterized as epic – at least in the forms in which they have come down to us.[13] But, all the same, they do evoke cultural circumstances which are not without significance for the study of a possible Arabic contribution to the Spanish epic – as well as to other forms of oral vernacular literature.

If indeed King Jaume's story is related to the Arabic one, it seems doubtful that the Aragonese king, or his collaborators, would have acquired it precisely by reading Yāqūt's geographical dictionary – or any other written Arabic account.[14] What both stories suggest, rather, is the richly intercultural ambience of medieval Iberia, in which narrative motifs, anecdotes, and episodes could easily have migrated, by word of mouth, from one linguistic community to another and from one body of oral literature to another.[15] The historical and cultural circumstances of the Iberian Peninsula in the Middle Ages suggest that our perspectives on the development of medieval Hispanic literature – and the epic in particular – cannot be complete unless, at very least, the possibility of such exchanges is taken into account and, in the fullness of time, exhaustively explored.[16]

For Professor L. Patrick Harvey, whose exemplary scholarship has done so much to illuminate the cultural contacts between Hispania and the Islamic world, I offer this brief note as an expression of sincere friendship and unlimited admiration.

University of California, Davis

3

NOTES

1. Martí de Riquer compares King Jaume's personal intervention in the redaction of his chronicle with that of Alfonso X, 'tot i que l'obra històrica d'Alfons el Savi sigui molt menys personal que la de Jaume I' (*Història de la literatura catalana*, I (Barcelona: Ariel, 1980), 399). Note also the crucial comments of L. Nicolau d'Olwer, 'La Crònica del Conqueridor i els seus problemes', *EUC*, XI (1926), 79-88, at 81-83.

2. *Les quatre grans cròniques*, edited by Ferran Soldevila (Barcelona: Selecta, 1971), p. 92 (Chap. 215); or in the edition of Josep Maria de Casacuberta, 4 vols (Barcelona: Barcino, 1926-60), IV, 54. On the King's having camped at El Puig, see Soldevila, p. 293a-b, n. 8. El Puig de Santa Maria corresponds to the Cidian *Çebolla*, a Castilian popular etymology for Arabic *Jubayla*. See Ramón Menéndez Pidal, *La España del Cid*, 2 vols (Madrid: Espasa-Calpe, 1947), I, 357; II, 909; *Cantar de Mio Cid*, 3 vols (Madrid: Espasa-Calpe, 1944-46), II, 569-71; also Soldevila, p. 291a-b. Today the town is known simply as El Puig (Valencia, *partido judicial*: Sagunto).

3. Riquer, *Història*, p. 419.

4. Soldevila, *Les quatre grans cròniques*, p. 293a, n. 8. Note also his comment: 'Així era de delicadament lleial l'ànima que s'amagava sota l'escorça del ferreny Conqueridor' (*Vida de Jaume I El Conqueridor*, second edition (Barcelona: Aedos, 1969), p. 204).

5. Menéndez Pidal, *La España del Cid*, I, 276-77. In the Cidian anecdote, the wife of the *Campeador*'s cook has just given birth and the hero refuses to break camp, insisting that the woman be allowed to rest the same number of days as was usual for the wives of Castilian noblemen. See Juan Gil de Zamora, *De preconiis Hispanie*, edited by Manuel de Castro y Castro (Madrid: Universidad de Madrid, 1960), pp. 135-36.

6. See Riquer, *Història*, pp. 406-07; for more details: Nicolau d'Olwer, 'La Crònica', pp. 79-81.

7. Concerning Yāqūt and his dictionary, see *The Encyclopaedia of Islam*, first edition, IV (Leiden: E.J. Brill, and London: Luzac, 1934), 1153-54; Clément Huart, *Littérature arabe* (Paris: Armand Colin, 1923), pp. 301-03; Reynold A. Nicholson, *A Literary History of the Arabs* (Cambridge: University Press, 1953), p. 357; and, especially, Friedrich J. Heer, *Die historischen und geographischen Quellen in Jāqūt's Geographischen Wörterbuch* (Strassburg: Karl J. Trübner, 1898).

8. *Jācūt's Geographisches Wörterbuch aus den Handschriften zu Berlin, St. Petersburg, Paris, London und Oxford*, edited by Ferdinand Wüstenfeld, 6 vols (Leipzig:

Deutsche Morgenländische Gesellschaft-F.A. Brockhaus, 1868), III, 896. The anecdote occurs in Yāqūt's entry on Fusṭāṭ (Old Cairo) and is offered as a popular etymological explanation of how the city came to receive its name; that is, for the tent (*fusṭāṭ*), which ᶜAmr left there because of the dove. I wish to express heartfelt thanks to my friend and colleague, Professor James T. Monroe, who generously located the Arabic passage for me; to him I am also indebted for the translation included here and for learned suggestions regarding the episode's context. I had originally encountered the anecdote in a paraphrase by Sir John Bagot Glubb, *The Great Arab Conquests* (New York-London: Quartet, 1980), p. 237, and subsequently in Alfred J. Butler, *The Arab Conquest of Egypt and the Last Thirty Years of the Roman Dominion*, edited by P.M. Fraser, second edition (Oxford: Clarendon, 1978), p. 281. Concerning ᶜAmr and his conquest of Egypt, see also *The Encyclopaedia of Islam*, second edition, I (Leiden: E.J. Brill, and London: Luzac, 1960), 451. The authentic etymology of *Fusṭāṭ* would seem to be Byzantine Greek *fossáton, fousáton* 'camp, encampment' (< Latin FOSSATUM – the Cid's *fonssado*). See *The Encyclopaedia of Islam*, second edition, II (Leiden: E.J. Brill, 1983), 957-58; N.P. Andriotis, *Etymologiko lexiko tēs koinēs neoellēnikēs* (Athens: Institut Français, 1951), s.v. *fousáto*. The name of the *Fussāṭū* district of the Jebel Nefusa in western Libya probably derives directly from Latin. See Tadeusz Lewicki, 'Une langue romance oubliée de l'Afrique du Nord,' *Rocznik Orientalistyczny* (Krakow), XVII (1951-52), 415-80, at 458.

9. Allusions to Arab hospitality are legion; note, for example, the detailed accounts in Wilfred Thesiger, *The Marsh Arabs* (London: Longman, 1964), pp. 8-9, 122, 198-99. Edward William Lane observes: 'Most Bedawees will suffer almost any injury to themselves or their families rather than allow their guests to be ill-treated while under their protection' (*The Manners and Customs of the Modern Egyptians* (London: J.M. Dent, and New York: E.P. Dutton, 1923), pp. 296-97). Commenting on the ᶜAmr episode in the light of his many years of experience with desert Arabs, Sir John Bagot Glubb notes: 'The tent has always been a place of refuge in the social system of the desert. To it any man or woman in want or danger could flee for protection to afford which the owner of the tent, even if a complete stranger, was bound to devote not only his best efforts but if need be his life. I have elsewhere told the story of a man who gave refuge in his tent to a sick wolf, and even killed a fellow tribesman to protect it. To us, it may seem curious that so ruthless a soldier as Amr ibn al Aasi should give up his tent rather than disturb a nesting dove' (*The Great Arab Conquests*, pp. 237-38). Butler too had observed: 'The appeal for protection, even on the part of an enemy, was sacred in the eyes of the Muslims' (*The Arab Conquest*, p. 281, n. 2). Concerning the terms *jiwār* and *jār* and their implications, see *The Encyclopaedia of Islam*, second edition, II, 558-59.

10. Notable exceptions are L.P. Harvey's review of Francisco Marcos Marín's *Poesía narrativa árabe y épica hispánica* (Madrid: Gredos, 1971), *BHS*, LI (1974), 280-83, and his articles 'Medieval Spanish', in *Traditions of Heroic and Epic Poetry*, edited by A.T. Hatto (London: MHRA, 1980), pp. 134-64, especially pp. 141-44, and '"(A)guisado" in the *Poema de Mio Cid*: the ghost of a pun in Arabic?', *BHS*, LXII (1985), 1-6; as well as Brenda Fish's contribution to the present volume.

11. On the sometimes striking parallels between Classical Arabic heroic narrative and the Spanish epic, see Álvaro Galmés de Fuentes, *Epica árabe y épica castellana* (Barcelona: Ariel, 1977) and Francisco Marcos Marín, 'El legado árabe de la épica hispánica', *NRFH*, XXX (1981), 396-419. Note also Juan Vernet, 'Antar y España', *BRABL*, XXXI (1965-66), 345-50. For other recent work, see my review of Galmés, *HR*, XLVIII (1980), 239-41.

12. On the modern Arabic oral epic, see, now, Bridget Connelly, *Arabic Folk Epic and Identity* (Berkeley and Los Angeles: University of California Press, 1986), which includes an extensive review and bibliography of previous work. Note also Serafín Fanjul García, *Literatura popular árabe* (Madrid: Editora Nacional, 1977), pp. 132-46.

13. As an example of *futūḥāt* or conquest literature, Yāqūt's story could easily have been drawn from oral heroic narrative. Concerning the relationship of the *Libre dels feyts* to Catalan epic poetry, see Manuel de Montoliu, *La cançó de gesta de Jaume I: nova teoria sobre la Crònica del Conqueridor* (Tarragona: Editorial Tarragona, 1922); 'Sobre els elements èpics, principalment arturians, de la Crònica de Jaume I', *Homenaje a Menéndez Pidal*, 3 vols (Madrid: Hernando, 1925), I, 697-712; 'Sobre la teoria dels poemes històrics cròniques rimades catalanes medievals', *Revista de Catalunya*, XXIII (1926), 401-11; 'Sobre el primitiu text versificat de la Crònica de Jaume I', *Anuari de l'Oficina Romànica*, I (1928), 253-336; also Riquer, *Història*, I, 380-92, 416-18. For additional epic elements – both narrative and stylistic – absorbed by Catalan chronicles, see Miquel Coll i Alentorn, 'Notes per a l'estudi de la influència de les cançons de gesta franceses damunt la Crònica de Bernat Desclot', *EUC*, XII (1927), 46-58; also Josep Miquel Sobré, *L'èpica de la realitat: l'escriptura de Ramon Muntaner i Bernat Desclot* (Barcelona: Curial, 1978). Concerning *futūḥāt* literature, see James T. Monroe, 'The Historical *Arjūza* of Ibn ᶜAbd Rabbihi . . .', *JAOS*, XCI (1971), 67-95, at 69.

14. Butler characterizes Yāqūt's narrative as a 'familiar story' (*The Arab Conquest*, p. 281, n. 2). Curiously, both Soldevila and Butler seem to accept their Catalan and Arabic accounts as historical. In arguing that the swallow episode occurred at El Puig, rather than at Burriana, Soldevila states: 'En el poc temps que el rei estigué a Borriana, no és possible que una oreneta pogué fer-hi niu. D'altra banda,

6

aquesta anada a Borriana devia tenir lloc, al més aviat, per l'agost, quan les orenetes ja fa temps que han fet el niu . . .' (*Les quatre grans cròniques*, p. 293a). Concerning Yāqūt's story, Butler likewise observes: 'It fits very well with the time of year when ᶜAmr left Babylon – the end of April – and it has the ring of truth' (p. 281, n. 2). All the same, the anecdote could very well be traditional in character. There is nothing quite like it in Stith Thompson's *Motif-Index of Folk-literature*, 6 vols (Bloomington: Indiana University Press, 1955-58). Compare, however, the following motifs: B365.2: *Animal grateful to hero for preventing destruction of nest* (no references listed); N261.1: *Train of troubles for seven brothers for having destroyed bird's nest*; Q285.1.2: *Punishment for breaking bird's nest*. In the light of the last two motifs, there can be little doubt concerning the story's relationship to a widely known folk-belief. Note José A. Sánchez Pérez, *Supersticiones españolas* (Madrid: SAETA, 1948): 'Quien destruye un nido de golondrina construido en casa de su propiedad, causará la desgracia de su familia' (p. 219); Mohammad Ibn Azzuz Akím, *Diccionario de supersticiones y mitos marroquíes* (Madrid: CSIC, 1958): 'Será desgraciado quien destruya el nido de una golondrina' (p. 39); *Popular Beliefs and Superstitions: A Compendium of American Folklore from the Ohio Collection of Newbell Niles Puckett*, edited by Wayland D. Hand et al., 3 vols (Boston: G.K. Hall, 1981): 'If birds build a nest under the eaves of your house, do not destroy the nest, because it is good luck to have them there' (no. 30494); 'If you move a sparrow's nest, it's bad luck' (30568); *Popular Beliefs and Superstitions from Utah collected by Anthon S. Cannon*, edited by W.D. Hand and Jeannine E. Talley (Salt Lake City: University of Utah Press, 1984): 'If you tear down a bird's nest, you'll have bad luck' (no. 12224). Conversely, the presence of a bird's nest on the roof of (or even near) someone's dwelling is widely held to bring good luck: Hand et al., *Ohio*, nos. 30491, 30493, 30580; Harry M. Hyatt, *Folk-lore from Adams County Illinois* (New York: Alma Egan Hyatt Foundation, 1935), no. 1528. For more on this, see Eduard Hoffmann-Krayer and Hanns Bächtold-Stäubli, *Handwörterbuch des deutschen Aberglaubens*, 10 vols (New York: Walter De Gruyter, 1987), s.vv. *Schwalbennest*, *Vogelnest*. The swallow, as in King Jaume's story, is particularly good luck. Known in German regional speech as *Muttergottesvogel* and *Herrgottsvöglein*, the swallow and its nest offer a variety of protections: 'Algemein ist der Glaube, das die S[chwalbe] das Haus, an dem sie nistet, vor Blitz, Streit, und Tod bewahrt' (Oswald A. Erich and Richard Beitl, *Wörterbuch der deutschen Volkskunde*, second edition (Stuttgart: Alfred Kröner, 1955), s.v. *Schwalbe*). In a Hispanic context: 'La casa en que anidan [las golondrinas], es por este hecho afortunada' (Sánchez Pérez, p. 145); 'En las casas donde anidan las golondrinas, nunca hay disturbios ni desgracias' (Félix Coluccio, *Diccionario de creencias y supersticiones [argentinas y americanas]*

(Buenos Aires: Corregidor, 1983), p. 206). For Morocco, identical beliefs are
listed by Ibn Azzuz Akím (pp. 29-30); also: 'There is *baraka* in the swallow . . .
They bring good luck to the house in which they nest' (Edward Westermarck,
Ritual and Belief in Morocco, 2 vols (New Hyde Park, New York: University
Books, 1968), II, 340; also *Survivances paiennes dans la civilisation mahométane*
(Paris: Payot, 1935), p. 135).

15. Similar circumstances doubtless attended the creation, or rather re-creation, in
Castilian of certain stories by Don Juan Manuel – to mention just one instance.
See John England, '*¿Et non el día del lodo?*': the structure of a short story in *El
Conde Lucanor*', and Celia Wallhead Munuera, 'Three Tales from *El Conde
Lucanor* and their Arabic Counterparts', both in *Juan Manuel Studies*, edited by
Ian Macpherson (London: Tamesis, 1977), pp. 69-86 and 101-17. Munuera notes:
'There are no important verbal parallels, which suggests that Don Juan was
recalling a tale in his own words rather than working from written models' (p.
117). Alan D. Deyermond has observed: 'No se debe pasar por alto la posibilidad
de una influencia árabe directa en algunos casos . . . ¿Es necesario, pues, pensar
en fuentes árabes escritas, mientras que las fuentes europeas fueron orales? No lo
creo' (*Libro del Conde Lucanor*, estudio preliminar de Alan Deyermond, edición
modernizada y notas de Reinaldo Ayerbe-Chaux, Clásicos Modernizados
Alhambra, II (Madrid: Alhambra, 1985), p. 28). For a review of scholarship on
Hispanic-Arabic literary contacts, see James T. Monroe, *The Art of Badīʿ az-
Zamān al-Hamadhānī as Picaresque Narrative* (Beirut: American University,
1983), pp. 9-12.

16. For a recent advance in such a direction, see María Rosa Menocal, *The Arabic
Role in Medieval Literary History* (Philadelphia: University of Pennsylvania Press,
1987). Note now also Francisco Márquez Villanueva, '*La Celestina* as Hispano-
Semitic Anthropology', *RLC*, LXI (1987), 425-53; S.G. Armistead and James T.
Monroe, 'Celestina's Muslim Sisters', *Celestinesca*, XIII:2 (1989), 3-27.

THE MORISCO EXPULSION AND DIASPORA: AN EXAMPLE OF RACIAL AND RELIGIOUS INTOLERANCE

Roger Boase

The expulsion of the last Muslims from Spain in the early seventeenth century was a key event not only in the history of Muslim-Christian relations but in the history of anti-Semitism. Much has been written about the exodus of the Spanish Jews in 1492 and about the plight of the many Jewish *conversos* who suffered at the hands of the Inquisition, but the Spanish Arabs or Moors – an equally significant religious minority whether one's criteria are demographic, economic or cultural – have still not received the kind of attention that they deserve. In most people's minds, the Spanish Inquisition is associated with the persecution of Jews.[1] It is not so widely known that Muslims were also terrorized by this institution[2] and that they too were the victims of an anti-Semitic theology. Racial and religious intolerance is nowhere more evident than in the reports of some of the meetings of Philip III's Council of State and in works written to justify the need for a policy of expulsion. The purpose of this paper is to consider the arguments used by these royal counsellors and apologists.

The use of the term 'Moriscos' requires no explanation. The word 'diaspora' could be applied to the displacement of these people on the Spanish mainland after the ruthless suppression of the Alpujarras uprising in 1570, but here it refers to their final expulsion to foreign lands in the years 1609-1614. By using this term, I wish to suggest not only a superficial similarity between the mistreatment of the Moriscos and that of the Jews (after all, both these religious minorities were persecuted and scattered abroad) but a similarity in the type of anti-Semitic prejudice and propaganda directed against them by Old Christians, even a similarity in the invective heaped upon them. In fact, the main strategy of contemporary apologists in their defence of the policy of expulsion was to fabricate an unorthodox racialist theology based upon biblical precepts and precedents: they sought to judaize Islam and to depict the Christian Spaniards as the new Chosen Race engaged in a crusade to recover their Promised Land from the Antichrist Muhammad. The five best-known anti-Morisco polemicists whose works were published between 1610 and 1618 use in their diatribes an explosive mixture of religious nationalism, popular eschatology, and racialist biblical exegesis, containing many traditional anti-Muslim and anti-Semitic ingredients. Jaime Bleda, Damián Fonseca, Pedro Aznar Cardona, Blas Verdú and Marcos de Guadalajara y Xavier were all Christian friars who had preached to the Moriscos.[3] All of them voiced the prejudices of the populace who criticized aristocrats for protecting their Morisco vassals and resented the professional and commercial skills displayed by certain members of this minority group. Here again one can perceive a parallel with the situation of the Jews and Jewish *conversos*.

To understand how Christian-Muslim relations deteriorated during the course of the sixteenth century until there was a climate of opinion favouring expulsion, it is necessary to sketch in the historical background from the year 1492. According to the capitulations drawn up by Ferdinand and Isabella when the Christian troops entered Granada, the new subjects of the Crown were promised that they would be allowed to preserve their mosques and religious institutions, to retain the use of their language and to continue to abide by their own laws and customs.[4] But within the space of seven years these generous terms had been broken. When the moderate missionary approach of Archbishop Hernando de Talavera was replaced by the fanaticism of Francisco Ximénez de Cisneros, who organized mass conversions and the burning of Arabic religious texts, these events resulted, not unnaturally, in the First Rebellion of the Alpujarras (1499-1500) and the assassination of one of Cisneros's agents, which in turn gave the Catholic Monarchs an excellent excuse for revoking their promises. In Andalusia after 1502, and in Valencia, Catalonia and Aragon after 1526, the Moors had to make a choice between baptism and exile. For the majority baptism was the easier and only reasonable option. Hence the Spanish Moors became New Christians subject to the jurisdiction of the Inquisition founded in 1481. For the most part, conversion was merely nominal: they paid lip-service to Christianity, but continued to practise Islam in secret.

The fall of Granada thus marked a new phase in Muslim-Christian relations coinciding with the emergence of the great nation-states in Europe and the beginning of what one might call the modern era. In medieval times the status of Muslims under Christian rule in Spain was similar to that of Christians under Islamic rule: they belonged to a protected minority which preserved its own laws and customs in return for tribute in money or in kind.[5] However, after the establishment of the Inquisition and the unification of Aragon and Castile under the Catholic Monarchs, there was no longer any possibility of *convivencia* between the three faiths. Not only had Spain become, at least in theory, an entirely Christian nation, but purity of faith came to be identified with purity of blood[6] so that all New Christians were branded as 'herejes en potencia'. As a member of a vanquished minority with an alien culture, every aspect of the Morisco's way of life – including his language, dress and social customs – was despised and condemned as uncivilized and the mark of a heathen. For example, in the eyes of the Inquisition and popular opinion, to eat couscous and to dance to the sound of Berber music were un-Christian activities for which, in the seventeenth century, a person might be obliged to do penance.[7] Even if a Morisco was a sincere Christian, he or she was bound to remain a second-class citizen and was exposed to criticism from Muslims and Christians alike. This was recognized by Pedro Fernández de Navarrete

10

when he observed that 'tengo por cierto, que si a los principios se huviera tomado algún modo de no tener señalados con nota de infamia a los Moriscos, huvieran procurado todos reduzirse a la Religión Católica: que si la tomaron odio y horror, fue por verse en ella abatidos y despreciados, de su baxo nacimiento'.[8] In other words, he believed that more Moriscos might have eagerly embraced Christianity if, by so doing, they could have expunged the memory of their despised origins.

In 1567 Philip II renewed an edict, which had never been very strictly enforced, making the use of Arabic illegal and prohibiting Islamic religion, dress, and customs. This edict resulted in the Second Rebellion of the Alpujarras (1568-70), which seemed to corroborate undoubted evidence of a secret conspiracy with the Turks.[9] The uprising was brutally suppressed by Don John of Austria. The town of Galera, for example, was rased to the ground and sprinkled with salt, and all its 2,500 inhabitants, including women and children, were slaughtered. To prevent organized opposition, tens of thousands of Moriscos in the region of Granada were dispersed to other parts of Spain and Old Christians were resettled on their lands. The conflict between the two communities had now reached a point of no return, and as early as 1582 expulsion was proposed by Philip II's Council of State as the only solution, despite some concern about the economic sacrifice which this measure would clearly entail owing to the decline of Moorish crafts and the shortage of agricultural manpower and expertise. But as there was strong opposition from some members of the nobility and the King was preoccupied by international events – subduing the Netherlands and preparing to invade England – no action was taken until 1609 and 1610 when Philip III issued edicts of expulsion on the advice of his favourite, the Duke of Lerma, and the Archbishop of Valencia, Juan de Ribera.

The decision to proceed with the expulsion was approved unanimously by the Council of State which met on 30 January 1608, although the actual decree was not signed by the King until 4 April 1609, five days before the conclusion of a peace treaty with England which enabled the Spanish to mobilize their army and navy to assist in the operation. Galleons of the Spanish fleet were secretly prepared, and they were later joined by many foreign merchant ships, including several from England.[10] On 11 September the expulsion order was announced by town criers in the Kingdom of Valencia, and the first convoy departed from Denia at nightfall on 2 October and arrived in Oran less than three days later. The Moriscos of Aragon, Castile, Andalusia and Extremadura received expulsion orders during the course of the following year. The majority of them settled in the Maghrib or Barbary Coast, especially in Oran, Tunis, Tlemcen, Tetuan, Rabat and Salé. Many travelled overland to France, but after the assassination of Henry IV in 1610, they were forced to emigrate to Italy, Sicily or Constantinople. Henri Lapeyre estimates from his study of census reports and embarcation lists that approximately 275,000 Spanish Moriscos emigrated in 1609-14, out of a total of 300,000 (pp. 204-06). This is perhaps an extremely conservative estimate, since it is not consistent with many of the contemporary accounts. Fray Marcos de Guadalajara, Pedro Aznar Cardona and the Valencian chronicler Gaspar Escolano all agree that there were approximately 600,000 emigrants.[11] The same figure is given in a letter of approbation preceding Damián Fonseca's *Justa expulsión de los moriscos de España*.[12] Pascual Boronat y Barrachina, in *Los moriscos españoles y su expulsión*,[13] also argues, on the basis of official statistics, that there must have been about half a million refugees. Bearing in mind that the total population of Spain at that time was only about seven and a half million, this must have constituted a serious deficit in terms of productive manpower and tax revenue. In the Kingdom of Valencia, which lost a third of its population, nearly half the villages were still deserted in 1638.[14]

There is an equal amount of disagreement concerning the large number of Moriscos who perished either in armed rebellion or on the journey into exile. Aznar Cardona states that between October 1609 and July 1611 over 50,000 died resisting expulsion, while over 60,000 died during their passage abroad by land or sea or at the hands of their co-religionists after disembarking on the North African coast (I, f. 190v). If these figures are correct, then about one-fifth of the Morisco population must have perished in the space of two years. Other writers, whose combined evidence cannot be lightly dismissed, put the figure at between two-thirds and three-quarters.[15] Most of those who survived the journey arrived at their destination starving and destitute because the bare necessities and money that they were permitted to take with them had been extorted from them by thieves and swindlers. Those travelling to France by land were cheated by farmers who demanded payment for the river water which they drank and for the shade of the trees under which they sat down to rest.[16] Many of those travelling by sea were forced to sell their own children to buy bread while waiting to board ship:

> Y quantos, a sus hijos queridos
> vendieron a los nuestros, solamente
> porque de pan les diessen un pedaço.[17]

It seems that it was a deliberate policy in some areas to starve the Moriscos in order to bribe them to part with their children, whose services would be required for agricultural purposes. With regard to those who boarded the ships in Denia in 1609, Antonio de Corral y Rojas writes: 'Se puede afirmar de dos años a catorce no embarcaron diez' (*Relación*, f. 39r). It was certainly Juan de Ribera's original intention, approved by the Council of State on 1 September 1609, that all children aged ten or under should remain in Spain to be educated by priests or trustworthy persons whom they would serve until the age of twenty-five or thirty in return for food and clothing, and that even suckling babes should be given to Old Christian wet-nurses on the same conditions (Boronat, II, 522-27). Later in the month the age limit was reduced to five years or under, and the embarcation lists show that in fact this policy was at least partially executed. If one looks at statistics for those Moriscos who embarked at Alicante between 6 October and 7 November 1609, one finds that the proportion of children to adults is exceptionally low (Lapeyre, pp. 232-37). Out of a total of 28,483 persons, there were 9,922 children of all ages (boys, girls, and young children) and 9,562 women. If all these women were married, which is a natural assumption in view of what we know about Morisco society, and if (as Lapeyre suggests) the average number of children per family was 2.5 (which is a conservative figure), one can calculate that there seem to be nearly 14,000 missing children, and thus, even allowing for infertility, infant mortality and underenumeration, one must conclude that about ten thousand from this batch of Moriscos had been sent to seminaries and convents or had been adopted by priests or Old Christian families. Yet, according to a document dated 17 April 1610, there were only 1,832 Morisco boys and girls aged seven or under in the Kingdom of Valencia, all of whom, against the wishes of their guardians, were to be sent to Castile to serve the prelates and other notables of the realm (Boronat, II, 575). In July 1610 the Church raised the age limit for Morisco children entitled and compelled to remain in Valencia to seven, and recommended to the King that all Morisco children above the age of seven should be sold as perpetual slaves to Old Christians. These included the orphans of rebels, children seized by soldiers and others concealed and cared for by people who believed they were doing an act of charity. The five theologians who signed this document argued that slavery was not only morally justifiable ('lícito en conciencia') but spiritually beneficial: these children would be less likely to become apostates, since their masters would ensure that they remained Roman Catholics for fear of forfeiting their right to retain them, and, as slaves rarely married, this would be another good method of ridding Spain of 'this evil race' (Boronat, II, 544).[18]

What, we may ask, was the significance of the age limit? It was thought that above the age of six or seven a child begins to lose his innocence and becomes more difficult to indoctrinate, whereas a younger child would have no real knowledge of his Muslim origins. The policy was justified on the theological grounds that innocent children baptized as Christians should not be punished for the sins of their fathers, although, paradoxically, the principle of hereditary guilt was found quite acceptable as a justification for expelling adults. Furthermore, it was said that to banish children with their infidel parents would be to guarantee their confirmation as Muslims and their consignment to hellfire in the hereafter. In the words of Juan de Ribera, 'no podemos entregar los corderos a los lobos' (Boronat, II, 707). But it was repeatedly emphasized that young Morisco children should not be educated above their proper station: apart from pupils preparing for the priesthood, they were to be brought up by artisans and farm labourers, otherwise there was a danger that they might aspire too high; and they should certainly not be allowed to study literature ('cosas de letras').[19] In this way it was hoped that all memories of Islam in Spain would be wiped out forever. In fact, not surprisingly, this policy was far more controversial than the actual decision to expel the Moriscos. It was finally decreed by a group of theologians, who had been instructed by Philip III to consider this question in October 1609, that baptized Morisco children beneath the age of reason should be expelled with their parents:

> Y porque el punto de los niños bautizados que aún no usavan de razón, tenía mucha apariencia y causa de dudar, mandó su Magestad que gravíssimos Theólogos y personas de santa vida le resolviessen, y fue decretado que podía y devía echarlos de España con sus padres, por las razones que allá propusieren (que no son de historia) y mayormente que la perversión que se temía dellos era accessoria y indirecta, como también el yrse sus padres a Berbería; pues la intención de su Magestad solo era echarlos de sus tierras y señoríos por sus delictos. (Escolano, *Década primera*, II, cols 1886-87)

Comparing the letters addressed to Philip III by Juan de Ribera and the decisions taken by the Council of State, one can appreciate to what an extent royal legislation concerning the Moriscos was dictated at every stage by the Church. The aging Archbishop of Valencia, who had initially been a firm believer in the efficacy of missionary work, became, in his declining years (no doubt through disillusion and frustration), the chief partisan of expulsion. The Duke of Lerma also underwent a change of heart when it was agreed that the lords of Valencia would be given the lands of the expelled Moriscos in compensation for their loss of their vassals.

In one of his letters to the King, Ribera quotes a passage from the apocryphal book of Ecclesiasticus (12.10-12):

> Quiero acabar con referir a Vuestra Magestad el consejo del Spíritu santo en las divinas letras. No te fíes jamás de tu enemigo, porque assí como el orín va secretamente labrando, y gastando el hierro, assí su malicia le va gastando el coraçón, y aunque lo veas pobre, y se finja humilde, no por esso te descuydes, antes está sobre ti, y no le pongas en buen lugar, porque sin duda te quitará a ti el tuyo, y se sentará en tu silla, y entonces conocerás, que te aconsejava bien, y te afligerás sin provecho de no aver tomado mi consejo. (Fonseca, *Justa expulsión*, p. 154)

There are two important points to note about this letter. First of all, it is a typical example of the way in which biblical passages were cited to lend authority to anti-

Morisco sentiments. Secondly, it suggests that the Moriscos were perceived as a security risk not merely in the political sense of plotting insurrection with the aid of the French or the Turks, but in the broader social sense: some Moriscos were clearly beginning to climb the social ladder and Old Christians felt that their positions were being threatened by this phenomenon.[20]

Together with the question of social mobility, one must consider the high fertility and comparatively low mortality of the Morisco population. In three memoranda to Philip III in 1602, Ribera had warned the King that, unless he took swift action, Christian Spaniards would soon find themselves outnumbered by Muslims. He believed that this might occur within the space of a few years because, he says, all Moriscos marry and have large families, whereas a third or a quarter of all Christians remain celibate: they enter the Church or remain bachelors for other reasons; many, for example, become soldiers and die in battle, while others travel to the Indies. The Moriscos, on the other hand, think only of reproducing and saving their skins; and their temperance in food and drink also gives them a high life expectancy (cited in Fonseca, pp. 161-62). Ribera's fears were prompted by a census of the Valencian population which he himself had supervised in this same year, which revealed that the Morisco population had increased by over one-third to 30,000 households within the space of twenty-nine years (Bleda, *Corónica*, p. 892; Lapeyre, p. 30), whereas the overall Christian population of Spain had declined during these decades partly, it is true, as a result of emigration, military service and ecclesiastical celibacy, but chiefly as a result of the plague epidemic of 1596-1602 which killed about 600,000 Spaniards, most of them in the heartland of Old Castile, leaving Valencia, with its dense Morisco population, untouched.[21]

The demographic factor was one of the decisive arguments in favour of expulsion employed by several speakers at the Council of State on 30 January 1608. The Comendador de León attributed the lower mortality of the Moriscos to three causes: their exemption from military service, their tendency to remain indoors, and their frugal eating and drinking habits. The only explanation that he could offer for the decline in the Old Christian population was their reluctance to shoulder the financial burden of marriage at a time of rising costs. He warned his listeners that, unless preventive measures were adopted, the Moriscos would be able to achieve their objective simply by means of a high population growth without either taking up arms or receiving assistance from abroad (Boronat, II, 464). He added that, with Turkey distracted by war with Persia and North Africa weakened by plague, drought and civil war, it was an opportune moment to take firm action. The Count of Alba de Liste then said, in a further twist of the demographic argument, that if the King, in his clemency, sent the Moriscos to North Africa, it would be a form of death sentence for them owing to sexual sterility caused by drought and starvation (Boronat, II, 473).

Pedro Aznar Cardona, who discusses the Morisco population explosion at some length, actually imagines that it was a deliberate strategy for domination: 'Su intento era crecer y multiplicarse en número como las malas yerbas.' Now that they can no longer be accommodated in their own districts, they wish to occupy the rest of Spain, thereby fulfilling a desire expressed in one of their ballads, which is an appeal to the Prophet Muhammad to grant them offspring:

> Tanto del Moro y Morica
> como mimbres en mimbrera
> y juncos en la junquera.

Whether they be rich or poor, healthy or crippled, the Moriscos all get married, and weddings usually take place by the age of eleven or twelve, whereas the Old Christian paterfamilias, with five or six children, would be content to marry off the eldest boy or girl, arranging for the others to become clerics, nuns, friars or soldiers (f. 36rv).

The fertility of the Morisco population is associated in the mind of Aznar Cardona with the myth of Islamic sensuality and licentiousness. Carnal vice, he says, is their chief topic of conversation and the object of all their thoughts (f. 35v). This is a stock theme in all anti-Morisco polemical works; it is also, of course, a characteristic feature of racialist abuse everywhere. Gross sexual promiscuity was, according to Bleda, the bait used by Muhammad to attract the common people to Islam:

> escondió el anzuelo de su falsa ley, y doctrina en el cevo dulce de los deleytes mundanos, permitiéndoles el ayuntamiento carnal a rienda suelta, y todos los regalos, y pasatiempos de la sensualidad: hasta darles la bienaventurança de la otra vida en deleytes carnales. (*Corónica*, p. 18)

In order to support this stereotype of Islam, Bleda then cites a Morisco proverb: 'Los Christianos gastan la hazienda en pleytos, los Iudíos en comidas, los Moros en fiestas.'

This alleged aspect of Islam is mentioned by Fray Antonio Sobrino as one of the reasons why the Church has been unsuccessful in its missionary efforts. Despite the Qur'ānic admission that Christianity and Judaism are also ways to salvation, Muslims prefer to abide by their own religion because it is more in keeping with their appetites. Christianity demands that we should love, not the material and visible world, but what is spiritual and invisible, whereas Islam promises carnal pleasures both here and in the hereafter. Thus the Devil makes their perverse and bestial religion easier to follow than any other (Boronat, II, 701-02). Like the figure of the Negro in the United States of America, the Morisco came to personify the sins of the flesh such as lechery, idleness and aggression, later romanticized in visions of oriental harems. But this does not imply that the Moriscos were considered less susceptible to what Gordon W. Allport calls 'the sins of the superego', such as pride, hypocrisy, cunning, avarice, and grasping ambition, all features traditionally ascribed to the Jews.[22] In fact Allport has observed that prejudiced people will not hesitate to use mutually exclusive stereotypes to justify their dislike (pp. 194-95), and this is certainly true of many Spanish writers in the seventeenth century: the Moriscos are lazy, yet industrious; abstemious, yet licentious; miserly, yet extravagant; cowardly, yet belligerent; ignorant, yet anxious to acquire learning in order to rise above their station.

There were, as we have seen, genuine grounds for fearing and envying the Moriscos: their numbers were increasing rapidly; some had become successful merchants and shopkeepers, despite attempts to exclude them from these professions; they exemplified in their conduct the virtues of thrift, frugality, and hard work; the majority outwardly conformed to the social and religious requirements imposed on them, but by subterfuge, according to the principle of *taqīya*,[23] they continued to practise the basic rituals of Islam, celebrating their own festivals and leading a seemingly carefree existence. However, there was, as I have already indicated, a far more sinister species of prejudice, for which there was no basis in reality, a prejudice based on a theory of the inherent superiority of Old Christians and the inherent guilt and sinfulness of the Moriscos, justified by passages of Old Testament scripture and supported by an entirely spurious and racialist interpretation of Muslim and biblical history.

The racialism of Pedro Aznar Cardona's *Expulsión iustificada de los moriscos españoles* (1612) is already evident in the letter of dedication to Pedro López, Canon of Huesca Cathedral, a graduate of the Colegio de San Bartolomé in Salamanca, who is praised both for his Christianity and his proven purity of blood ('provada limpieza de todos quatro costados'). San Bartolomé is here adorned with the epithet 'crucible of lineages' because it was the first university college to introduce rules, shortly after 1482, forbidding admittance to any but those 'of pure blood'.[24] The author boasts that he is the legitimate son of Old Christian parents, whose Christianity is older than the estates which now belong to them by inheritance, from the family of Embides Cardona in the village of Moros and from the ancient family of Aznares in the village of Aniñón (near Calatayud) where he was born (f. 4r). His upbringing in an impecunious family with aristocratic pretensions and his close association with the Moriscos of Aragon makes the idea of intermarriage between Moriscos and Old Christians particularly abhorrent to him. He is disgusted that some Old Christians, who claim to be of noble birth, should sully what little purity of lineage they possess by marrying Moorish girls, and he prays to God that the stain will not reach their souls ('y plegue a Dios, no llegase la mancha al alma'). Anyone, he says, who bows down so low for the sake of the things of this world will need the strength of a camel to rise up again (f. 37r). Later, using a string of animal images, he utters a tirade of abuse against the departed Moriscos. Here is a short sample: 'Estos eran los lobos entre las ovejas, los zánganos en la colmena, los cuerbos entre las palomas, los perros en la Iglesia, los Gitanos entre los Israelitas, y señalmente, los herejes entre los Católicos' (f. 63v). Since true nobility means freedom from vice, the author argues that it is Philip III's task, following the example of King David, to banish the perpetrators of vice, leaving not a trace behind of this evil infidel race (ff. 65r, 102r). In these references to David and the Children of Israel, Christian Spaniards are clearly identified as God's Chosen People.

The same doctrine of racial and religious purity was expounded, with even greater fanaticism, by the Royal Chaplain and Confessor Jaime Bleda in his *Defensio fidei* (1610),[25] and in his *Corónica de los moros de España* (1618). In *Defensio fidei*, Bleda advocated a policy of complete segregation between Moriscos and Old Christians because he maintained that any intermingling of either customs or lineage would lead to the contamination of religion: women of Old Christian families should not be permitted to marry Moorish converts; Moriscos should be forbidden to employ Old Christian servants; they should only practise medicine on their own people, lest they harm Old Christians or perform the last rites according to Islam; they should be excluded from holding any religious office; their corpses should not be brought into churches; if they die without making confession, half their goods should go to the Crown; they should not be admitted as witnesses in a lawsuit if the accused is a Christian; their women should not perform the work of midwives; they should be compelled to breed and eat pigs; and the use of Arabic should be outlawed (Boronat, II, 454-55).

In his *Corónica de los moros de España*, Bleda develops, by means of biblical analogies, the idea of the Spaniards as God's chosen race. He refers his readers to Deuteronomy 20, concerning what purport to be the laws of God delivered by Moses to the Israelites (20.16-18):

In the cities of these nations whose land the Lord your God is giving you as a patrimony, you shall not leave any creature alive. You shall annihilate them – Hittites, Amorites, Canaanites, Perizzites, Hivites, Jebusites – as the Lord your God commanded you, so that they may not teach you to imitate all the abominable things that they have done for their gods and so cause you to sin against the Lord your God.

Bleda correctly informs us that when the Children of Israel entered the Promised Land, they did not slaughter all the Canaanites and other native peoples, nor did they drive them out; instead they retained them as a subject race, because, contrary to God's wishes, they wished to exploit them for their tribute and services (p. 869). The parallel with the situation of the Moriscos is self-evident. He then adds that subsequently, in fact after the death of Joshua, it was God's decree that the Canaanites should remain for a time on the frontier in order to dissipate the effeminate and cowardly spirit of the Hebrew people. In the Bible it is simply stated that God allowed these nations of Canaan to remain so that the Israelites would not forget how to wage war (Judg. 3.1-2). It is also said that through them God wished to test Israel (Judg. 2.22). Bleda here seems to be alluding to the regrets with which many Spaniards viewed the conquest of Granada, because it was thought that without a Moorish Granada there would be no stimulus to noble exploits.[26] Philip III is again likened, in his religious zeal, to King David who, in Psalm 83 (82 in the Vulgate), appealed prophetically for the destruction of the Ishmaelites, Hagarenes and other ancestors of the Moriscos. One wonders what Bleda's reaction would have been to the fact that the very next Psalm, 84, contains a highly flattering, albeit indirect, reference to Hagar and Ishmael: 'Blessed is the man whose strength is in Thee; in whose heart are the ways of them who passing through the valley of Baca make it a well' (5-6). It was in Becca or Mecca, as it later came to be called, that Abraham and his son Ishmael are said to have built the Ka'bah, the focal point of Muslim pilgrimage, close to the spring of Zamzam which God had caused to well up out of the sand when Hagar and her son were dying of thirst (Gen. 21.17-20). The interpretation of the story of Hagar and Ishmael by St Paul and its adaptation to the aims of anti-Morisco polemics will be discussed later.

The same biblical analogies and many others are employed by the Portuguese Dominican Damián Fonseca in his *Justa expulsión de los moriscos de España* (1611), a book which is also packed with letters, official reports, papal bulls and other useful documentary evidence. Philip III's supposedly heroic enterprise is compared with Moses's entry into the Promised Land and David's expulsion of the Jebusites (prologue, sig. + + 6v-+ + 7r). Not only are the Spanish Old Christians God's special elect, but the God whom they worship would seem to be the jealous Lord of the Old Testament who expects a burnt offering from His Catholic Majesty to appease His divine wrath: the unfortunate phrase which Fonseca uses in this context is 'el agradable holocausto' (p. 169). The Moriscos, with whom the author spent twenty years as a missionary, are depicted as an inherently inferior and irredeemably evil race, who have imbibed treachery with their mothers' milk: 'les venía de casta ser traydores . . . con la leche mamavan esta rebelión' (p. 152). One of his favourite images for them is that of the seven-headed Hydra slain by Hercules: when one head is cut off, another grows in its place; and this monster appears in the engraved frontispiece.

Fray Marcos de Guadalajara, in his *Memorable expulsión y iustíssimo destierro de los moriscos de España* (Pamplona: Nicolás de Assiayn, 1613), even sought biblical authority for the view that, with God's approval, kings have a right to punish children, some say to condemn them to death, for the sins of their fathers. Therefore he does not believe in the innocence of the Morisco children. As we know from experience, he says, children are as bad as or even worse than their parents. In order to purify his realm, Philip III had to extract the evil seed ('mala semilla'), otherwise it would have choked the good corn in God's house. Like a good farmer, he had to throw out the buds with the roots (f. 148r). Aznar Cardona even calls the King 'nuestro Católico Galeno de Galenos': he was a Catholic Galen purging the poison or pestilential corruption which existed in the mystical body of Christian Spain (ff. 62v-63r). Juan de Ribera uses the more obvious surgical metaphor: sometimes the arm has to be cut off to preserve the health of the body (Boronat, II, 708).

A conceit of one contemporary poet of Portuguese origin, Juan Méndez de Vasconcelos, presents the expulsion of the Moriscos as a reversal of the Hebrew Exodus:

> O vil canalla pérfida Morisma,
> que gozando la tierra, santa y pura,
> aborrecéys de Dios la gloria misma,
> y al poder de quien soys propia hechura . . .
> No ha de abrir para vos el mar camino,
> ni en la tierra estaréys, santa, y sagrada,
> mas en tablas de robre, y tosco pino,
> a la Egipto infernal y desdichada.[27]

The other Old Testament story which was said to prefigure the expulsion of the Moriscos was that of Hagar, the Egyptian slave-girl, and her son Ishmael, from whom several Arab tribes, including the Quraysh, claim descent. According to Genesis (21.9-13), Sarah persuaded Abraham to banish Hagar and her son because she was jealous and did not want Ishmael to be an heir with her newly-born son Isaac. That Ishmael could be regarded as a rightful heir indicates that he was Abraham's legitimate and first-born son, and it is stated in Genesis (16.1-3) that Sarah, fearing lest she would remain infertile, gave Hagar to Abraham as a *wife*. St Paul, however, allegorized the story in his Letter to the Galatians as the conflict between Judaism and Christianity, between the Old Law and the spiritual emancipation brought by Christ. Hagar represents the covenant from Mount Sinai while Sarah is the heavenly Jerusalem, the mother of free men:

> And you, my brothers, like Isaac, are children of God's promise. But just as in those days the son born after the flesh persecuted the spiritual son, so it is today. But what does Scripture say? 'Drive out the slave-woman and her son, for the son of the slave shall not share the inheritance with the free woman's son'. (4.28-30)

Jaime Bleda interprets St Paul's words to mean that Ishmael and Isaac play a fratricidal game called persecution: the elder brother, renowned for his skill as an archer, made the younger stand still so that he could aim his arrows at him, intending to murder the holy child, thereby making himself his father's sole heir. Others say, adds Bleda, that Ishmael was teaching Isaac to worship idols, and that this was the reason why he and his mother had to be sent into exile. Thus, according to his highly original exegesis, Sarah's appeal to Abraham prefigures the Church's appeal to the Catholic Monarchs to banish the Moriscos. Since the Moriscos were the native 'sons of the soil' ('hijos de la tierra, nacidos en casa') and since it was hoped that they would multiply and cultivate the land as good Christians, Ferdinand and Isabella did not comply with this request. But, like Ishmael, the Moriscos continually directed their arrows against the Christians. Hence Hagar, symbolizing infidelity and heresy, had to be punished by banishment (pp. 907-08). Blas Verdú and Guadalajara, following the same chain of reasoning, describe Philip III as a second Abraham who was obliged to banish his illegitimate son, that is to say the Moriscos, the descendants of Hagar.[28]

All the authors whose works I have studied in some detail share the view that Ishmael was banished by God for the sin of idolatry, although there seems to be no warrant for this theory in the Old Testament. They also concur that the Prophet Muhammad's mother and uncle were Jewish and that he was a precursor of the Antichrist, if not the Beast of the Apocalypse himself, with the two horns of a lamb and the voice of a dragon.[29] In the first book of his *Corónica de los moros*, Bleda introduces the Prophet of Islam as follows:

> Mahoma engañador del mundo, Profeta falso, nuncio de Satanás, el peor precursor del Anti-christo . . . Este tan grande monstruo parió, y crió el Oriente. (p. 1)

After explaining the origin of the word 'alarbe', from a Hebrew word for 'thief', he discusses and dismisses as incredible the Prophet's alleged descent from Abraham. Is it possible, he asks, that such a barbarous race could have kept such long and detailed genealogical records while Spaniards can hardly tell you the names of their great-grandfathers? Besides, as Guadalajara also remarks, the Prophet's lowly profession as a muleteer seems inconsistent with noble birth. Therefore he asserts: 'fue hombre de mala raça, de baxa casta, *Filius terrae*' (pp. 4-5). Bleda then seeks to establish his Jewish connections. His mother Emina (Āminah) was, he claims, Jewish by race and religion, and his Jewish uncle Baeyra, an astrologer who predicted that the child would be the founder of an empire – a clear reference to the Christian hermit Baḥīra – instructed him in the Jewish rites and had him circumcised. Some authorities say that Muhammad was the incestuous, adulterous offspring of Emina and her brother Baeyra, and thus entirely Jewish, in fulfilment of the prediction that the Antichrist would be born of a dishonest woman (p. 5). The fact that many Jews joined Muhammad and welcomed him as their Messiah is for Bleda another feature linking him with the Antichrist who, according to many Church Fathers, would be received by the Jews as King and Messiah (p. 16). Bleda states correctly that Muhammad had a Jewish scribe (whose name he transcribes as Abdalla Cerralle (p. 15), not Zayd ibn Thābit) and a Jewish wife (by whom he means Ṣafiyyah, whose first husband was one of the leaders of the Banū al-Naḍīr). We are informed that she considered herself superior to the other wives, saying that her father was Aaron, her uncle Moses, and her husband Muhammad. Her husband, says Bleda, approved of her words because he too was a Jew and was not ashamed of it (p. 19). These anecdotes, and many others, serve to illustrate the Jewish character of Islam. The Qur'ān is described as a profane anti-Gospel ('Anti Evangelio'), containing a diabolical mixture of Jewish, Arian, Nestorian, Sabellian, Manichaean and Epicurean elements, a syncretic blend of Christianity, Judaism and idolatry designed to deceive the world and to please everybody (pp. 12, 17).

Much the same hideously deformed account of Muslim history is given in the works of Guadalajara, Aznar Cardona, Verdú and Fonseca. It would be an arduous task to disentangle the many different fallacies and to trace their various lines of transmission. Very few of the stated sources are even listed in the index of Norman Daniel's *The Image of Islam in the West*,[30] which is one of the standard works on the subject. And there is still so much material in the works of these five authors which is worth investigating. I have said nothing, for example, about numerology, astrological prophecies and the interpretation of omens, nor have I discussed the dress and eating habits of the Moriscos.

This study of anti-Morisco polemical literature at the time of the expulsion shows that, by the early seventeenth century, prejudice against the Moriscos, compounded of fear, envy, hatred and contempt, backed by a racialist theology, had reached almost epidemic proportions. All the prose works in this genre were written by missionaries who obviously voiced the sentiments of the populace. Fonseca actually states in his letter of dedication that his patron, Don Francisco de Castro, who was the Spanish ambassador at Rome, has received 'el común aplauso del pueblo, cuya boz, es boz de Dios.'[31] There was no attempt on the part of these writers to understand the culture of the Moriscos – the mere fact that it was different from that of Christian Spaniards was taken as a threat to the Spanish nation and a sign of their hostility to Christ. If one compares these works to sixteenth-century examples of anti-Islamic propaganda, for example the works of Juan Andrés, Bernardo Pérez de Chinchón, and Lope de Obregón,[32] one realizes how much the status of the Moriscos had fallen in the intervening period: their religion and culture no longer deserved to be studied and taken seriously; any slanderous anecdote, any insulting remark, any distortion of the truth was acceptable if it served what these Christians considered to be the laudable aim of denigrating Islam. Not only was cultural diversity a phenomenon which these clerics found impossible to stomach, but the concept of assimilation, which is surely the theoretical basis of all missionary endeavour, was equally uncongenial to them. This paradoxical situation illustrates the truth of Allport's pronouncement: 'A prejudiced dominant majority will favour neither cultural pluralism nor assimilation. It says in effect, "We don't want you to be like us, but you must not be different"' (p. 240).

Racialist biblical exegesis provided ample evidence for the inherent and thus incorrigible sinfulness of the descendants of Ishmael, even though strong doubts were expressed about this long pedigree, and for the inherent superiority of Spanish Old Christians, the spiritual heirs of the Children of Israel. What is still more extraordinary is that, in the sixteenth century, anti-Jewish theologians such as Diego de Simancas and Balthasar de Porreño defended the need for statutes of purity of blood by citing how the Moabites and Ammonites were excluded by the Israelites from the Temple (Deut. 22.3; Neh. 13.1). An anonymous inquisitor during the reign of Philip IV wondered how such Old Testament passages could serve as a just precedent for the mistreatment of New Christians in Spain since the law of Moses was a harsh law, inspired by fear of God, whereas the Gospel was a law of grace and love.[33] Indeed it is ironic that both anti-Jewish and anti-Muslim polemicists had to rely so much on the Old Testament to justify their racialist theories.

It seems that, in the minds of these anti-Semites, the Israelites were dissociated from the Jews, who were regarded as the descendants of Judas, the murderer of Christ, not Judah, the son of Jacob (Aznar Cardona, f. 178v). It was conveniently forgotten that it was Pilate who permitted the Crucifixion; that, according to the Gospels, Christ's executioners were Roman soldiers; and that the mob of bystanders was not entirely Jewish. For Bleda and his colleagues, then, there could be no better method of vilifying the last remnants of Arab Spain than to depict Islam as a form of pseudo-Jewish heresy. Bleda even suggests that the Moorish invasion of Spain was a divine punishment for the pro-Semitic policies of the Visigothic King Wittiza (698-710), who revoked the decrees of his father King Egica (687-702) by liberating the Jews from slavery and restoring to them their lands and privileges in contravention of the Sixth Council of Toledo held in 638 (pp. 873-74). At this Church Council, and at the Fourth Council of Toledo in 633, over which St Isidore presided, it was decreed that all Jews baptized by King Sisebut in 612 should be compelled to live as Christians, whether or not baptism had been performed by force. This was officially cited as a legal precedent applicable to the Moriscos at the Council of State on 30 January 1608 (Boronat, II, 461). However, the immediate historical precedent for expelling the Moriscos was, of course, the expulsion of the Jews from Spain in 1492. In a letter dated 10 April 1605, Bleda urged Philip III to follow the example of his royal predecessors Ferdinand and Isabella, who had been persuaded by Fray Thomás de Torquemada to banish the Jews from their realm and would have done the same to the Moors had they refused baptism. God, he says, rewarded the Catholic Monarchs for their Christian zeal by giving them the New World (Boronat, II, 452). By this analogy Bleda was clearly emulating the example of the fanatical Grand Inquisitor. Thus, despite its universalistic creed and its doctrine of the brotherhood of man, Christianity was converted into a repressive racialist ideology. It was in the name of this perversion of Christianity, and in the alleged interests of the state, that the Moriscos were persecuted, segregated, and finally expelled.

Queen Mary and Westfield College, London

NOTES

1. Paul J. Hauben, for example, omits 'the Morisco problem' as a theme in his anthology of texts on *The Spanish Inquisition* (New York: John Wiley & Sons, 1969) because he feels it does not 'merit such attention' (p. 11). But some recent books do consider and compare the sufferings of both minorities: *L'Inquisition espagnole, XVe-XIXe siècle*, edited by Bartolomé Bennassar (Paris: Hachette, 1979); *Les Problèmes de l'exclusion en Espagne (XVIe-XVIIe siècles)*, edited by Agustín Redondo (Paris: La Sorbonne, 1983); and Henry Kamen, *Inquisition and Society in Spain in the Sixteenth and Seventeenth Centuries* (London: Weidenfeld & Nicolson, 1985).

2. The best general book on the Moriscos based on Inquisition material is still Henry Charles Lea, *The Moriscos of Spain: their conversion and expulsion* (London: Bernard Quaritch, 1901).

3. Four of these writers are mentioned in Miguel Angel de Bunes, *Los moriscos en el pensamiento histórico: historiografía de un grupo marginado* (Madrid: Cátedra, 1983).

4. Miguel Garrido Atienza, *Capitulaciones para la entrega de Granada* (Granada: Ayuntamiento, 1910), pp. 269-95.

5. Francisco Fernández y González, *Estado social y político de los mudéjares de Castilla* (Madrid: Real Academia de la Historia, 1866), pp. 118-28; Robert I. Burns, *Muslims, Christians and Jews in the Crusader Kingdom of Valencia* (Cambridge: Cambridge University Press, 1984), pp. 12, 57.

6. See, with special reference to the Jews, Albert A. Sicroff, *Les Controverses des statuts de 'pureté de sang' en Espagne du XVe au XVIIe siècles*, Études de Littérature Étrangère et Comparée, XXXIX (Paris: Didier, 1960).

7. Cf. Louis Cardaillac, *Morisques et chrétiens: un affrontement polémique (1492-1640)* (Paris: Klincksieck, 1977), p. 19.

24

8. *Conservación de monarquías. Discursos políticos sobre la gran Consulta que el Consejo hizo al Señor Rey don Filipe [sic] Tercero* (Madrid: Imprenta Real, 1626), Discurso VII, p. 53. As he says on an earlier page, both the Jews and the Moriscos were driven to despair: they behaved badly because nothing better was expected of them (p. 51). The same point was made at about the same time by an anonymous inquisitor (*Discurso de un Inquisidor*, BNM, MS 13043, ff. 159v-160r; see Sicroff, p. 176). Despite his reputation as a liberal, Fernández de Navarrete still uses the conventional racialist image of Jews and Muslims infecting the good blood in the mystical body of the Spanish monarchy (p. 51).

9. K. Garrad, 'The Causes of the Second Rebellion of the Alpujarras (1568-1571)' (unpublished Ph.D. thesis, University of Cambridge, 1955).

10. Some embarcation lists with the names of ships and captains are given in Henri Lapeyre, *Géographie de l'Espagne morisque*, Démographie et Sociétés, II (Paris: SEVPEN, 1959), pp. 230-37.

11. Marcos de Guadalajara y Xavier, *Prodición y destierro de los moriscos de Castilla, hasta el valle de Ricote. Con las dissensiones de los hermanos Xarifes, y presa en Berbería de la fuerça y Puerto de Alarache* (Pamplona: Nicolás de Assiayn, 1614), Dedication to Philip III and f. 73r; Pedro Aznar Cardona, *Expulsión iustificada de los moriscos españoles y suma de las excellencias de nuestro rey don Felipe el Católico Tercero deste nombre*, 2 parts (Huesca: Pedro Cabarte, 1612), I, f. 190v (over 590,000), f. 57r (250,000 in Aragon, 136,000 in the Kingdom of Valencia), II, f. 7r (over 600,000); Gaspar Escolano y Perales, *Década primera de la historia de Valencia*, 2 vols (Valencia: Pedro Patricio Mey, 1610-11), II, col. 1989.

12. *Justa expulsión de los moriscos de España: con la instrucción, apostasía y trayción dellos: y respuesta a las dudas que se ofrecieron acerca desta materia* (Rome: Iacomo Mascardo, 1612), approbation by F. Iuan González de Albeda, Maestro y Regente del Colegio de la Minerva.

13. 2 vols (Valencia: Real Colegio de Corpus Christi, 1901), II, 305. This is a useful work of scholarship despite the author's racialism and his explicitly apologetic intentions. Bleda's *Defensio fidei*, for example, is described as 'el esfuerzo de un teólogo de primer orden al servicio de una causa justa' (II, 89). For him, Bleda's reasoning is solid and brilliant, his intention healthy, his style eloquent, and his enthusiasm sincere (II, 90). Contrast this with Lea's judgment: 'I have met few books more calculated to excite horror and detestation than *Defensio Fidei*' (*The Moriscos*, p. 289n).

14. Henry Kamen, *Spain 1469-1714. A society of conflict* (London: Longman, 1983), pp. 221-22.

15. Lea, *The Moriscos*, p. 364, cites the following sources: Archivo de Simancas, Inquisición de Valencia, Legajo 205, f. 2; Luis Cabrera de Córdoba, *Relaciones de*

las cosas sucedidas en la Corte de España desde 1599 hasta 1614 (Madrid: publicadas de Real Orden, 1857), pp. 391, 396; Juan Ripoll, *Diálogo de consuelo por la expulsión de los moriscos de España* (Pamplona: Nicolás de Assiayn, 1613), f. 20r; Jaime Bleda, *Corónica de los moros de España* (Valencia: Felipe Mey, 1618), p. 1021. To this list may be added: Juan Luis de Rojas, *Relaciones de algunos sucesos célebres, nuevos y postreros. Salida de los moriscos de España y entrega de Alarache* (Lisbon: Iorge Rodríguez, 1613), ff. 24v-25v; and Fonseca, *Justa expulsión*, p. 185. The latter writes: 'y se sabe por cosa cierta, y lo asseguran todos los que buelven de Berbería, y lo escriven los Christianos de Orán, que no quedan vivos la quarta parte de los que salieron del Reyno de Valencia' (p. 343). Bleda is of the same opinion, but adds, with characteristic venom, that it would have been better if they had all perished.

16. Aznar Cardona, *Expulsión iustificada*, II, f. 6r. They were also prevented from picking fruit from the trees: 'les negavan los arboles frondosos / la fruta de sus ramas estendidas', Gaspar Aguilar, *Expulsión de los moros de España por la S.C.R. Magestad del Rey Don Phelipe Tercero nuestro Señor* (Valencia: Pedro Patricio Mey, 1610), p. 188.

17. Aguilar, p. 189; 'no han quedado sino los muchachos que los padres vendían por remediar la hambre que padecían encerrados en corrales esperando la embarcación', Cabrera de Córdoba, *Relaciones*, p. 371. Cf. Antonio de Corral y Rojas, *Relación del* [sic] *rebelión y expulsión de los moriscos del Reyno de Valencia* (Valladolid: Diego Fernández de Córdova y Oviedo, [1613]), f. 39r.

18. These measures are very similar to those proposed by the Archbishop of Valencia a few years earlier in his third *memorial* to Philip III: 'vendiendo los niños, y niñas menores de siete años (que serán más de treynta, y cinco mil) a Christianos viejos, serán todos Cathólicos, olvidarán la lengua, y el hábito, aprenderán oficios, y artes, y vendrán necessariamente a olvidar las ceremonias de Mahoma, y a guardar las de nuestra santa Fe' (Fonseca, *Expulsión*, p. 187). He adds that some children might be sold as slaves to work in the galleys and mines.

19. This is the tenth point in Juan de Ribera's report dated 27 August 1609 (Boronat, II, 523). Philip III's commentary on it is as follows: 'En el décimo punto que pues el exemplo de lo que se hizo con los moriscos de Granada mostró que el repartir los niños para criarlos y servirse dellos hasta la edad de 25 años por sólo el comer y vestir salió bien, se haga agora lo mesmo dándolos a officiales mecánicos que no sean armeros ni les enseñan cosas de letras o a labradores para la cultura de los campos, porque quando sean grandes no aspiren a más que aquello que les huvieron enseñado' (p. 527).

20. 'Trátase de vedar a los moriscos que no sean arrieros, ni tratantes mercaderes, ni tenderos, sino que todos se ocupen en la labor del campo, porque se han

averiguado grandes daños e inconvenientes de andar por el reino y hacer oficio de mercaderes', Cabrera de Córdoba, *Relaciones*, p. 371 (June 1609).

21. Kamen, *Spain 1469-1714*, p. 223.

22. *The Nature of Prejudice*, 25th anniversary edition (1st edition, 1954; Reading, Mass.: Addison-Wesley, 1979), p. 199.

23. In reply to an inquiry made in 1563, the Mufti of Oran sent a *fatwā* (legal decree) to the Spanish Moriscos, which was soon translated into Aljamiado, permitting them, when necessary, to dissimulate and lead a double life. See L.P. Harvey, 'Crypto-Islam in Sixteenth-Century Spain', *Actas del Primer Congreso de Estudios Árabes e Islámicos* (Madrid: Comité Permanente del CEAI, 1964), pp. 163-78.

24. Kamen, *Inquisition and Society*, p. 117.

25. *Defensio fidei in causa neophytorum sive morischorum regni Valentiae totiusque Hispaniae* (Valencia: I.C. Garriz, 1610). Bleda originally intended to publish this work in Castilian but he was forbidden to do so in 1601 by the Jesuit Father Luis de la Puente, who had been commissioned to examine the work by the Consejo Real. This is stated in a letter dated All Saints' Day 1610, addressed to the Duque de Lerma (*ibid.*, pp. 579-80). Pope Clement VIII read the work in manuscript at the suggestion of his confessor Cardinal Baronius, probably in 1603 when Bleda visited Rome, and was so favourably impressed that he urged Philip III to do the same (Bleda, *Corónica*, p. 957). Pope Pius V, who receives a letter of appeal in the printed edition of the *Defensio*, was less enthusiastic.

26. See remarks by Juan Ginés de Sepúlveda and Fray Alonso de Cabrera in Roger Boase, *The Troubador Revival: a study of social change and traditionalism in late medieval Spain* (London: Routledge and Kegan Paul, 1978), pp. 113-14.

27. *Liga deshecha por la expulsión de los moriscos de los Reynos de España* (Madrid: Alonso Martín, 1612), f. 44v.

28. Verdú, *Engaños y desengaños del tiempo, con un discurso de la expulsión de los moriscos de España* (Barcelona: Sebastián Matheuad, 1612), ff. 141v-142r; Guadalajara, *Memorable expulsión*, f. 154v. The same argument was used by Fray Juan de Grijalba in a sermon preached in Mexico in 1621: see Robert Ricard, 'Les Morisques et leur expulsion vus du Méxique', *BH*, XXXIII (1931), 252-54.

29. 'Et vidi aliam bestiam ascendentem de terra, et habebat cornua duo similia Agni, et loquebatur sicut draco' (Rev. 13.11), cited by Aznar Cardona, *Expulsión iustificada*, f. 22v. The two horns are interpreted as Muhammad's two titles, that of Prophet and that of promulgator of a new divine law.

30. (Edinburgh: University Press, 1960; reprinted 1980).

31. The same phrase, proclaiming the infallibility of the populace, occurs in John Gower's *Mirour de l'omme* (*ca.* 1378), 'Au vois commune est acordant la vois de dieu' (l. 12725) and in the Bachiller de la Palma's *Divina retribución sobre la caída*

de España en el tiempo del noble rey Don Juan el Primero (*ca*. 1479), edited by J.M. Escudero de la Peña, Sociedad de Bibliófilos Españoles, XVIII (Madrid: SBE, 1879), pp. 29-30. It was, in fact, a well-known proverb. Two Judeo-Hispanic examples are cited in Eleanor S. O'Kane, *Refranes y frases proverbiales españolas de la Edad Media*, Anejos del *Boletín de la Real Academia Española*, II (Madrid: RAE, 1959), s.v. *voz*. For further examples in Latin and English, see *The Oxford Dictionary of English Proverbs*, 3rd revised edition (Oxford: Clarendon, 1970), s.v. *voice*.

32.   Andrés, *Libro nuevamente imprimido que se llama confusión dela secta mahomatica y d'l alcorà* (Valencia: Juan Joffre, 1515); Pérez, *Libro llamado Antialcorano* (Valencia: [Juan Joffre], 1532); Obregón, *Confutación del Alcorán y Secta Mahometana, sacado de sus proprios libros: y dela vida del mesmo Mahoma* (Granada: [Sancho de Lebrija?], 1555).

33.   *Discurso de un Inquisidor* (see note 8 above), discussed in Sicroff, *Les Controverses*, p. 174.

DIVINATION FROM SHEEP'S SHOULDER BLADES: A REFLECTION ON ANDALUSIAN SOCIETY[1]

Charles Burnett

In the description of his native land, written in 1188, Gerald of Wales refers to certain Flemish immigrants in Haverfordwest in Pembrokeshire (Dyfed) who 'from the inspection of the right shoulders of rams, which have been stripped of their flesh and not roasted but boiled, can discover both future events and those which have passed and remained long unknown . . . They also declare most confidently from the signs of certain little cracks and marks [on the blade] the symptoms of approaching peace and war, murders and fires, adulteries in the house, the fortune of the king, his life and his death.' They benefited considerably from this skill, for many of them foresaw in the blade the destruction of the land after the death of King Henry I up to a year and a half before this event. Consequently they sold their possessions in good time and left the land without suffering any loss.[2]

In 1921 a mad White-Russian General who styled himself His Excellency Chiang Chün Major-General Baron Roman Fyodorovich von Ungern-Sternberg, believing himself to be a reincarnation of Tzagan Burkhan, the Mongolian God of War, mounted a campaign to liberate Mongolia and the 'living Buddha' from the Chinese. He made no move, however, without first consulting his soothsayers, who read the omens from cracks on sheep's shoulder blades.[3]

These two references to divination from sheep's shoulder blades – of which the technical name is scapulimancy – come from two widely different areas and cultures. But, as the tenth-century Arabic traveller al-Masᶜūdī says: 'Whereas the art of [astrological] prognostication is common to the Arabs and certain cultivated societies, and geomancy is proper to the Berbers, all human races have the gift of practising scapulimancy'.[4] From the wider perspective afforded by modern scholarship we can say that al-Masᶜudi is substantially correct. Historians and anthropologists have discovered and investigated instances of scapulimancy from Shang China in the third millenium B.C., throughout central Asia in historic and into modern times, and, sporadically, amongst American Indian tribes, in Arabic North Africa, among the Bushmen of South Africa, and in several parts of Europe.[5] Anthropologists are undecided as to whether diffusion from one centre, independent invention in several centres, or a mixture of both, accounts for the spread of the art. Amongst nomadic peoples or societies whose livelihood depends on herding, it is natural that the skeleton, along with every other part of the animal, should be put to some use, and, of all the bones in the skeleton, the shoulder blade presents the largest flat area. Just as the femur was converted into a fipple-flute, so the spatula was used as a primitive writing-tablet.[6]

Cultural diffusion seems to account for the spread of two principal kinds of scapulimancy which are clearly distinct from each other. Anthropologists refer to these as 'calcinating' and 'non-calcinating' scapulimancy respectively. The first is the kind practised in Central Asia and the Far East, and among the American Indians. The shoulder blade, previously extracted from the animal, is heated on a fire until cracks appear, and these cracks are then 'read' by the seer. In Shang China notches were artificially gouged out of the blade before heating, the question was inscribed on the blade, and the direction of the crack resulting from the firing in relation to the notch gave a 'yes' or 'no' answer. The number of shoulder blades with inscriptions on them – which amounts to over 100,000 – is a valuable source for Shang history.[7] It seems that the Mongols might have been responsible for spreading the calcinating method. It was observed amongst them by William Rubruck in 1253, and two treatises in Mongolian on the practice were found by a Danish expedition to Central Asia in 1938.[8] Affairs of state and the fortunes of the ruler seem to have been the main subjects covered, and the seer was a courtier who, typically, carried his bones around with him.

In Western Europe most references to scapulimancy suggest that the non-calcinating variety was the norm. The meat was boiled until it fell off the shoulder blade, which was then 'read' without any further preparation. In the Arabic world we find examples of both methods, but in Islamic North Africa the non-calcinating form is prevalent.

Eisenberger, to whom we are indebted for collecting a wealth of literary and folk material on scapulimancy, cites several references to its practice from European sources. Michael Psellos in the eleventh century writes a short attack on divination by sheep's shoulder blades and bird flight, and describes the practice as he knew it in Byzantium. We find Thomas Aquinas[9] and Chaucer[10] condemning its use, along with that of other forms of divination, such as gazing into a dish of water or finding significance in the crackling of a fire. But there are also non-polemical references. We read that Eustache Lemoine, a semi-legendary Robin-Hood-like figure of the thirteenth century, whose exploits generated a series of romances, went to Toledo to learn all kinds of wisdom, including, naturally, the science of shoulder-blade divination. The most objective and thorough account of its practice is given by Gerald of Wales with whose description this article opened. Gerald inserts a little novella concerning an adulterous affair revealed by the blade.[11] The domestic character of the message of the shoulder blade, and especially its accuracy in detecting adultery, is a feature of the scapulimancy practised by the 'minor seers' amongst the Gaelic speakers of Scotland, according to *The Secret Common-Wealth of Elves, Fauns, and Fairies* written in 1692 by Robert Kirk, Presbyterian minister of Aberfoyle.[12] Eisenberger mentions several other post-medieval cases of its use in the British Isles: amongst the 'Dutch-made-English' in the seventeenth century, and in Scotland and Ireland in that and the following century.[13]

However, neither Eisenberger, nor any other anthropologist or historian in discussing scapulimancy, has used the evidence of several Arabic and Latin texts concerning the art. The rituals prescribed in these texts correspond very closely to the recorded examples of the practice in Islamic North Africa and Western Europe.

In bibliographies of Arabic literature three works on *ᶜilm al-katif* ('the science of the shoulder blade') are mentioned. One of these is attributed to the possibly apocryphal author of Hermetic works, Ṭumṭum al-Hind. Another is anonymous and exists in only one manuscript.[14] The third is attributed to Yaᶜqūb ibn Isḥāq al-Kindī, the ninth-century 'Philosopher of the Arabs' who was the first Muslim to attempt to assimilate Greek philosophy to the modalities of Islamic thought. However, both in Arabic and Latin several magical and astrological works are attributed to him falsely, and we have reason to doubt this attribution. This text exists in several manuscripts.[15] Of the two manuscripts seen by me, both contain 'al-Kindī's' work. One, written in A.D. 1538 in Cairo (now Istanbul, MS Şehid Ali Paşa 1812), contains a complete text, but no diagram. The other, written in *maghribī* script and now in Tunis (National Library, MS 18848), contains only a fragment of 'al-Kindī's' work, but includes a detailed diagram of the shoulder blade – the Tunisian chart (Plate I) – which provides a valuable key to the text.[16] Both manuscripts corroborate the attribution to al-Kindī, and the dedication to Yūhannā ibn Māsawaih,[17] a physician, who, with al-Kindī, was patronized by the Caliph Muᶜtaṣim at Baghdad. It must be noted, however, that, in the complete text of the Cairo manuscript, the regular chapter incipit '*qāla Yaᶜqūb*' – 'Yaᶜqūb said' – ceases half-way through the text, and the rest of the work is ascribed to a certain 'Abū Ru'ais' of whom nothing further is known.

There are three Latin manuscripts containing between them four works on scapulimancy.[18] All three manuscripts are of the thirteenth to fourteenth centuries. Two of them contain diagrams of the blade. Sections of two of the texts (*De spatula I* and *De spatula III*) can be shown to be independent translations of a portion of the Arabic treatise attributed to al-Kindī. *De spatula I* is entitled *Liber Amblaudii et Hermetis* and it is tempting to see Amblaudius/Amblandius, who is later called 'of Babylon', as a corruption of 'Alkindius' who came from Baghdad (*latine* Babylon) and at the beginning of his work does indeed claim to pass on the wisdom of Hermes.[19] *De spatula II* on the other hand includes many passages corresponding to sections of the Arabic work attributed to Abū Ru'ais, and again, the Latin name of the alleged author – 'Arbissi' – may be a corruption of Abū Ru'ais. *De spatula III* and *IV* provide neither the name of the original author (or supposed author) nor the name of a translator. The former is written by someone who attempts to write good Latin, but who retains the Arabic terms for the parts of the shoulder blade. The latter is an extremely literal translation of an Arabic work and is hardly comprehensible in its Latin form. It may have been a crib made by someone whose first language was Arabic to enable a

Christian author, whose Arabic was poor or non-existent, to produce an elegant Latin version.

Only *De spatula I* and *II* give indications of their origin. They are both translations made by Hugo of Santalla, who was a *magister* in the service of Michael, the first bishop of Tarazona after its reconquest; he held the see from 1119 to 1151. Hugo, who probably originated from one of the several villages with the name of Santalla in León, translated some ten works on astronomy, astrology and cosmology for his ecclesiastical patron. In the preface to one of these – that of Ibn al-Muthannā"s commentary on al-Khwārizmī's astronomical tables – he states that Bishop Michael found the Arabic manuscript of the work in 'Rotensi armario et inter secretiora bibliotece penetralia', i.e., in the library at Rota, which, as is now commonly believed, is Rueda de Jalón, the last outpost of the Banū Hūd, the rulers of the *tā'ifa* kingdom of Zaragoza.[20] It seems likely that the Arabic texts on scapulimancy used by Hugo were also found here. Thus we have evidence that works similar to extant Arabic texts on scapulimancy attributed to al-Kindī and Abū Ru'ais may have been available in a *tā'ifa* kingdom on the Ebro in the early twelfth century. Moreover, when we look at the contents of these texts we find that this evidence receives considerable support.

The messages of the shoulder blade are conveyed through the marks, such as lines, grooves, hollows, and pieces of meat sticking to the bone, which are discerned in different places (*mawāḍiʿ, loci*) on the shoulder blade.[21] The bulk of the Arabic text is taken up with explaining the significance of each of these marks in each place. In the manuscript from Tunis, and associated with two of the Latin texts, there are schematic diagrams of the shoulder blade in which the places are mapped out. A full description of the significance of each place is written on the Tunisian chart so that it can almost be used independently of an explanatory text. We discover from the texts and the chart that the shoulder blade has a private and a public side.

The private side can only be read by close members of the family. And with good reason. The spine indicates the land or region of the 'master of the blade'. It is divided into three. The division where the spine joins the flat part of the shoulder blade belongs to the owner of the blade's family. Half-way along the spine is his house, and at the tip of the spine is the place of his 'bed'. His bed is divided into a further three parts: 'the *umm walad* (the female slave who bore her master a child)', 'the daughters and sisters' and 'the free-born woman or wife'. It is from the tip of the spine that the 'adulteries in the house' mentioned by Gerald of Wales can be investigated. Other domestic details include the physical characteristics of the *umm walad*: whether she has black hair, is of moderate height, or is a white girl, or has blemishes such as scars from smallpox or from a dog-bite. Another sign shows that the wife now goes to her husband, now to her lover. We gain some insight into the domestic life of the society using these sheep bones. Concubines and free-born wives are clearly differentiated. Servants in the house are black or white, Christian or Berber. The person who cooks the sheep is of significance, and could be a woman or a man. Questions of dominance of husband over wife, or *vice versa*, are regarded as important. The children might rebel against their father. Wheat is stored in underground granaries. A thief may dig through the walls of the house. Wind might bring down trees in the owner's courtyard. Locusts may devastate his crops.

The area round the socket also concerned the 'master of the shoulder blade', and, in particular, his health and the health of his family. However, the front of the shoulder blade, the flat part, concerns questions of relevance rather to the community. It is here that we get some idea of the political concerns of the people using the shoulder blade.

We read that the 'big column' of the blade – i.e. the thickened bone forming the lower edge of the blade on the side away from the spine – is divided into several parts. At its extremity is the place of the seat of the Emir. Then come, in order, the place of the family of the Emir, his children, his slaves, his viziers, his governors and his secretaries. After this come the places of the family of Fihr and the family of Marwān. These are the two most important Arabic tribal divisions in Spain. The Umayyads descended from Hishām ibn ᶜAbd al-Malik ibn Marwān, and when they were overthrown from the caliphate in Damascus by the ᶜAbbāsids, one of their number, ᶜAbd al-Rahmān, fled to the West, entering Spain in A.D. 755. He was opposed by the incumbent governor of Spain, Yūsuf al-Fihrī, who supported the ᶜAbbāsid faction. The friction between the Marwanids and the Fihrites, which also represented the ancient division into Yemeni and Mudarī Arabs, continued throughout Andalusian history.[22] On the Tunisian chart the places of 'Yemen and the tribe of Qudāᶜa' and (possibly) 'the Mudarī . . . and its region' are adjacent to each other.[23]

The slender column – the edge of the blade running along the top of the shoulder – belongs to the *mushrikūn* – 'the polytheists'. This term covers any disbelievers against whom a Holy War must be directed. Christians were commonly referred to as *mushrikūn* in that they appeared to worship a triumvirate of Gods. The seat of the 'Emir' of the polytheists is towards the end of the slender column opposite that of the Emir of the Muslims. Other ranks within the kingdom of the polytheists are not specified. Instead, as one goes along the slender column, one finds out whether the price of commodities – specifically butter and fruit – is going up or coming down.

The space between the the two columns, as one can easily observe, is divided into a light and dark area, in that the spine prevents light from penetrating the blade. The light area, on the side of the big column, belongs to the Muslims, the dark area to the polytheists, and in their respective areas one can see their success or failure in battles on land or at sea, the death or illness of their rulers, and who will succeed to the rulership. Within the area belonging to the Muslims is 'the place of Córdoba'. Here one can see famine or abundance in the city, or an army invading, or the Emir setting out on an expedition.[24] The only other Andalusian city mentioned in the Arabic texts is

33

the capital of the Banū Hūd (Zaragoza), which is next to the place of Córdoba on the Tunisian chart. This place is specifically described in the Arabic text as being between 'the people of opposition' and 'the people of obedience' – i.e., between the Polytheists and Muslims – and here, one is told, one can see the outcome of a Holy War. In one of the Latin diagrams of the shoulder blade, however, further Spanish cities are mentioned: Sevilla, Jaén, and Toledo.[25] The significance of these places is not clear, since they do not figure in the text. All three places, however, were capitals – along with Zaragoza and Córdoba – of the small *ṭā'ifa* kingdoms which arose after the break-up of the Andalusian caliphate in A.D. 1031. This could suggest that the Arabic chart from which this Latin one was taken might have been adapted for use by *ṭā'ifa* rulers.

In the treatise of Abū Ru'ais specific mention is made on occasion of the Emperor of Rūm[26] and of a 'Christian' (*naṣrānī*). Elsewhere Christians appear to be designated simply as 'polytheists' or 'the people of opposition'. However, another major division of Andalusian society is also found in both the Arabic and Latin texts: that is, the Berbers. The largest Muslim element of Arabic Spain was the Berbers from North Africa. However, the Berbers and the pure Arabs kept apart from each other socially and geographically and were frequently in conflict. In 1085 the *ṭā'ifa* kingdoms were swept away by an invasion of austere Berber Muslims (the Almoravids), but these in turn were subdued in 1146 by another Berber invasion, that of the Almohads. One of the Latin treatises mentions the *moabite* ('Moabites'), which is the biblical tribe with which the Almoravids were identified, because of the similarity of the sound of the two words. Like the pure-blooded Arabs the Berbers had their own tribal divisions, and were, in particular, divided into two clans, the Butr and the Barānis. The places of 'the Butr, who are the Berbers' and 'the Barānis, who are the Negroes' are marked on the Tunisian chart opposite the places of the Yemeni and Muḍarī (?) Arabs. The two clans of the Berbers and the two clans of the Arabs continually changed their allegiances. Frequently the Arabs would be in league against the Berbers, but, in A.D. 889, for example, Kuraib ibn Khaldūn of Sevilla led a confederation of Barānis Berbers and Yemeni Arabs against another confederation of Butr Berbers and Muḍarī Arabs.[27] It would be interesting to know whether he consulted a shoulder blade.

In general the shoulder-blade manuals give us a picture of the racial mix which characterized Andalusian society. The Barānis are described as 'Negroes', and the *umm walad* herself might have frizzy hair. The wife might be a desert Arab (*badawīya*). The kingdom of Rūm is beyond the borders of the land of the Emir, but there are also Christians within Muslim territory – e.g., a Christian may have cooked the sheep whose shoulder blade was used.[28] There is a panoply of government officials, including a chief of police and a chief of the post.[29] From the prominence of Córdoba in the Arabic texts and the use of the title Emir, one might guess that the works in their present form were composed before A.D. 929, when the Emir took up the title Caliph. To refer to the

Caliph as Emir after A.D. 929 would be a case of *lèse majesté*. However, occasionally our Arabic authors insert the title Caliph as an alternative to Emir, and Abū Ru'ais, in one passage, uses the word *malik* ('king'). Moreover, 'emir' could be taken as a title for any ruler or military commander, and we have seen evidence that the texts translated by Hugo of Santalla were probably used by the rulers of the ṭā'ifa kingdom of Zaragoza. In the Tunisian chart the reference to *āl al-khilāfa* (Appendix, no. 11) could suggest any date before 1031, since the ᶜUmmayads, both before and after they had established the Western Caliphate in 929, were referred to as *banū al-khilā'if* (= 'the descendants of the [Eastern] Caliphs'). A pre-ṭā'ifa date is also suggested by the reference to 'provincial governors' (ᶜ*ummāl*) in Appendix, no. 7.

In the Latin translations many of the details of Arabic society have been lost. We find the same division of the shoulder blade between the Muslims and the Christians (with whom the polytheists are positively identified), and the Emir has become the 'rex Saracenorum'. But the families of Marwān and Fihr are disguised under the title 'reges Latinorum', and 'Baranis' and 'Butr' have been taken over into the Latin text as obscure synonyms for Christians and Saracens. The hierarchy of the Arabic court is missing altogether, and no attempt has been made to replace this by concepts familiar to Christian Europe.

It is quite conceivable that the Arabic texts, which are clearly products of an Andalusian soil, were adorned with the names al-Kindī and Ibn Māsawaih to give them an air of authority. Al-Kindī was popularly known in Andalusia above all as 'the easiest to use and most reliable judge amongst astrologers',[30] and the text on which his reputation rested appears to have been translated at least twice, once by Hugo of Santalla himself.[31] Ibn Māsawaih, on the other hand, was known for several works of medicine, including a pseudepigraph on pharmacy which became popular in its Latin translation.[32] The dedication gains some credence from the fact that al-Kindī and Ibn Māsawaih were contemporaries, and a work on the soul is said to have been addressed by the philosopher to the physician.[33] It is possible that al-Kindī composed a generalized work on scapulimancy which was then adapted to suit the situation in al-Andalus. The origin of al-Kindī's work is said to have been a sheet or plan (*ṣaḥīfa*, *carta*) found in Athens, and written in Greek. There is no evidence of scapulimancy in Greece in Antiquity, but a Byzantine work on scapulimancy was discovered by Delatte in a thirteenth-century manuscript.[34] This Greek work prescribes the same method for preparing the shoulder blade as the Arabic and Latin works, and divides the blade in the same way into parts concerning the household, the master of the shoulder blade, and political affairs. However, no proper names are given; the text has not been adapted to suit any particular political situation. In this Greek text we probably see an example of the basic form of a shoulder-blade manual which could be amplified and adapted to the needs of specific societies and situations. Such a work might have been brought to al-Andalus and amplified there. That Arabic scapulimancy originated from a sheet or a plan might also have some truth. This plan would have been a diagram of the shoulder blade such as the Tunisian chart and the diagrams in the Latin manuscripts. These give information which is not in the text, and could in themselves be sufficient *aides-mémoire* for the practitioner.

Whatever the ultimate origins of Arabic scapulimancy might be, our shoulder-blade texts clearly reflect the specific society of the Maghreb. The Arabic texts have become 'frozen', as it were, in the Latin translations made in the twelfth century, and, together with the two Arabic texts surviving in later manuscripts discussed here, they give us a precious glimpse of the private affairs and public concerns of men and women living in medieval Andalusia.

The Warburg Institute

APPENDIX

The 'Places' on the Shoulder Blade
(Tunis, National Library, MS 18848)

What follows is a provisional translation of the Arabic script in each of the 'places' on the diagram of the shoulder blade attached to a copy of 'al-Kindī''s text on scapulimancy in Tunis, National Library, MS 18848 (not foliated). It must be emphasized that because of both the poor state of the manuscript and the peculiarities of the subject-matter, the interpretation of the text is highly tentative. Some of the readings should become clearer when the Arabic treatises on scapulimancy, which describe the 'places', have been studied in more detail.

A. The Big Column.

1. This is the big thick column. It is divided into all these parts. It pertains to the Emir and his companions and his jurisdiction (*khāṣṣīya*), and what happens to them (?) in it.
2. This is the tomb of the Emir, in which he sees his tomb.
3. The place of the family (*ahl*) of the Emir and his bed and his bedstead (*sarīruhu*),[35] and what happens in it.
4. The place of the progeny of the Emir and his sons and what happens to them in it.
5. The place of the slaves of the Emir and what happens to them in it of good and bad.
6. The place of the viziers of the Emir – the closest of them – and what happens to them in it.

7. The place of the provincial governors (*ᶜummāl*) of the Emir and what happens to them in it of good and bad.
8. The place of the secretaries (*kuttāb*) of the Emir and the administrators (*aṣḥāb al-khuṭṭa*).
9. The place of the family of Fihr and what happens to them in it.
10. The place of the family of Marwān and what happens to them in it.
11. The place of the family of the Caliphate (*āl al-khilāfa*) and what happens to them in it. ·
12. The place of the Arabs in their totality and what happens to them in it.

B. The Slender Column.

13. The place (of the Polytheists) and their companions, and what happens to them in the presence of their king.
14. The place of the destruction of the Polytheists because of famine and their tribulations and their unnatural ways, and what happens to them in it.
15. The place of the rise and fall of price and what happens in it, and the place of . . . and butter (*saman*) and fruit.
16. The place of the livestock of the master of the shoulder blade, and the place of the losses and gains accruing to him and the like.

C. The Big Cartilage.

17. (Unreadable).
18. (. . .) in illness and what happens in it.
19. (. . .) and its perishing.
20. The place of the difficulty of the sea and the perishing of the people on it.
21. The place of the difficulty of the sea of the Polytheists.

D. The Small Cartilage.

22. The place of the spies, the wayfarers (*ṭāriqīn*) and enemies, and these are inside the country.
23. The place of the rise and fall of price and what occurs of drought, and this is the small cartilage, which is the edge of the spine.
24. The hump (*sanām*). This is the place of the bed of the man and his bedstead, which include both good and ill-fortune for him, and the door of his house and those who live with his family (*asbāb*).
25. The house of the man, in the vicinity of the bed.[36]
26. The country (*al-balad*).[37] This is the middle of the spine.
27. The village (*al-qarya*) from which the sheep are taken.[38]
28. The place of the horse of the man and his saddle and (. . .).

E. The 'Sea'.

29. This is the place of the sea – the big cartilage – and one sees in it the battles of the Muslims with the Polytheists and . . . and what happens between them.

30. This is the place of the dark sea,[39] shared (?) between the Polytheists and the Muslims.

31. The place of the Polytheists [and their sea and their trumpets][40] and the place of their sea, which is shared.

32. The place of the sea, and the fleets and the boats and the banners and he sees what happens to them in it of good and bad.

33. The place of the departures of boats and what happens between them and the enemy.

34. The place of the sea of the Polytheists, and their boats and fleets and their going out (to the) Muslims and their wars and what happens between them in it.

35. The place of the tombs of the Polytheists on the sea[41] and their banners and their going out from their region, and what happens to them.

F. Other Places on the Flat Part of the Shoulder Blade.

36. This is the place in which one sees the Emir's good or ill fortune.

37. The place of the treasure-house (*khizāna*) of the Emir and his clothes and his weapons.

38. The place of the castle of the Emir.

39. The place of the capital (*qāᶜida*) of the Emir and the place of the prison and what happens in it.

40. The place of the chamberlain (*hājib*) of the Emir.

41. The place of the Friday-mosque of the Emir and his country and his region and what happens in it.

42. The place of the killing and the tombs and the battle and the affliction (?) of the Polytheists and what happens in it.

43. The place of the Emir of the Polytheists and his capital and his base and his tomb and what he sees in it for him.

44. The place of the retainers of their Emir and what happens to them in it.

45. The place of the frontier province and of Zaragoza and of those who beguile (others) away from the Emir, and what happens between them, and he sees for them in it (change) from good and bad to the opposite.

46. The place of the path of cavalry and armies and soldiers and their departure to the Polytheists and what happens between them of wars and harmful calamity, and this is the place of Córdoba.

47. The place of the fighting of the Polytheists with the Muslims and their wars and their boats and what happens in it.

48. The place of the enemy of the Polytheists and the killing and capture of them, and what happens to them in it.

49. The place of the wars of the Polytheists and their going out from their country and their spreading into (various) regions and countries.

50. The place of the cavalry of the Polytheists and their battle and the rout over them, (. . .) always.

51. The place of the wars of the Polytheists and what is planned among them, and the death of their greatest (leaders), and the place of the faults among them, and what happens in them.

52. The place of Yemen and the tribe of Quḍāᶜa (. . .).

53. The place of the Muḍarī (?) and the . . . (?) and its region, and what happens in it.

54. The place of abundant rain and its floods, and what happens in it of good and ill fortune.

55. The place of the Butr – and these are the Berbers – and what happens to them in it.

56. The place of the Barānis – and these are the Negroes – and their region and what happens to them in it.

57. The place of the sea – all of it – its exterior and interior (. . .).

G. The Socket.

58. The place of the socket. All of it – on the inside and outside – belongs to the master of the shoulder blade. In it he sees his good and bad.

59. And the socket is the household of the man and the place of his family and his property and his clothes and his livestock and all the people of his house.

60. The place of meat (*laḥm*), and this is the root of good fortune in the head of the socket.

61. Root of misfortune, and what he sees in it.

62. The hollow of the socket, and this is the place of the domestic animals and his granaries and the places of his slaves and servants and paternal aunts and maternal aunts and all relatives.

H. The Small Column.

63. The small column, and in it he sees the tomb of his family and relations.

64. The place of the tomb of the man, particular to himself.

65. The place of the master of the shoulder blade and his tomb when he is aged (?),[42] and the place of the tomb of his sons and his family.

66. The place of the tombs of his daughters with their family.

67. The place of the tomb of the wife, with her ancestors and her family.

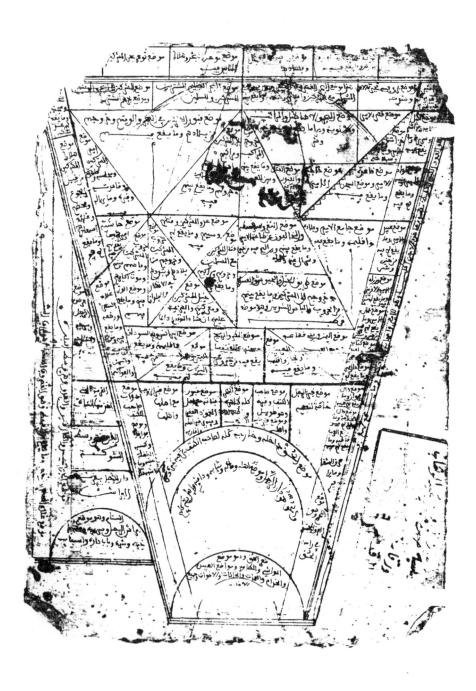

Plate I: The Tunisian Chart (Tunis, National Library, MS 18848)

40

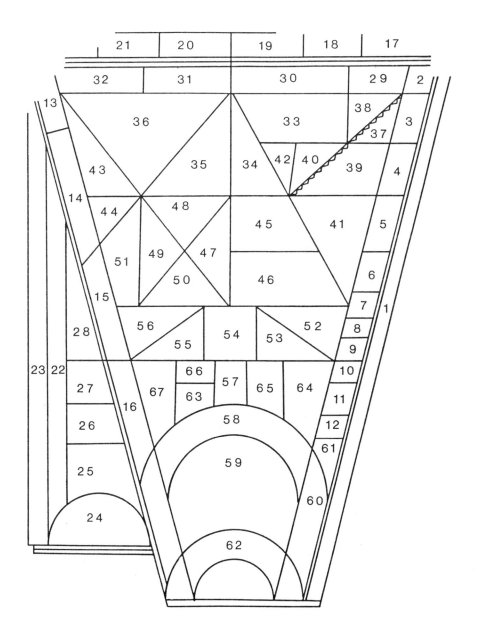

Fig. 1: Key to the Tunisian Chart (Tunis, National Library, MS 18848)

NOTES

1. I am grateful to several audiences in England, Spain and America who have patiently sat through and commented on various versions of an illustrated talk on which this article is based, to Larry Conrad, Dimitri Gutas, Ahmed al-Hamdi and P. Sj. Van Koningsveld, who have helped me interpret the Arabic; and especially to Professor Harvey who has kindly corresponded with me on some aspects of the topics covered here. This article is complementary to my 'Arabic Divinatory Texts and Celtic Folklore: a comment on the theory and practice of scapulimancy in Western Europe', *Cambridge Medieval Celtic Studies*, VI (1983), 32-42, in which the recorded instances of scapulimancy in Wales, Scotland and Ireland are discussed, the Arabic and Latin texts on scapulimancy are summarized and compared, and a list of known texts describing the practice of scapulimancy (from six languages) is given. To this list may be added four Persian works, including one ascribed to Naṣīr al-Dīn al-Ṭūsī, listed in C.A. Storey, *Persian Literature*, II.3 (London: Royal Asiatic Society, 1977), 493, and an Arabic text attributed to Ṭumṭum (M. Ullmann, *Die Natur- und Geheimwissenschaften im Islam* (Leiden: E.J. Brill, 1972), p. 381, n. 4). See also *The Encyclopedia of Islam*, new edition (Leiden: E.J. Brill, 1978), IV, 763 (s.v. *katif*). Two chapters on scapulimancy in Georgio Anselmi's *Divinum opus de magia disciplina* are discussed in my 'An Islamic Divinatory Technique in Medieval Spain', to be published in *The Arabic Influence upon Medieval Europe*, Al-Masaq Monograph, I, edited by D.A. Agius and R. Hitchcock. This article includes an edition and translation of *De spatula IV*.

2. *Giraldi Cambrensis Opera*, VI, edited by James F. Dimock, Rolls Series (London, 1868), 87-89 and *Gerald of Wales: The Journey Through Wales and The Description of Wales*, translated by Lewis Thorpe (Harmondsworth: Penguin, 1978), pp. 145-47.

3. Fitzroy Maclean, *To the Back of Beyond* (London: Jonathan Cape, 1974), pp. 121-24.

4. *Les Prairies d'or*, edited by Barbier de Meynard and Pavet de Courteille, revised edition by Charles Pellat, Publications de l'Université Libanaise, Section des Études Historiques, XI (Beirut: Université Libanaise, 1966-79), II, 302.

5. The fullest anthropological account of scapulimancy is that of E.J. Eisenberger, 'Das Wahrsagen aus dem Schulterblatt', *Internationales Archiv für Ethnographie*, XXXV (1938), 49-116.

6. I have seen examples of this in the National Museum of Ireland in Dublin and in the Museum of Aleppo. The revelations of the Koran were originally written on camels' shoulder blades, as well as on other natural objects.

7. D.N. Keightley, *Sources of Shang History. The Oracle Bone Inscriptions of Bronze Age China* (Berkeley: University of California Press, 1978).
8. C.R. Bawden, 'On the Practice of Scapulimancy among the Mongols', *Central Asiatic Journal*, IV (1958), 1-44; *idem*, 'A Tibetan-Mongol Bilingual Text of Popular Religion', in *Serta Tibeto-Mongolica. Festschrift für Walther Heissig zum 60. Geburtstag am 5.12.1973*, edited by R. Kaschewsky, K. Sagaster and M. Weiers (Wiesbaden: Otto Harrassowitz, 1973), pp. 15-32.
9. *Summa theologiae*, 2, 2, q. 95, art. 3 (Turin: Petrus Mariettus, 1922), III, 545: 'Divinatio vero ex quibusdam signis in spatula alicuius animalis apparentibus spatulamantia vocatur'.
10. *Parson's Tale*, line 603: 'horrible swering of adiuracioun and coniuracioun, as doon thise false enchauntours or nigromanciens . . . in a shulder-boon of a sheep' (*The Complete Works of Geoffrey Chaucer*, edited by W.W. Skeat, IV, second edition (Oxford: Clarendon, 1900), 607).
11. See my 'Arabic Divinatory Texts', p. 33.
12. *The Secret Common-Wealth and A Short Treatise of Charms and Spels*, edited by Stewart Sanderson, Mistletoe Series (Cambridge: Folklore Society, 1976), pp. 67-68.
13. Further examples, kindly furnished by Patrick Sims-Williams, are given in my 'Arabic Divinatory Texts', p. 32.
14. I have seen neither of these works.
15. For full descriptions of the Arabic and Latin works and the manuscripts in which they occur see my 'Arabic Divinatory Texts', pp. 39-40.
16. See Plate I; a tentative English translation of the legible portions of this chart is given above in the Appendix.
17. The Tunis MS gives 'Yahyā ibn Māsawaih khādim al-Muᶜtasim'; the Cairo MS gives 'Yahyā ibn Māsūm khādim al-Muᶜtasim'. 'Yūhannā' and 'Yahyā' are variant Arabic forms for the name 'John'.
18. These were first mentioned by C.H. Haskins, in his *Studies in the History of Mediaeval Science*, second edition (Cambridge, Mass.: Harvard University Press, 1927), p. 79. A relationship between the Latin and Arabic texts was suggested by M.T. d'Alverny in 'Al-Kindī, *De Radiis*', *Archives d'Histoire Doctrinale et Littéraire du Moyen Age*, XLIX (1975), 152.
19. It is less likely that Amblaudius is a corruption of the Arabic corruption of Ptolemy's cognomen Klaudios, which appears in other Latin translations from the Arabic as Phludensis.
20. Burnett, 'Some Comments on the Translating of Works from Arabic into Latin in the Twelfth Century', *Miscellanea Mediaevalia*, XVII (1985), 161-71, at 169.

21. See my 'Arabic Divinatory Texts', pp. 35-38, for descriptions of the justification of the practice and the preparation of the blade, and for some of the passages from the Arabic and Latin text relevant to the following discussion.
22. See E. Lévi-Provençal, *Histoire de l'Espagne musulmane*, I (Leiden: E.J. Brill, 1950), 96, 101-4, 360 and 396 and T.F. Glick, *Islamic and Christian Spain in the Early Middle Ages* (Princeton: Princeton University Press, 1979), pp. 139-40.
23. See nos. 52 and 53 in the Appendix above. In the case of the second 'place' the reading is highly conjectural.
24. Cairo MS, p. 49b: 'When you see below the seat of the Emir near the place of Córdoba a black film or black point, then there is abundance for Córdoba and the army is powerful and bringing happiness and joy. And if it happens that there is in the above-mentioned place a red or black stripe, then booty will come to the Emir and benefits and properties. And if you see in the place of Córdoba yellowness or a white point, then battles occur to the people of Córdoba and epidemics and troubles and starvation'; ibid., p. 51a: 'And if the blackness spreads to the white part of the shoulder blade – to the place of Córdoba – then the Emir is going out by himself'.
25. Oxford, Bodleian Library, Canon. Misc. 396, f. 112r.
26. Cairo MS, p. 48a: *Sulṭān al-Rūm*. By 'the Emperor of Byzantium (the usual meaning of *Rūm*)' probably any Christian king is meant.
27. Lévi-Provençal, *op. cit.*, p. 360. In the Cairo MS other nations are mentioned in passing: e.g., on p. 46b there is a list including the *barbar, al-yaman, miṣr* ('Egypt'), *turk* and *rūm*; on pp. 47a-b there are references to 'Christians or Tartars'.
28. Cairo MS, p. 36b: 'the cook is not a Christian (*naṣrānī*)'.
29. Abu Ru'ais mentions a *ṣāḥib al-madīna, ṣāḥib al-shurṭa*, and a *ṣāḥib al-bārid*, whilst both Arabic authors refer to 'the governor' (*wazīr*), the *wālī* and 'the master' (*mawlā*).
30. 'Commodissimum et veracissimum inter astrologos'. This is the judgement of Hermann of Carinthia in recommending al-Kindī's *Iudicia* as a work that Robert of Ketton should translate (Haskins, *op. cit.*, p. 121).
31. See Burnett, 'A Group of Arabic-Latin Translators Working in Northern Spain in the mid-12th Century', *JRAS* (1977), pp. 62-108 (see p. 67, n. 51). *Pace* Richard Lemay, 'The True Place of Astrology in Medieval Science and Philosophy', in *Astrology, Science and Society*, edited by P. Curry (Bury St. Edmunds: The Boydell Press, 1987), p. 67, n. 14, the two translations of al-Kindī's *Iudicia* – one by Robert of Ketton, the other appearing in the *Liber trium iudicum* and *Liber novem iudicum* and apparently by Hugo of Santalla – are unrelated to each other.
32. M. Ullmann, *Die Medizin im Islam* (Leiden: E.J. Brill, 1970), pp. 112-15, 304-06.

33. See G.N. Atiyeh, *Al-Kindi: The Philosopher of the Arabs* (Rawalpindi: Islamic Research Institute, 1966), p. 194.

34. A. Delatte, *Anecdota Atheniensia*, I, Bibliothèque de la Faculté de Philosophie et Lettres de l'Université de Liège (Liège: Université, 1927), 206-09.

35. This, one may presume, is the place in which one sees the Emir's relationship with his concubines.

36. I.e., the quarters of his womenfolk.

37. The reading is unclear, but the place seems to correspond to the place of this name in the Cairo MS, f. 4b.

38. Cf. Cairo MS, f. 4b: 'the place of the sheep (*al-ghanam*) and their grazing and the village (*al-qarya*)'.

39. The chart gives *al-bahr al-ẓalīm* = 'the dark sea', but one should note that the related term *bahr al-ẓulma* = 'the Atlantic Ocean'.

40. The words in brackets appear to have been crossed out.

41. P. Sj. Van Koningsveld has suggested that this may be an allusion to the Vikings, who raided al-Andalus several times during the Emirate, and whose practice was to 'bury' their dead by sending them out to sea on burning ships. On the other hand 'the sea' here could be the name of the place on the shoulder blade (as implied in no. 29 above).

42. The Arabic gives only *ṭawīl* ('long'), which might be assumed to be *ṭawīl al-ʿumr* ('long in life' or 'aged').

USES OF THE BIBLE IN THE *POEMA DE FERNÁN GONZÁLEZ*

Alan Deyermond

Any attempt to give an account of the *Poema de Fernán González* – whether on the level of plot, of literary structure, of folkloric or figural analysis, or of ideology – depends on two assumptions: first, that the verse text in the unique extant manuscript (Escorial b.IV.21, copied in the fifteenth century) is incomplete, and second, that the *Estoria de España* fully and with relative fidelity supplies what is missing in the manuscript. Luckily, the evidence for both assumptions is very strong. This is not a case analogous to the phantasmagoric lost ending of the *Auto de los reyes magos*, or even to the hypothetical lost beginning of the *Cantar de Mio Cid*; neither is it analogous to the *Mocedades de Rodrigo* or *Elena y María*, where the ending is clearly lost but we lack the evidence that could tell us what that ending was. Unfortunately the evidence of the *Estoria de España* is ambiguous in one respect: how far beyond the end of the extant manuscript did the *Poema* continue? Did it end with the independence of Castile, as is believed by, among others, Alonso Zamora Vicente and Miguel Ángel Pérez Priego, or did it continue until Fernán González's death and burial, as María Eugenia Lacarra argues?[1] Either would make a satisfying conclusion to the story, though the kind of poem we contemplated would differ significantly according to the hypothesis we accepted. It seems to me more likely that the *Poema* ended with the hero's death and burial, though it does not necessarily follow that all the intermediate episodes believed by Lacarra to have formed part of the text did in fact do so.

The abrupt ending of the extant text of the *Poema* is one of the most obvious difficulties that is presented to the reader.[2] The other is that what begins as a poem about the history of Spain, concentrating increasingly on Castile, becomes in stanza 173 a poem about Fernán González, whose birth had been mentioned only six stanzas earlier.[3] It is true that in the extant manuscript Fernán González is said at the outset to be the poem's subject ('del conde de Castiella quiero fer una prosa', 1d), but it is easy to understand why a prosified quatrain at the beginning of the *Sumario de crónicas hasta el año 1368*, which is very similar to stanza 1 of the *Poema de Fernán González* but concludes 'de los reyes e enperadores quiero fablar una breve cosa',[4] should be taken by Lacarra (p. 14n) as a possible reading from a lost manuscript of the *Poema*. The poet's apparent uncertainty about the subject matter of his poem is, however, resolved when we realize that he has a figural vision of Spanish history: not only does the early history of Spain have a clear figural relationship to that of Israel in the Old Testament, while significant New Testament parallels are to be found in the poet's treatment of Fernán González, but the Count is presented as the culmination of Castile's history just as that of Israel culminates in Jesus as Messiah.[5]

The resolution of these two immediate and obvious hindrances to the reading of the poem leads, unfortunately, to two further and more intractable ones. If, as all modern scholars agree, Fernán González's career as hero of the *Poema* reaches a triumphant climax in the attainment of Castilian independence from León, a large section (stanzas 14-121) loses most of its point, since the story of the Visigothic kingdom, its overthrow by the Moors, and Pelayo's initiation of the Reconquest is – while clearly relevant to Fernán González's battles with the Moors – largely irrelevant to his outwitting of the King of León. The shift of emphasis from Moors to Leonese as the main threat to Castile is as disconcerting as the shift from Spanish history to an individual hero had seemed to be.[6] And a figural reading of the *Poema*, necessary to restore coherence to what had seemed a work with double focus, seems to clash with the frequent references to Fortune's wheel. These assume a cyclical, rather than a linear and providential, view of history; in C.A. Patrides's terms, the references to Fortune's wheel depict history as a phoenix, while a figural reading depicts it as a ladder.[7]

I shall return to these problems at the end of this article, since I believe that the only hope of resolving them lies in an analysis of the ways in which the poet uses the Bible. Any work by a medieval Christian would, of course, presuppose the Christian view of history and an awareness of the Bible, but these platitudes become useful critical knowledge only when there is active reference to that view and clear allusion to the Bible within the work. In the *Poema de Fernán González*, unlike, say, the *Siete infantes de Lara*, the Bible and Christian historiography are consistently active as subtexts.

The *Poema* opens with an invocation which refers explicitly to the Creation and the Incarnation: 'En el nonbre del Padre que fizo toda cosa, / del que quiso nascer de la Virgen preciosa' (1ab). A more extensive series of explicit references to passages of the Old and New Testaments is to be found in stanzas 105-12, the prayer of the Christians suffering at the hands of the Muslim invaders. Both invocation and narrative prayer are found in a number of other medieval works, both in Spanish and in other languages, and it is not my intention to suggest that their use makes the *Poema* a uniquely biblical composition.[8] They do, however, tend to show that less explicit allusions to the Bible elsewhere in the text should not be dismissed as mere coincidence. The same is true of the poet's use of characteristically biblical vocabulary, which has been extensively documented by Olegario García de la Fuente.[9]

Five studies published in the past thirty years have, directly or indirectly, shed light on the *Poema*'s use of the Bible, and it is to be hoped that a sixth study will soon appear. J.P. Keller's analysis of ternary structures overstates the case at times, but reveals beyond doubt the poet's consistent tendency to arrange his material in sets of three.[10] It is not easy to estimate how much of this is due to folklore patterns (quite possibly inherited from the lost *Cantar de Fernán González*), but some of the ternary structures have a clearly religious base. Samuel G. Armistead's brief but influential article about line 80c opened up the question of the poet's view of history, and it poses questions that still challenge all interpreters of the *Poema*.[11] The problem of figural patterns in the *Poema*, implicit in Armistead's article, is dealt with explicitly by David William Foster.[12] Foster's book has its faults, but the section on the *Poema* makes some telling points and opens the way to further investigation. María Eugenia Lacarra's historical and ideological analysis, already referred to, shows how secular and religious interests may have helped to shape the *Poema*, and gives an illuminating account of the poet's Neogothic ideology which, as we shall see, is closely allied to his use of the Bible. Colbert I. Nepaulsingh's pages on the *Poema* in his book on medieval Spanish literature stress its apocalyptic aspect (entirely compatible with a political objective), and reveal a number of hitherto unsuspected biblical allusions.[13] Finally, David Hook's unpublished paper on pagan elements in the Spanish epic shows clearly that some aspects of the *Poema* may with equal plausibility be attributed either to deep-rooted pre-Christian traditions or to biblical influence.[14]

Hook's paper draws renewed attention to the fact that the *Poema*, like any literary work, may have two or more simultaneously functional subtexts: biblical and folkloric patterns may coexist.[15] The present article's restriction to the biblical subtext does not imply a suggestion that it is the only one.

Old Testament allusions predominate in the first part of the *Poema* (stanzas 1-172, dealing with the history of Castile and before that of all Hispania), whereas allusions to the New Testament are more frequent once Fernán González has become the centre of interest, though we must not exaggerate the extent of the change.[16] There is a steadier, more consistent pattern in the first part, no doubt because it is easier for the poet to portray the Spaniards, and then specifically the Castilians, as God's chosen people than to present the military and political struggles of a secular ruler as being, in any consistent way, either an *imitatio Christi* or the antitype that the Old Testament types had imperfectly prefigured.[17]

The poet's prologue sets out a pattern of fall and restoration, of sorrow that gradually becomes joy in a triumphant climax to history's progress:

Contar vos he primero *en* cómmo la [tierra] perdieron
nuestros antecessores, en quál coyta visquieron:
commo omnes deserrados fuydos andodieron;
essa rabia llevaron que *luego* non morieron.

Muchas coytas passaron nuestros antecessores,
muchos malos espantos, muchos malos sabores,
sufrién frío e fanbre e muchos amargores;

estos vicios¹⁸ d'agora estonz heran dolores.

Entanto deste tienpo yr vos he *yo* contando
cómmo fueron la tierra perdiendo e cobrando;
[*line missing*]
fasta que todos fueron al conde don Fernando. (3-5)

The four essential elements in this passage are: (a) an ancestral calamity, as a result of
which (b) the land is lost and (c) cold, hunger and other sufferings afflict the people
until (d) a gradual recovery begins, culminating in the narrative present. The most
obvious analogue is the Biblical narrative of the Fall, whose effects are to be undone
only by the coming of the Messiah. The disobedience of Adam and Eve ('nuestros
antecessores' to Jews and Christians alike) leads to expulsion from Eden: 'Et emisit eum
Dominus Deus de paradiso voluptatis, ut operaretur terram de qua sumptus est.
Eiecitque Adam' (Genesis 3.23-24).¹⁹ God warns the guilty couple that hardship and
misery await them and their descendants:

> Mulieri quoque dixit: Multiplicabo aerumnas tuas, et conceptus tuos: in dolore
> paries filios, et sub viri potestate eris, et ipse dominabitur tui. Adae vero dixit.
> Quia audisti vocem uxoris tuae, et comedisti de ligno, ex quo praeceperam tibi ne
> comederes, maledicta terra in opere tuo: in laboribus comedes ex ea cunctis
> diebus vitae tuae. Spinas et tribulos germinabit tibi, et comedes herbam terrae.
> In sudore vultus tui vesceris pane, donec revertaris in terram de qua sumptus es
> [. . .] (3.16-19)

The transformation of this inherited burden of sorrow into joy becomes a recurrent
theme of the Old Testament once the historical narrative and the long passages of law-
giving are past: 'quia in ipsis diebus se ulti sunt Iudaei de inimicis suis, et luctus atque
tristitia in hilaritatem gaudiumque conversa sunt' (Esther 9.22). What may be seen in
such passages as a foreshadowing becomes explicit prophecy of a final and irreversible
transformation in 'Gaudium et laetitiam obtinebunt, et fugiet dolor et gemitus' (Isaiah
35.10); 'Converte, Domine, captivitatem nostram, sicut torrens in austro. Qui seminant
in lacrymis, in exsultatione metent' (Psalm 125.4-5): and 'Audite verbum Domini, _
gentes, et annuntiate in insulis quae procul sunt, et dicite: Qui dispersit Israel
congregabit eum, et custodiet eum sicut pastor gregem suum [. . .] Tunc laetabitur virgo
in choro, iuvenes et senes simul; et convertam luctum eorum in gaudium, et consolabor
eos, et laetificabo a dolore suo' (Jeremiah 31.10 & 13). These prophecies are echoed in
Jesus's promise: 'Et vos igitur nunc quidem tristitiam habetis, iterum autem videbo vos,
et gaudebit cor vestrum, et gaudium vestrum nemo tollet a vobis' (John 16.22). There is

of course no verbal borrowing from the Bible in the passage of the *Poema de Fernán González* that I have quoted, but the biblical pattern is unmistakable. It might be objected that this is no more than the pattern of exile and return found in many epics that are unconnected with the Judeo-Christian tradition, but in those epics the hero who returns is generally the one who was himself exiled; the emphasis on exile and hardship as the result of an ancestral calamity, together with the explicit statement of Christian purpose in stanzas 1-2, put the Biblical filiation of stanzas 3-5 beyond doubt.

The calamity is then located in the reign of Rodrigo:

> Cómmo es muy luenga desde el tienpo antigo,
> cómmo se dio la tierra al buen rey don Rodrigo
> cómmol' ovo ganar el mortal enemigo;
> de grand honor que hera tornol' pobre mendigo. (6)

The words 'el mortal enemigo' are to some extent ambiguous, but the ambiguity is one that enriches the meaning rather than weakening it by uncertainty. Their primary meaning is, as some editors note, 'the Devil', but they may also refer to the Muslim invaders, who are associated with the Devil at a number of points in the poem.[20] Also, the mention of the Devil so soon after the reference to the disaster that befell 'nuestros antecessores' tightens the connection with the third chapter of Genesis. The connection becomes still closer by veiled allusions to the story of Rodrigo's seduction of Count Julian's daughter. The main emphasis in the poet's account of the causes of the fall of Visigothic Spain is on dynastic dissension (this was of course the reason that historically led one faction to invite the Muslim army to cross the Straits),[21] which is used by the Devil to inspire treason:

> Fyjos de Vautyçanos [Wittiza] non devyeran nascer,
> que essos començaron trayción a fazer,
> volvyó lo el diablo e metyó ý su poder,
> esto fue el escomienço de Espanna perder. (41)

Nevertheless, the legend of la Cava was by this time very widely known, and despite the poet's praise for Rodrigo's qualities in stanza 35 there is a reference which must be (as Victorio says, p. 50) to the King's lust:

> Fynó se Vautyçanos, reynó rey don Rodrigo;
> avýan en él los moros un mortal enemigo,
> era de los cristianos sonbra e grrand abrygo,
> por culpa *en* que era non le era Dyos amigo.

Seven stanzas later there is a reference to the story of Count Julian as one that is well
known ('El conde don Yllán, byen avedes oýdo / cómmo ovo por las paryas a
Marruecos trocido', 42ab), and even though the seduction of his daughter is not
mentioned his anger ('Fyzo *le* la grrand yra trayción volver', 43a) is sufficient reminder.
These allusions to Rodrigo's sin thus reinforce the biblical pattern of the poet's account
of the fall of Spain. A similar pattern, it may be worth recalling, is found at the
beginning of the *Libro del cavallero Zifar*: the sin of Zifar's ancestor Tared led to the
loss of the kingdom and to a curse on his descendants.[22]

Julian deceives Rodrigo into disarming Spain, quoting Scriptural precedent:

¿Las armas, qué las quieres? pues non as pelear.

Manda por *tod* el reyno las armas desatar,
dellas fagan açadas pora vyn*n*as labrar,
e dellas fagan rejas pora panes senbrar,
cavallos e rocines todos fagan arar.

Todos labren por pan, peones e caveros,
syenbren cuestas e valles e todos los oteros,
enrryquesquan tus reynos de pan e de dineros,
ca non as contra quien poner otros fronteros. (50d-52)

This is an obvious quotation of one or both of two texts:

Et iudicabit gentes, et arguet populos multos; et conflabunt gladios suos in
vomeres, et lanceas suas in falces. Non levabit gens contra gentem gladium, nec
exercebuntur ultra ad praelium. (Isaiah 2.4)

Et iudicabit inter populos multos, et corripiet gentes fortes usque in longinquum;
et concident gladios suos in vomeres, et hastas suas in ligones: non sumet gens
adversus gentem gladium, et non discent ultra belligerare. Et sedebit vir subtus
vitem suam et subtus ficum suam, et non erit qui deterreat [. . .] (Micah 4.3-4)

Micah is, of course, drawing directly on Isaiah, but adds the vision of the people
enjoying the fruits of peace. This addition (which underlies, for example, part of
Cranmer's prophecy at the end of *King Henry VIII*) may be recalled by stanza 52 of the
Poema de Fernán González. Julian's treacherous exhortation becomes, in amplified
form, the credulous Rodrigo's order to his subjects (62-67), and there is an ironic
reversal by which anyone who, loyal to Spain's interests, refuses to disarm is threatened

with a traitor's death (66d, 67d).[23] How can the following of Scripture be so disastrous? The explanation is simple: Isaiah, and Micah after him, present the beating of swords into ploughshares as part of an apocalyptic vision, where earthly history comes to an end: 'Et erit in novissimis diebus praeparatus mons domus Domini in vertice montium, et elevabitur super colles' (Isaiah 2.2; cf. Micah 4.1). Julian's treachery is thus, in the *Poema*'s account, compounded by blasphemy: he brings about prematurely something that was reserved for the Apocalypse. While the Spaniards disarm, the Muslims prepare for war; it may be worth noting that another apocalyptic vision, that of Joel, includes an ironic reversal of the Isaiah passage:

> Clamate hoc in gentibus, sanctificate bellum, suscitate robustos; accedant, ascendant omnes viri bellatores. Concidite aratra vestra in gladios, et ligones vestros in lanceas. Infirmus dicat: Quia fortis ego sum. (Joel 3.9-10)

The Devil is shown in the Gospels (e.g. Matthew 4.6) quoting Scripture for his purpose; here his work is done by Julian, whose complicity with him is stressed: 'vyo lo el diablo que tyende tales redes' (68b), and 'el diablo antyguo en esto travajava' (70c).[24]

The fall of Visigothic Spain to the Muslims, with the attendant and vividly-described sufferings of the Spaniards (89-97), is presented as the result not only of Count Julian's treachery and the Devil's machinations but of the sins of the Visigothic rulers, as we have already seen. The Spaniards, in the depths of their misery, recognize this:

> Nós a Dios falesciendo á nos él falescido,
> lo que otros ganaron emos todo perdido,
> partyendo nós de Dios á se de nós partydo,
> *tod* el byen de los godos por end es confondido. (100)

This, the familiar Augustinian concept of the *flagellum Dei* – the heathen used by God to chastise an erring Christian people –, is also the familiar pattern of the book of Judges and other parts of the Old Testament, in which Israel turns away from God and is punished by being abandoned to her enemies. A typical passage – which I cite merely as one example among many, and not because I believe it to be a direct source of the *Poema* – reads: 'Fecerunt autem filii Israel malum in conspectu Domini: qui tradidit illos in manu Madian septem annis' (Judges 6.1). There are some similarities between the Muslim conquest of Spain and the Babylonian conquest of Jerusalem (II Kings 25), and, although the two narratives are not close enough to establish a direct link, Foster's reference to Spain's Babylonian captivity (p. 50) is not fanciful. The prayer of the distraught Spaniards (105-13), mentioned above, is concerned in all but its

last stanza with God's miracles of deliverance in the Old and New Testaments. Three
of the stanzas deal wholly or in part with miracles performed during the Babylonian
captivity and narrated in the book of Daniel: 'quitest a los jodíos del rey de Babilón'
(107c), 'Libreste a Susanna de los falsos varones, / saquest a Daniel de entre dos
leones' (108ab), and:

> Librest a los tres ninnos de los fuegos ardientes,
> quando ý los metieron los pueblos descreyentes,
> cantaron en el forno cantos muy convenientes,
> otra vez los libreste de bocas de serpyentes. (109)

Prayers recalling a series of miracles are, as is well known, common in medieval
literature, but the *Poema de Fernán González* gives greater prominence to miracles of
deliverance during the Babylonian captivity than does the average of the thirteenth- and
fourteenth-century Spanish poems from which I have taken samples. Moreover, the
Muslims are called 'la gent descreýda' (102d) and 'los pueblos descreýdos' (117c), while
the Babylonians are 'los pueblos descreyentes' (109b). We must, as A.C. Spearing
reminds us, be careful not to assume that every repetition in medieval poetry is
designed to establish a parallel;[25] and we must bear in mind that the lecherous
Archpriest is, much later in the poem, called 'el falso descreýdo' (647c); yet the three
references in 102-17 are so close together, and arranged so symmetrically, that it seems
highly likely that the poet intends to make a point.

The biblical pattern continues in the first phase of the Reconquest, which
immediately follows the description of the Spaniards' sufferings and their plea for
deliverance:

> oyó les Jesu Cristo a quien *seién* llamando.

> Dyxo les por el ángel que Pelayo buscassen,
> quel' alçassen por rey e que a él catassen,
> en manparar la tierra todos le ayudassen,
> ca él les daría ayuda por que la anparassen.

> Buscaron a Pelayo commo les fue mandado,
> fallaron lo en cueva fanbrryento e lazrado,
> besáronle las manos e dieron le el rreygnado,
> óvolo rescebyr pero non de su grrado. (114d-16)

This passage combines three narrative elements from the Old Testament. Time after time, when the apostate people of Israel repent their sins, God appoints a deliverer (for example, Judges 1.1-2, 2.16, 3.15), and on occasion the message is brought by an angel:

Venit autem angelus Domini, et sedit sub quercu, quae erat in Ephra, et pertinebat ad Ioas patrem familiae Ezri. Cumque Gedeon filius eius excuteret atque purgaret frumenta in torculari, ut fugeret Madian, apparuit ei angelus Domini et ait: Dominus tecum, virorum fortissime. Dixitque ei Gedeon: Obsecro, mi domine, si Dominus nobiscum est, cur apprehenderunt nos haec omnia? ubi sunt mirabilia eius, quae narraverunt patres nostri, atque dixerunt: De Aegypto eduxit nos Dominus? Nunc autem dereliquit nos Dominus et tradidit in manu Madian. Respexitque ad eum Dominus, et ait: Vade in hac fortitudine tua, et liberabis Israel de manu Madian: scito quod miserim te. (Judges 6.11-14)

Secondly, the deliverer is frequently of humble birth (this is also a folk-motif: see Deyermond and Chaplin, p. 43), and is pursuing a rustic occupation when the call comes, as in the passage just quoted or the story of David (I Samuel 16.19). Neither Pelayo nor Fernán González is of humble birth, but circumstances make them both appear to be: Pelayo is 'fanbrryento e lazrado', and Fernán González is kidnapped by a poor charcoal-burner[26] and brought up as his son (176). Thirdly, Pelayo taking refuge from the Muslims in a cave recalls the episode of David and his followers in the cave Adullam (I Samuel 22.1-2). (It should be noted in passing that the *Poema*'s other Pelayo, the monk who prophesies Fernán González's victories, has his hermitage near a cave (226) and is named six stanzas later.) Thus stanzas 114-16 and their echoes later in the poem bind King Pelayo, the monk Pelayo, and Count Fernán González together in a network of associations, a kind of secular prefiguration. Fernán González is shown as Pelayo's rightful heir both through narrative patterning and by divine approval mediated through the prophecies of the second Pelayo.[27]

Yet much of Old Testament history is concerned with a great ruler who is briefly succeeded by an unworthy son (for instance, Gideon succeeded by Abimelech, Judges 9), and this pattern too is found in the *Poema*:

Fynó el rey Pelayo, don Cristo lo perdón,
reygnó su fijo Vavilla que fue muy mal varón,
quiso Dios que mandaſſe poco *en* la región,
ca vysquió rey un anno e más poca sazón. (122)

Murió est rey Alfonso, sennor aventurado
– sea en paraýso tan buen rey heredado –,

55

reygnó su fijo Fabya que fuc malo provado,
quiso Dios que vysquiesse poco en el reygnado. (125)²⁸

Despite such temporary setbacks – swiftly remedied by God's providence working itself
out in history – the general tendency is upwards, as the kingdom of Asturias-León
drives the Muslims back and Castile is formed in three stages:

D'un alcaldía pobre fyzieron la condado,
tornaron la después cabeça de reynado. (172cd)

The poet's location of the by now traditional Praise of Spain is very interesting.²⁹ It
occupies stanzas 144-57, being inserted into the historical narrative of the late eighth
century. This is unusual: the usual place for such a passage is in a prologue or in
combination with a lament for the fall of Visigothic Spain to the Muslim invaders.
There is, however, an anticipation of the passage immediately after the poet narrates
Rodrigo's accession to the Visigothic throne:

Era estonce Espanna toda d'una creencia,
al Fyjo de la Virgen fazían obediencia,
pesava al diablo con tanta reverencia,
non avýa entre ellos envydia nin *entencia*.

Estavan las yglesias todas byen ordenadas,
de olio e de cera estavan abastadas,³⁰
los diezmos e premiencias leal *miente eran dadas*,
e eran todas las gentes en la fe arraygadas.

Vesquían de su lazeryo todos los labradores,
las grrandes potestades non eran rovadores,
guardavan byen sus pueblos com leales sennores,
vesquían de sus derechos los grrandes e menores.

Estava la fazienda toda en ygual estado [. . .] (37-40a)

José Antonio Maravall comments on this account of Visigothic Spain as a political and
religious golden age.³¹ Its separation from the Praise of Spain in stanzas 144-57 is at
first sight surprising, but, while it may be a simple oversight by the poet, I believe that it
is a part of his figural plan. The combination of social harmony, piety and natural
abundance (the ecclesiastical context of 38b does not invalidate the importance

attached to these products of the Spanish countryside) recalls the Garden of Eden. It is
true that 'Vesquían de su lazeryo' (39a) suggests imperfection more proper to post-
lapsarian humanity, but the overall impression given by this passage is of a lost paradise,
especially when it is followed by:

avýa con este byen grran*d* pesar el pecado,
revolvyó atal cosa el mal aventurado,
que el gozo que avýa en llanto fue tornado. (40bcd)

Then comes the reference to the 'fyjos de Vautyçanos' and to Count Julian (41-42; the
relevance of their treason to the theme of fall and restoration is discussed above,
pp. 51-53). What, then, of the later Praise of Spain? This gives most emphasis to
natural abundance (145-51), but it goes on to mention piety and God's special favour
(152-54) and social harmony (155). The implication is that Pelayo and his successors
have recreated the earthly paradise that had been lost by ancestral sin, and that Old
Castile is both the foundation ('el cimiento') and the triumphant culmination of this
process (156-57). Far from being a defect in the *Poema*'s structure, therefore, the
unusual division of the Praise of Spain reinforces the biblical pattern of loss and
restoration.

References to that pattern are not confined to the first part of the *Poema*. Soon
after the introduction of Fernán González, they occur in the hero's speech:

Quando entendió que era de Castyella sennor,
alçó a Dios las manos, rogó al Cryador:
'Sennor, tú me ayuda – que só muy pecador –,
que yo saque a Castyella del antygo dolor.' (184)

'Antygo dolor', taken in isolation, is not an obvious allusion to a disaster typologically
linked to the Fall and the expulsion from Eden, but of course the words do not occur in
isolation. Given the way in which the overthrow of Visigothic Spain was treated in the
first part of the *Poema*, these two words are enough to trigger recollections of an
ancestral disaster and its Biblical counterpart. Speaking to his men some time later,
Fernán González refers explicitly to the Devil's role in that disaster, and rewrites history
so that Old Castile, not Pelayo in the Asturian mountains, becomes the saving remnant:

Assy guisó la cosa el mortal enemigo,
quando perdió la tierra el buen rey don Rodrygo,
non quedó en Espanna quien valiesse un fygo,
sy non Castyella Vieja un logar muy antygo. (216)

57

The great majority of the biblical elements in the second, or Fernán González, part of the *Poema* are concerned not with the pattern established in the first part but with resemblances – some vague and questionable, others clear – between the hero and the earthly life of Jesus. These resemblances belong to an extension of Pauline and patristic typology which has, as far as I know, no accepted technical term, but which I have elsewhere called postfiguration: events in the life of an individual Christian, or in the history of the Church or of a Christian nation, are presented as imperfect reflections of events in the life of Christ.[32] An early example in the poet's account of Fernán González's deeds comes in the monk Pelayo's prophecy: 'Antes de tercer día serás en grrand cuydado' (239a). This is part of the pervasive threefold structuring analysed, and to some extent exaggerated, by J.P. Keller, and by itself it would not establish a postfigurative link. A more striking case is in the description of the battle of La Era Degollada, against the Navarrese:

> El conde fue del golpe fyera miente llagado,
> ca tenía grrand lançada por el diestrro costado;
> llamava 'Castellanos', mas ningún *fue ý viado*,
> de todos sus caveros era desanparado. (317)

A lance-wound in the side, temporary abandonment by dismayed followers, and unexpected victory evoke the last part of the Passion followed by the Resurrection.[33] The resemblance is clear, but is it deliberate and relevant? The likelihood is strengthened when the hero tells his followers of his vision of the dead monk Pelayo before the battle of Hacinas against the Muslims:

> Esta es la razón que la voz me dezía:
> 'Conde Fernán González, lieva dend, ve tu výa,
> tod el poder de Áfryca e de Andaluzía,
> vencer lo has en canpo deste tercero día.' (426)

and warns them that anyone who surrenders to the Muslims 'con Judas en infyerno yaga quando moriere' (444d; cf. 445d; see Foster, p. 59, and Valladares Reguero, p. 131).[34] Fernán González tells his men that the devil who has taken the form of a fiery serpent has no power to harm them because Christ broke his power in the Harrowing of Hell (477). When the hero is tricked by the Navarrese Queen Teresa of León into going to Navarre under safe conduct, the King of Navarre promises to bring only five men with him, but:

el rey y los navarros *aqu*el pleyto falsaron,
en lugar de los seys más de treynta llevaron. (584cd)

When in the next stanza Fernán González exclaims 'yo mesmo só vendido' (585d), the
association of this act of treachery with Judas and the thirty pieces of silver is likely to
have suggested itself to at least some members of the poet's contemporary public. All
of this, I recognize, is speculative and tenuous, but what follows is unmistakable.

King García of Navarre besieges the church in which Fernán González has taken
refuge, and, in violation of sanctuary ('non la quiso dexar maguer era sagrada', 590b), he
presents a choice between prison and death (591cd). The Count surrenders under safe
conduct, and God's displeasure is shown by two supernatural happenings:[35]

Oyeron una voz commo voz de pavón,
partió se el altar de somo a fondón. (592cd)

The 'voz de pavón' (which echoes Fernán González's great cry when he knows he has
been betrayed: 'El conde dio grrand voz com sy fues a tronido', 586a) has been shown
by Néstor A. Lugones to derive from *Libro de Alexandre* 1727; Lugones draws attention
to the connotations that both works inherit from the bestiary's account of the peacock.[36]
In the context in which the *Poema de Fernán González* places it, however, the loud cry
takes on different and more emotive connotations:

Et circa horam nonam clamavit Iesus voce magna, dicens: Eli, Eli, lamma
sabacthani? hoc est: Deus meus, Deus meus, ut quid dereliquisti me? [. . .] Iesus
autem iterum clamans voce magna, emisit spiritum. Et ecce velum templi scissum
est in duas partes a summo usque deorsum: et terra mota est, et petrae scissae
sunt [. . .] (Matthew 27.46 & 50-5l; cf. Mark 15.34 & 37-38)

There can be no question here of accidental resemblance, or even of unconscious
reminiscence: the same phenomena, in the same order, in the Gospels and the *Poema*,
and the verbal detail ('de somo a fondón', 'a summo usque deorsum') mark this as a
deliberate allusion.[37] If any doubt remained, it would be dispelled by the threefold
echo of Christ's words from the Cross:

dixo: 'Sen*n*or del mundo ¿por qué me as fallido?' (594d)

'e por esto me tengo de ti desanparado' (595d)

'nunca fiz por que fue*s*se de ty desanparado' (596b)

This is not the first time that Fernán González has reproached God for abandoning him: a similar, though less emphatic, reproach was uttered in 545-46, and Foster describes that as 'a frank accommodation of Christ's lament on the cross' (p. 55); in that case, the resemblance may be unintended, but in 594-96 it must be deliberate.[38] We have, then, a series of clear allusions to the Passion: betrayal for money (metaphorical in the *Poema* – it is significant that the poet chooses this metaphor), two loud cries, the altar split from top to bottom, the bitter complaint of abandonment by God. The sequence is not exactly the same in Gospels and *Poema*: notably, the first cry is separated in the *Poema* from the words of complaint; but this is far outweighed by the close verbal similarities. In the light of these allusions, more distant resemblances may seem to form part of a pattern: 'El sol era ya baxo' (591a) may be a distant reminiscence of 'tenebrae factae sunt super universam terram' (Matthew 27.45; cf. Mark 15.33 and Luke 23.44-45); the distress of the Castilians at hearing the news and their ritual gestures of mourning ('rascadas muchas fruentes, rota mucha mexylla', 600c) recalls 'Et omnis turba eorum, qui simul aderant ad spectaculum istud, et videbant quae fiebant, percutientes pectora sua revertebantur' (Luke 23.48); and the close imprisonment in Castroviejo:

> Tornemos en el conde dol' avemos dexado,
> era en Castro Vyejo en *la* cárcel echado,
> de gentes de Navarra era byen aguardado,
> nunca fue omne *nado* en presyón más coytado (605)

bears more than a passing resemblance to: 'Illi autem abeuntes, munierunt sepulchrum, signantes lapidem, cum custodibus' (Matthew 27.66).[39] Taken in isolation, none of these three parallels could reasonably be presented as evidence for a biblical subtext to this part of the *Poema*. Even the three together do not advance the argument very far. But in the context of the much closer parallels discussed above, these more distant ones take on a very different aspect. They are not necessarily conscious parallels, and the third – the reminiscence of the guarding of the Sepulchre in stanza 605 – may be a case of what Albert B. Lord has labelled 'thematic attraction'.[40] (It is true that Lord refers to 'the subconscious forces of attraction that are operative in oral tradition', but such a process is not confined to oral tradition.) It may be significant that when Princess Sancha frees the hero from prison (rather mysteriously: we are told only that 'luego sacó la duenna al conde don Fernando', 636b) and the couple reach Castile, a resurrection image is used to describe the joy of the Castilians at their recovery of their lost leader:

Todos e ella con ellos con grrand gozo lloravan,
tenién que eran muertos e que resucitavan,
al Rey de los cielos bendezían e laudavan,
el llanto que fazían en grrand gozo tornavan. (680)

One other passage requires comment. After Fernán González's imprisonment the Castilians do not know what to do without a leader, until Nuño Laínez advises them in what is described as a mysterious speech:

Los unos queryén uno, los otrros queryén ál,
commo omnes syn cabdiello avenién se muy mal;
fabló Nunno Laýnez de seso natural,
buen cavallero d'armas e de sennor leal.

Començó su razón muy fuerte e oscura:
'Fagamos *nos* sennor de una pyedrra dura,
semejable al conde, dessa mesma fechura,
sobre aquella pyedra fagamos todos jura.

Assý commo al conde las manos le besemos,
pongamos la en carro, ante nós la llevemos,
por amor del buen conde por sennor la ternemos,
pleito e omenaje todos a ella faremos.' (654-56)

David Hook (see n. 14) draws attention to Mediterranean and Germanic pagan rituals that closely resemble this substitution of a roughly-carved stone image, carried on a waggon, for the missing leader. He is undoubtedly right to conclude that the resemblance is too close to be dismissed as mere coincidence, but I wonder whether this may be an example of pagan and biblical subtexts combining to form a puzzling episode of the *Poema*. The biblical element that I have in mind is not the Old Testament making of a graven image (see Valladares Reguero, pp. 134-35), since there is no suggestion that the Castilians' action provokes divine wrath – on the contrary, their predicament is, as we have seen, joyfully resolved by Fernán González's return with Sancha. The operative parallel is from the New Testament:

Et ego dico tibi, quia tu es Petrus, et super hanc petram aedificabo ecclesiam meam, et portae inferi non praevalebunt adversus eam. Et tibi dabo claves regni caelorum. (Matthew 16.18-19)

Jesus says that He will leave as His representative on earth a strong stone ('Sy el conde es fuerte, fuerte sennor llevamos', says Nuño Laínez, 658a).[41]

I shall not attempt to trace biblical elements in the part of the *Poema* that is preserved in the *Estoria de España*'s prosification, because of the uncertainties involved in such a procedure, and also because the biblical dependence of the *Poema*, from the beginning of its historical introduction to near the end of the extant verse text, has already been sufficiently demonstrated.[42] The nature of that dependence changes, as we have seen: the predominantly Old Testament subtext of the historical introduction establishes the Spaniards, and then specifically the Castilians, as the antitype of the Israelites: a people chosen by God to fulfil His purpose, and carrying out that mission despite disastrous lapses, whereas the largely New Testament subtext of the greater part of the *Poema* cannot without impiety show Fernán González as another Christ. The chief purpose of the New Testament allusions is to fix in the mind of the reader or hearer the impression that those who betray or oppress Fernán González and Castile are to be associated with the betrayers and persecutors of Christ.

I must now return to the two problems left unresolved at the beginning of this article: the shift of emphasis from Moors to Leonese, and the incompatibility of a figural view of history with the frequent references to Fortune's wheel.

Lacarra argues (pp. 13-14) that the lost part of the *Poema* included a further invasion of Castile by the Moors, but even if her view is correct it does not go very far towards resolving the first difficulty, since only a final and climactic battle against the Moors would satisfactorily link the end of the *Poema* to its beginning, and there is no suggestion that the *Poema* ended in this way. A more promising approach is to see the change from military struggle against Moors and Navarrese to political struggle against León in the light of Biblical history. Just as the narrowing focus from Hispania to Castile and then to Fernán González as the triumphant culmination of Spanish history reflects the development of Biblical history from all mankind to Israel and then to the single figure of the Messiah, so the change from a people's battles against the enemy to the betrayal of an individual and his imprisonment (first in Navarre and then in León), leading to his liberation and the triumphant establishment of a new political order, reflects the Biblical pattern. Moors, Navarrese and Leonese share their hostility to Castile and to Fernán González personally, his struggles against these three adversaries are interwoven in the narrative, and the final political defeat of León sets the seal on the military defeats of the Moors and Navarrese. Lacarra shows that the poet condemns the Moors and the Navarrese with a vigour that is not directed against León, and she argues that this reflects the Alfonsine political ideology of the 1270s (pp. 25-30). However, the loss of the last part of the *Poema* impedes a definitive judgment of the poet's attitude to León, and against the anti-Navarrese feeling emphasized by Lacarra we must set the fact that Princess Sancha, bride and rescuer of the hero, is Navarrese.

The case for seeing the three antagonists of Castile and of Fernán González as in some sense one is strengthened by the links that the poet establishes between them. Queen Teresa of León does not merely plan Fernán González's capture in Navarre; she is herself Navarrese. And the hero's envoy to King Sancho of Navarre accuses him of collaboration with the heathen and of enmity to Christendom:

Por fer mal a Castyella e destruyr castellanos,
feziste te amigo de los pueblos paganos,
feziste guerra mala a los pueblos cristianos,
porque non querién *ellos* meter se en las tus manos. (288)

As Claude Allaigre points out, the accusation is made more explicit in the *Estoria de España*, when the King (here García, not Sancho) is said to assemble 'muy grandes huestes de los suyos et de agenos, gascones et moros'.[43] One other factor helps to link the beginning and end of the poem: we have seen (p. 56, above) that the last stanza of the historical introduction describes Castile's growth from 'alcaldía pobre' to 'condado' and then, looking to the future, 'cabeça de reynado' (172cd). The kingdom of which Castile is to be the head – already was the head, when the poem was composed in the second half of the thirteenth century – is the most important in the Peninsula, with claims to hegemony. Thus Fernán González's political defeat of León is a major step towards the restoration of the paradisal Hispania overthrown by the Moors because of the sins of its rulers and people. The Biblical pattern thus links not only the history of Castile with the deeds of Fernán González, but also the Moors of the eighth century with the Leonese king who tries to frustrate Fernán González's divinely-ordained mission.

As to the second difficulty, the references to Fortune's wheel are insistent:

era de mala guisa la rueda trastornada,
la cautyva d'Espanna era mal quebrantada. (74cd)

Sennor, ya tienpo era, sy fuesse tu mesura,
que mudasses la rueda que anda a la ventura [. . .] (179ab)

Contesce esso mismo con la gent renegada,
heredan nuestra tierra e tienen la forçada;
mas mudar s'á la rueda que era trastornada,
serán ellos vencidos, la fe de Cristo onrrada.

Non es dicho fortuna ser syenpre en un estado,

uno ser syenpre ryco e otrio ser menguado;
camia estas dos cosas la fortuna pryado,
al pobre faze ryco e al ryco menguado. (438-39)

There is a general difficulty for a Christian writer in using the image of Fortune's wheel – whether as random operation or as inevitability – for anything more than the pattern of an individual's physical life, or, by analogy, the rise and fall of an empire. Once the question of merit, of sin and punishment, is allowed to enter the picture, the image breaks down, as Juan de Mena soon discovered. Yet, as Howard R. Patch's study amply demonstrates, the temptation to use the image is very strong.[44] Does its use by the *Fernán González* poet clash irretrievably with his figural view of history? At first sight it would appear so. It is not merely that his references to the wheel imply a cyclical concept of history. Such a concept, as Armistead shows, explains the otherwise baffling mention of 'los duennos primeros' (80c) – a previous Moorish conquest. And that mention does not stand alone: 'iMal grrado a los moros que la solían tener!' (59d) says the same thing, and when we are told that Almanzor 'coydó a Espanna syn falla conqueryr' (388b) it seems that the wheel is to turn again. Yet this time things will be different, for Fernán González's Castile, unlike Rodrigo's Hispania, stands firm against the Moorish onslaught. The hero's reference to the wheel in stanzas 438-39, already quoted, occurs in a long speech to his men before the battle of Hacinas. He goes on to tell them that the wheel must now, for good or ill, stop:

Amigos, lo que digo bien entender devedes,
sy fuéremos vencidos, ¿qué consejo prendredes?
Morredes commo malos, la tierra perderedes,
sy esta vez caedes non vos levantaredes. (442)

The cycle of fall and recovery is, as we have seen, fundamental to the historical books of the Old Testament, though it occurs within the context of the linear working-out of God's purpose for His people. With the Incarnation, that cycle ends. In Northrop Frye's words:

If we follow the narrative of the Bible as a sequence of events in human life, it becomes a series of ups and downs in which God's people periodically fall into bondage and are then rescued by a leader, while the great heathen empires rise and fall in the opposite rhythm. At a certain point this perspective goes into reverse, and what we see is something more like an epic or romantic hero descending to a lower world to rescue what is at the same time a single bride and a large host of men and women. In this perspective the *sequence* of captivities and redemptions disappears and is replaced by a unique act of descent and return.[45]

Fernán González will break out of the cyclical pattern, making Castile secure from the perils of transience. This was made clear by the poet at the outset:

Entanto deste tienpo yr vos he *yo* contando
cómmo fueron la tierra perdiendo e cobrando;
[*line missing*]
fasta que *todos* fueron al conde don Fernando. (5)

The figural view of history depends, of course, on the perception of partial repetitions, but in each case the repetition is at a higher level (or, in the case of postfiguration, at a lower one). As Patrides observes, the 'concern with types had the threefold purpose of confirming that historical events are non-recurring and irreversible, that they imply a design according to which the created order advances onward, and that they are meaningful only in so far as they are seen to relate to the advent of the Messiah' (p. 7). The *Poema de Fernán González* relates the sins and travails of Spain to those of Israel, and then shows how its hero, by courage, endurance, resourcefulness and divine favour, moves history to a new level. He is not a Christ figure, but as Christ is to sacred history, so Fernán González is to the secular history of Spain. The message fits the mood of the poet's times, whether he was writing at the end of Fernando III's triumphant reign or during Alfonso X's long struggle to attain his imperial ambition.[46]

Queen Mary and Westfield College, London

NOTES

1. *Poema de Fernán González*, edited by Zamora Vicente, Clásicos Castellanos, CXXVIII, 2nd edition (Madrid: Espasa-Calpe, 1954), p. 225; *Poema de Fernán González*, translated by Pérez Priego, Clásicos Modernizados Alhambra, VII (Madrid: Alhambra, 1986), pp. 16, 135; Lacarra, 'El significado histórico del *Poema de Fernán González*', *Studi Ispanici* (1979), 9-41, at 13-14.
2. This cannot be due to loss of folios from the extant manuscript. See *Historia del Conde Fernán González: A Facsimile and Paleographic Edition with Commentary and Concordance*, edited by John S. Geary, Spanish Series, XXXV (Madison: HSMS, 1987).

3. My quotations are from Zamora Vicente's edition, with the following regularizations: accents according to modern scholarly usage; initial *rr* transcribed as *r* ; *i* and *u* when vocalic, *j* and *v* when consonantal; punctuation altered when necessary. Italics represent Zamora Vicente's emendations (or those of earlier editors that he has adopted).

4. *Poema de Fernan Gonçalez*, edited by C. Carroll Marden (Baltimore: The Johns Hopkins Press; Madrid: M. Murillo, 1904), p. 163.

5. For a definition and authoritative account of figural (typological) patterns, see Erich Auerbach, 'Figura', translated by Ralph Manheim, in Auerbach, *Scenes from the Drama of European Literature: Six Essays* (New York: Meridian Books, 1959), pp. 9-76.

6. Lacarra's contention (pp. 22-25) that the poet avoids hostility to León does not diminish this difficulty.

7. *The Grand Design of God: The Literary Form of the Christian View of History* (London: Routledge & Kegan Paul, 1972), pp. 7, 9.

8. For the background to the narrative prayer, see Peter E. Russell, 'La oración de doña Jimena *(Poema de Mio Cid*, vv. 325-367)', in his *Temas de 'La Celestina' y otros estudios del 'Cid' al 'Quijote'*, Letras e Ideas, Maior, XIV (Barcelona: Ariel, 1978), pp. 113-58. While this article was in press I was able, thanks to the kindness of Professor Nicasio Salvador Miguel, to see Aurelio Valladares Reguero, *La Biblia en la épica medieval española* (Úbeda: the author, 1984), in which chap. 5 (pp. 127-35) deals with the *Poema de Fernán González*. I have inserted parenthetical references at the appropriate points.

9. 'Estudio del léxico bíblico del *Poema de Fernán González*', *Analecta Malacitana*, I (1978), 5-68. See also his 'Coincidencias entre *Alexandre* y *Fernán González* en temas bíblicos', in his *El latín bíblico y el español medieval hasta el 1.300*, II: *El libro de Alexandre*, Colección Centro de Estudios Gonzalo de Berceo, XI (Logroño: Instituto de Estudios Riojanos, 1986), pp. 133-36.

10. 'The Structure of the *Poema de Fernán González*', *HR*, XXV (1957), 235-46.

11. 'La perspectiva histórica del *Poema de Fernán González*', *Papeles de Son Armadans*, no. 21 (April 1961), 9-18.

12. *Christian Allegory in Early Hispanic Poetry*, Studies in Romance Languages, IV (Lexington: University Press of Kentucky, 1970), pp. 45-59.

13. *Towards a History of Literary Composition in Medieval Spain*, University of Toronto Romance Series, LIV (Toronto: University Press, 1986), pp. 84-90. Beverly West's promisingly-titled *Epic, Folk, and Christian Traditions in the 'Poema de Fernán González'* (Potomac, Maryland: Studia Humanitatis, 1983) – an abridgement of her University of North Carolina doctoral thesis '*Poema de Fernán González*: The Role of Tradition in the Growth of the Legend through Epic, Folklore and

Christianity' (1982) – is disappointing, largely because she appears unfamiliar with some of the basic bibliography of the subject and misunderstands key terms like 'martyred' and 'resurrected' (pp. 111-12).

14. 'Paganism in the Medieval Spanish Epic', paper read to the King's Epic Seminar, London, February 1987. I am grateful to Dr Hook for allowing me to consult the typescript of his paper.

15. For folkloric elements, see A.D. Deyermond and Margaret Chaplin, 'Folk-Motifs in the Medieval Spanish Epic', *PQ*, LI (1972), 36-53.

16. I use the word 'allusion' in a much narrower sense than Northrop Frye, whose fascinating book *The Great Code* begins with the alarming statement that 'Blake's line "O Earth, O Earth return" [. . .], though it contains only five words and only three different words, contains also about seven direct allusions to the Bible' (*The Great Code: The Bible and Literature* (London: Routledge & Kegan Paul, 1982), p. xii).

17. There is, of course, no such difficulty in the comparison of Fernán González with David (267cd) or Samson (414c): on such comparisons, which are found also in the *Poema de Almería* and other heroic verse in medieval Latin, see H. Salvador Martínez, *El 'Poema de Almería' y la épica románica* (Madrid: Gredos, 1975), pp. 210-22 and 227-29. On Castile as Israel, see Nepaulsingh, pp. 86-87.

18. *Vicios* has here its normal thirteenth-century meaning of 'pleasures', not 'vices'.

19. I quote from *Biblia sacra iuxta vulgatam Clementinam*, ed. Alberto Colunga & Laurencio Turrado, Biblioteca de Autores Cristianos, XIV (Madrid: Editorial Católica, 1977). The choice is to some extent arbitrary, since we do not know what text or texts of the Bible may have been available in San Pedro de Arlanza in addition to the Vulgate. The problem is common to all studies of the use of the Bible in medieval literature, as Peter Dronke shows in 'The Song of Songs and Medieval Love-Lyric', in *The Bible and Medieval Culture*, ed. W. Lourdaux & D. Verhelst, Mediaevalia Lovaniensia, Series I, Studia, VII (Louvain: University Press, 1979), pp. 236-62; repr. in his *The Medieval Poet and his World*, Storia e Letteratura, CLXIV (Rome: Edizioni di Storia e Letteratura, 1984), pp. 209-36, at pp. 209-10. The chief advantage of quoting the Vulgate is that it is in the language in which the Arlanza poet read the Bible; the disadvantage is that it may give a false impression of precision, and there is thus a good case for following Northrop Frye's example by quoting the Authorized Version (Frye gives his reasons, *The Great Code*, p. xiv).

20. *Poema de Fernán González*, edited & translated by Erminio Polidori (Roma: Giovanni Semerano, 1962); *Poema de Fernán González*, edited by Juan Victorio, Letras Hispánicas, CLI (Madrid: Cátedra, 1981). For the secondary meaning, cf. stanza 35b, quoted below.

21. Louis Chalon, 'L'Effondrement de l'Espagne visigothique et l'invasion musulmane selon le *Poema de Fernán González'*, *AEM*, IX (1974-79), 353-63, compares the *Poema*'s account with the historical reality and with historiographic tradition. The comparison is also made in the last section of the article by Pedro Valdecantos García, 'Los godos en el *Poema de Fernán González'*, *Revista de la Universidad de Madrid*, VI (1957), 499-530, whom Chalon does not cite. Chalon's article is much superior to that of his predecessor, who, although he offers a good deal of useful information, reflects too obviously the political attitudes of official Spain in the 1950s (e.g., 'Con su vida colectiva, intrigante en revuelo perpetuo, [los judíos] dan al pleito dinástico un cariz esencialmente trágico. Es el problema hebreo el mayor peligro que tenía planteado el estado visigodo; problema muy antiguo', p. 519).

22. James F. Burke, *History and Vision: the figural structure of the 'Libro del Cavallero Zifar'* (London: Tamesis, 1972), pp. 57-58.

23. Nepaulsingh (p. 86) suggests another Biblical source for part of the amplification: 'The melting of the Gothic weapons in a huge fire (st. 63) probably echoes Ezekiel 39:9 ("et succendent et comburent arma").'

24. I discuss the equivalent passage of the *Estoria de España* in 'The Death and Rebirth of Visigothic Spain in the *Estoria de España'*, *RCEH*, IX (1984-85), 345-67, at p. 358.

25. *Criticism and Medieval Poetry* (London: Edward Arnold, 1964), p. 23.

26. West (p. 37) translates *carbonero* as 'coal-miner', but I remain convinced that 'charcoal-burner' is the correct rendering.

27. See Claude Édouard Allaigre, 'Des Rapports de l'histoire, de la légende et de la chanson de geste: le saint moine-ermite du *Poema de Fernán González'*, in *Les Genres littéraires et leurs rapports avec l'histoire: Actes du XIVe Congrès de la Société des Hispanistes Français* (Nice: SHF, 1978), pp. 17-31; the discussion that followed this paper is recorded, pp. 33-48.

28. Graciela Brevedán, 'Estudio estructural del *Poema de Fernán González'* (unpublished doctoral thesis, University of Kentucky, 1976), pp. 30-31, compares this pattern with an example in Visigothic Spain: Wamba's successor (*Poema*, st. 33).

29. On the development of this topos, see Stephen Reckert, *The Matter of Britain and the Praise of Spain: the history of a panegyric* (Cardiff: University of Wales Press, 1967). See also Josefina Nagore de Zand, 'La alabanza de España en el *Poema de Fernán González* y en las crónicas latino-medievales', *Incipit*, VII (1987 [1988]), 35-67.

30. The abundance of oil and wax is again mentioned – in its traditional place and without ecclesiastical connections – in st. 147.

31. *El concepto de España en la Edad Media*, 2nd edition (Madrid: Instituto de Estudios Políticos, 1964), p. 323. Lacarra suggests political reasons for the poet's choice (pp. 36-40).

32. For a somewhat more extensive discussion, see my 'Death and Rebirth of Visigothic Spain', p. 356.

33. The hero's men think he is dead; the threefold occurrence of 'muerto' in st. 321-22 strengthens the resemblance.

34. This is also, as Zamora Vicente points out in his note to st. 444, a formula in legal malediction clauses (see also David Hook, 'On Certain Correspondences between the *Poema de Mio Cid* and Contemporary Legal Instruments', *Iberoromania*, n.s., XI (1980), 31-53, at 50). There is clearly a convergence of influences here.

35. Nepaulsingh suggests (p. 88) that God's displeasure is caused by Fernán González's surrender rather than the King's treachery and violation of sanctuary. He points out that the Count had said in st. 444 that anyone who surrendered to the Moors would go to Hell. Surrender to a Christian king, however wicked he may be, is in a different category, and the figural references that follow show that Fernán González is not the object of God's wrath.

36. '"Commo voz de pauon" en *El libro de Alexandre* y en el *Poema de Fernán González*', *Meridiano 70* (Austin, Texas), no. 4 (Spring, 1977), 25-33, at 31-32.

37. The poet adds (st. 593) that the church is still split, and will remain so until the Last Judgment ('fasta la fin complida'). This may be aimed at pilgrims: Cirueña is just south of the Camino Francés.

38. Carolyn Bluestine, 'Heroes Great and Small: Archetypal Patterns in the Medieval Spanish Epic' (unpublished doctoral thesis, Princeton University, 1983), suggests (pp. 229-30) that 'this time Fernán González has overstepped the bounds of the permissible' and that henceforth he 'will receive aid only from human helpers'.

39. Bluestine refers to Fernán González's prison as a 'figurative tomb' (p. 230), and comments on its mythical connotations (pp. 280-81 n. 86), but does not mention its figural aspect.

40. *The Singer of Tales*, Harvard Studies in Comparative Literature, XXIV (Cambridge, Mass.: Harvard University Press, 1960), p. 206.

41. An interesting analogue (A.D. 1067) occurs in *The 'Carmen de Hastingae proelio' of Guy, Bishop of Amiens*, ed. and trans. Catherine Morton and Hope Muntz (Oxford: Clarendon, 1972): 'Autumat insipiens uulgus se posse tueri / regali solo nomine, non opere. / In statuam regis puer est electus ab illis, / cuius presidium contulit exicium' (ll. 649-52). The editors translate 'In statuam regis' as 'the shadow of a king' (p. 43), but it is likely that the words should be rendered literally, as a reflection of the tradition that is used by the *Fernán González* poet and that is discussed by Hook. I hope to deal with this question elsewhere.

42. I make no claim to a complete coverage. For other possibilities, see e.g. Foster, pp. 45-59; Bluestine, p. 258 n. 28; Valladares Reguero, pp. 127-35; Ricardo Arias y Arias, *El concepto del destino en la literatura medieval española* (Madrid: Ínsula, 1970), pp. 144-63; and Connie L. Scarborough, 'Characterization in the *Poema de Fernán González*: Portraits of the Hero and the Heroine', in *Literary and Historical Perspectives of the Middle Ages: Proceedings of the 1981 SEMA Meeting*, edited by Patricia W. Cummins *et al.* (Morgantown: West Virginia University Press, 1982), pp. 52-65, at pp. 54-57.

43. 'De la perspective poétique et du traitement de l'histoire dans le *Poema de Fernán González*', *LNL*, no. 222 (1977), 4-17, at 12.

44. *The Goddess Fortuna in Mediaeval Literature* (Cambridge, Mass.: Harvard University Press, 1927). Patrides says: 'But it was one thing to denounce the cyclical view and another to evade its mazes' (p. 14).

45. *The Great Code*, pp. 192-93. Cf. Patrides, pp. 3-9.

46. I am grateful to Professor Claude Allaigre, Dr David Hook, Professor Aurelio Pérez Jiménez, and Srta Eugenia Ramos Fernández for supplying me with copies of elusive bibliographical material, to Ms Katharine Kearsey for a discussion that helped me to clarify my ideas on a number of points in this article, and to Dr Hook and Dr Barry Taylor for their close and constructive editorial scrutiny. Shortly before correcting proof of this article (written in 1988), I received, thanks to the kindness of Professor José Fradejas Lebrero, a copy of *Poema de Fernán González: edición facsímil del manuscrito depositado en el Monasterio de El Escorial*, edited by César Hernández Alonso (Burgos: Ayuntamiento, 1989). The excellent colour facsimile supersedes the black-and-white one mentioned in n. 2, above, and the volume contains important articles on various aspects of the *Poema* as well as a regularized transcription, with modern Spanish version, by José Manuel Ruiz Asencio. It is clearly indispensable for all future studies of the *Poema*. José Fradejas Lebrero, 'Significado e intención del *Poema de Fernán González*', pp. 13-36, deals with a number of issues mentioned in the present article (for instance, he supports Menéndez Pidal's date of *ca.* 1255, but rejects San Pedro de Arlanza as the place of composition, arguing instead for a poet commissioned by Nuño González de Lara, a powerful noble of Alfonso X's court). As an example of Biblical influence on the poet, he argues convincingly (pp. 32-33) for the Moors' attack on Tierra de Campos and Fernán González's reaction to it (st. 713-24) as a re-creation of David's reaction to the Amalekites' attack on Ziklag (Samuel 30), though without verbal borrowings.

BISHOP JUAN ARIAS DÁVILA OF SEGOVIA: 'JUDAIZER' OR REFORMER?

John Edwards

On 28 October 1497, in the reign of Pope Alexander VI Borja, Bishop Juan Arias Dávila of Segovia died in Rome, at the age of eighty-seven.[1] By then, the Bishop had been out of Castile for seven years, not as a visitor to the Eternal City on routine ecclesiastical business, but rather as one who, under investigation by the inquisitorial tribunal of his own city, had taken his case to Rome for judgment. The explanation of the events involving the Bishop which took place, in Segovia and elsewhere, in the years 1486-97, contributes much to a proper understanding of various issues concerning both Church and monarchy in the reign of Isabella and Ferdinand. Despite the picturesque claim of Pablo Alvarez Rubiano that the Arias Dávila descended from a Leonese family known as the Arias de Argüello, it is clear that they were in fact a dynasty of converts from Judaism.[2] Indeed, the Bishop was not alone among his relatives in being subject to the Inquisition's scrutiny. Much of the investigation by the Segovian inquisitors concerned his parents, Diego Arias Dávila and Elvira González, both by that time deceased. Also accused were Bishop Juan's nephew, Francisco Arias, *regidor* of Segovia and son of Pedro Arias I 'el Valiente' and María Ortiz Cota, as well as the Bishop's sister Isabel Arias, her husband Gómez González de la Hoz, and their four sons, Diego Arias, Pedro Arias, Juan de la Hoz and Alonso Arias, though not their daughter Isabel Arias, who was a Poor Clare. The results of the Segovian activity, in the form of 230 statements by witnesses and a number of procedural documents, provide the main source for the study of the trial. However, these papers may be supplemented from royal diplomatic correspondence, the Registro General del Sello of Castile and other royal administrative papers, as well as papal documents.[3]

The earliest statements by witnesses which survive in the records of the Segovian investigation of the Arias Dávila family date from 1 January 1486, while succeeding statements, divided into eight books numbered from one to nine with no number eight, stretch from January 1486 to April 1491. These documents are supplemented by further statements collected by the Ávila tribunal of the Inquisition between December 1490 and May 1492.[4] These pre-trial statements by witnesses, in Segovia and elsewhere, are followed by undated procedural documents, which indicate that the actual process against the Bishop and his relatives began in 1490, and probably in May or June, although the procurator fiscal's charges against Juan Arias's mother, Elvira González, are not dated. In any case, a defence lawyer was engaged, apparently in June 1490, in accordance with normal Spanish inquisitorial procedure. The defence questionnaire for its own witnesses was thus drawn up by a cleric, Antón Rodríguez, and this survives, together with the replies of eleven witnesses, whose testimony was collected in mid-June 1490. The surviving documents also include an undated attack on the credentials of the prosecution witnesses, made by Juan de San Juan, on behalf of Elvira González, and counter-statements by the prosecution, as well as a prosecution statement, made before the Valladolid tribunal of the Inquisition, by Pedro Maldonado against Diego Arias, the Bishop's father.[5] At this point, the succession of trial documents in the source in the Archivo Histórico Nacional comes to a halt, but it is necessary to look at the obstacles which lay in the path of the Segovia inquisitors, at least as early as 1489, in their pursuit of both investigation and trial. Some of this evidence is to be found in their own records. On 27 July 1489, for instance, the Supreme Council of the Inquisition issued a block or *carta inhibitoria* to prevent further moves in the Arias Dávila case, while earlier in the same month a series of documents indicates moves by the Bishop, then still in Segovia, to obstruct the local tribunal's activities against him and his relatives.[6] However, it was by now clear that Juan Arias did not intend to confine his resistance to the boundaries of his own diocese. By April 1490, the Catholic Monarchs were instructing their ambassadors in Rome, the Bishops of Astorga and Badajoz, not only to stop the trial in Rome and have the Arias Dávila case returned to Castile, but even to have Bishop Arias dispossessed of his see.[7] In January 1493, the Segovian inquisitors interrogated the apostolic protonotary and public notary Alvaro de San Juan, whom they accused of having forged documents to help the Bishop with his case.[8] Intelligence-gathering by royal agents in Rome appears to have resulted in two reports, which survive in Simancas. One concerned the possibility of securing a sentence against Bishop Juan in the Roman trial, while the other purported to give details of the bribes which the Bishop had offered to Pope Innocent VIII, nine cardinals, six curial officials and various witnesses, in order to secure a verdict in his favour.[9] In addition, Roman sources indicate that Innocent and his Curia had already been concerned with the case since May 1488, but the implications of this interest, as well as those of the other trial documents, need to be examined in the context of the overall significance of the case.[10]

In contrast with inquisitorial, royal and papal documents, more recent historians have firmly placed the Arias Dávila trial in the context of investigations of the 'judaizing' activities of *conversos*. Immediately before mentioning that Juan Arias obtained the bishopric of Segovia, Yitzhak Baer refers to his father as one whose attitude 'towards his fellow Jews' (*sic*) was unknown, though his enemies had accused him of starting life as a pedlar in the villages, 'where he had ingratiated himself with the peasants by singing Moslem songs for them'. Diego was described by his enemies 'as a contemptible courtier of depraved sexual habits, who sucked the blood of the citizenry and undermined the economic strength of his country'.[11] Baer is clearly not impressed either by Diego Arias or by his Judaism, having not come across the trial documents used here, but he might have followed more closely the contemporary sources which not

72

only accuse Diego of economic corruption, but also refer in the bluntest terms to his and his family's Jewish origins.[12] Although he appears to have taken due notice of the attacks made on Diego Arias by the chronicler Alonso de Palencia, he did not remark the many 'poetical' comments on Henry IV's *contador mayor* and his ancestry. The author of the *Coplas de Mingo Revulgo* restricted his comment to the conventional image, used elsewhere by Palencia, of the royal official as a wolf which seized the sheep, or people, of Castile.[13] Similarly, the *Coplas del Provincial* highlighted the irony that the Cross should appear on the coat-of-arms of the *contador*, a descendant of the 'Christ-killers', referring to him as a Jewish whore, a circumcised Jew, and even as the captain of the soldiers who carried out the Crucifixion.[14] Given the nature of these contemporary sources, it is hardly surprising that authors from Lea up to the latest writer of a general survey of the Spanish Inquisition, Juan Blázquez Miguel, should assume that the Arias Dávila trial was simply concerned with 'judaizing' by *conversos*.[15] Nonetheless, there are obvious difficulties in holding such a view. For one thing, whatever the deeds and misdeeds of his relatives, assessments of Bishop Juan as a diocesan, from the sixteenth-century historian of Segovia, Colmenares, to more modern writers such as Lea and Tarsicio de Azcona, are so positive that it is hard to explain how a model prelate could have fallen under such suspicion.[16]

In order to try to solve the puzzle, modern writers have placed Juan Arias's troubles firmly in the context of his *converso* origins, and, on the face of it, there is ample evidence to support such a view. Azcona points, as background, to the bull *Ut officium inquisitionis*, issued by Sixtus IV on 25 May 1483 and directed at Archbishop Alfonso de Fonseca of Santiago de Compostela, which forbade any of his suffragans of Jewish descent to act as an inquisitor, except through the medium of an Old Christian official. For this author, the bull was most probably directed at Bishop Juan of Segovia, seeing that he was the only clearly *converso* bishop in the province of Santiago.[17] Later, in May 1488, Innocent VIII commissioned Bishop Juan Meneses of Zamora to admonish his brother of Segovia for his lack of zeal in pursuing Inquisition cases, while, during the investigation of his own parents and relatives, an Aragonese royal document states that he 'went in the dead of night to the churchyard of the Convent of La Merced, dug up the bones of his ancestors, and hid them in a place where they could not be found', this before proceeding to Rome.[18] Against the view of Juan Arias as a protector of Jews may be adduced his harsh action, according to Colmenares, in a supposed 'ritual murder' case in Sepúlveda in 1468. The Bishop had sixteen Jews brought to Segovia, some of them being burnt and others hanged in the enclosed pasture (*dehesa*) beside the Franciscan Convent of San Antonio, of which more will be heard in due course.[19]

In the case of Juan Arias's relatives, however, the enquiries of the Segovia inquisitors appear to have found ample evidence of what was conventionally regarded, in that period, as 'judaizing'. During the 1480s and 1490s, the Inquisition in Spain steadily developed its expertise in identifying, at least to its own satisfaction, continuing Jewish belief and practice among converts from Judaism and their descendants. It is not always possible to disentangle the different charges which were included in the lists compiled by prosecutors on behalf of the different local tribunals. However, for the purpose of the present analysis, a list of forty-one charges has been used, and these have been divided into three main categories, which may be generally defined as, firstly, positive adherence in thought and action to Judaism, secondly, hostility in thought and action towards Christianity, and, thirdly, a category of religious 'dissidence' which does not fit into any specific religious orthodoxy. This last category includes such things as blasphemy, materialistic attitudes, scepticism, anticlericalism, magic and sexual immorality, such as male homosexuality and bigamy.[20] An analysis, in these terms, of the charges made by witnesses against the main persons accused in the Segovia investigations produces interesting results, and particularly so given that the bulk of the evidence comes from pre-trial documents and has not therefore been sifted and organized by professional lawyers.

In the case of the *contador* Diego Arias, there is no doubt that the bulk of the charges concern continued adherence to Judaism. They involved Sabbath observance, the keeping of dietary laws and the continuance of close social relations with Jews, some of them his relatives. However, he was also accused of failing to observe the Christian Sunday, of defying the Inquisition, of abusing the Christian faith and, more generally, of irreverence, scepticism, blasphemy, and even the strange offence of 'melancholy' (which may have been seen by the witness concerned as a sign of unbelief). Over all, though, most witnesses, either by direct testimony or by hearsay, concentrate on the bringing of pre-cooked food (*adafina*) for the Sabbath from the Jewry to his house.[21] The same accusation inevitably loomed large in the offences for which the *contador*'s wife, Elvira González, was brought to account. Indeed, apart from vague accusations of being a 'heretical' or 'bad' Christian, and, according to a single witness, of having practised magic, all the charges against Elvira concerned adherence to the Jewish faith. They included not only dietary laws, Sabbath observance and the giving of charity to Jews, but also observances associated with 'rites of passage', that is, births, marriages and deaths. Elvira was also commonly accused of having regularly given oil to help keep synagogue lamps burning.[22] In the case of the Bishop's sister, Isabel Arias, who died during the inquisitorial investigations, all the accusations concerned continued adherence to Judaism. They included fasting and dietary laws, customs concerning childbirth and burial, alms-giving to Jews and the donation of oil for synagogue lights, but also knowledge and speaking of Hebrew.[23] However, only seven witnesses gave evidence against Isabel, compared with over seventy against the *contador* and over thirty against his wife, although in the latter two cases much of the evidence consisted of hearsay, while all the evidence against Isabel was claimed to be first-hand, she presumably being a less public figure. All the other cases against Bishop Juan's relatives seem to have been built upon fairly limited evidence. Thus his brother-in-law, Gómez González de la Hoz, who was denounced by eight witnesses, some of them citing hearsay, was accused of offences concerned with Jewish practice, including the observance of dietary laws and the giving of charity to Jews.[24] Isabel and Gómez's four sons had varying amounts of evidence given against them. The apostolic protonotary Diego Arias Dávila was mainly accused, not of keeping Jewish dietary laws (though four of the fifteen witnesses mentioned this) but rather of giving charity to Jews, of showing general hostility towards Christianity including failing to observe Christian feasts and fasts, and of opposing and obstructing the work of the Inquisition.[25] Diego's brother Pedro Arias, or 'Pedrarias', was the object of more diverse accusations, including worshipping privately in the Jewish way, and even having been circumcised (a rumour which also attached itself to the Protonotary), and also general hostility to Christianity and obstruction of the Inquisition. He was also accused of irreverence and scepticism, a charge so frequent also in the Soria-Osma area of Castile, as elsewhere in Europe in this period.[26] Only two people gave evidence against Juan de la Hoz, and, like his brothers, he was accused vaguely of continued adherence to Judaism and hostility to the new faith, and particularly the Holy Office.[27] The remaining nephew of the Bishop, Alfonso Arias Dávila, had a similar pack of charges levelled against him, by six people, including his own mother, before his death.[28]

On the face of it, these Segovian investigations fit well into the established pattern of inquisitorial trials of 'judaizing' *conversos* in many parts of Spain in the 1480s and 1490s. The charges brought against members of the Arias Dávila family, by witnesses and prosecutors alike, parallel those found by Beinart and others in Ciudad Real, Trujillo and other parts of New Castile and Extremadura, as well as in Córdoba and Soria-Osma.[29] However, there is a major difficulty in the way of interpreting this particular Segovian trial wholly in terms of Jewish belief and practice among *conversos*. This is the nature of the charges against the Bishop himself. The fact is that the surviving Segovia documentation contains not a single charge in this category. Instead, Juan is accused, by a mere three witnesses, all on the basis of hearsay, of general (and vague) hostility towards Christianity (!), Old Christians and the Inquisition, and more specifically by two men of homosexuality, a charge said to have originated with the Bishop's former chaplain, Juan de Escalona, and a canon of Segovia, Juan Vázquez.[30] One of those who accused the Bishop of obstructing the Inquisition was a Jewish jeweller, Abraham Meme, who claimed to have the information from Mosén Zaragoza. Here, in the acceptance and use by the Inquisition of Jewish witnesses, there is a further parallel with practice elsewhere, for example in Extremadura and Teruel.[31] Nonetheless, if the Bishop of Segovia was indeed the target, as a judaizer, of the papal legislation referred to earlier, as well as the Segovia Inquisition, it seems quite extraordinary that no such charge was made against him. Clearly the causes of the Arias Dávila trial require further investigation.

To begin with, it is obvious that Bishop Juan's family had achieved political fame, and for many notoriety, long before the period of the inquisitorial investigations. As Baer remarked concerning Henry IV, 'one of the most hated courtiers was the king's secretary and auditor of the royal accounts, Don Diego Arias Dávila . . . His enemies described Diego Arias as a contemptible courtier of depraved sexual habits, who sucked the blood of the citizenry and undermined the economic strength of his country'.[32] In making such statements, Baer stresses the line adopted by the acerbic commentator Alonso de Palencia, a strong critic of Henry IV, rather than that of the writer of glosses on the *Coplas del Provincial*, included in a manuscript in the Real Academia de la Historia. For the latter author, Diego's 'position as a favourite ['la privanza'] did him more harm than his blood'.[33] Nonetheless, Palencia, in his *Decades*, took full advantage of Diego Arias's humble and *converso* origins to discredit both him and his master. According to the chronicler, Diego was born in Ávila, but came to Segovia while John II was still alive. He was 'un converso de oscuro linaje', and an 'hombre de bajas inclinaciones', who at first made his living by selling spices, 'cambiando especias de escaso valor e vendiendo a bajo precio otra de mayor estimacion', such as pepper, cinnamon and cloves. However, the future *contador mayor* tired of touring the villages and became a farmer and collector of taxes. According to Palencia, he acquired his nickname of 'el Volador' from his series of escapes, on a horse 'de miserable traza y de ínfimo precio', from irate peasants 'cuando le perseguían para vengar el atropello cometido contra algunos de ellos'. Palencia claimed that Prince Henry made Diego his secretary only after he had freed him 'ya en camino de suplicio' from execution for an unknown capital crime. The chronicler, in his lurid and persuasive prose, appears to ascribe many of the ills of the subsequent reign of Henry IV to the evil and misconduct of his *contador* Diego Arias, including what he regarded as endemic corruption of the kingdom's laws and customs, as well as the failure to prosecute war against the Muslim kingdom of Granada.[34] Thanks to the political and economic importance of Segovia in the mid- to late fifteenth century, the Arias Dávila dynasty, founded by the *contador* Diego, was, in Eleazar Gutwirth's words, 'una de las más obvias y visiblemente influyentes'.[35]

Indeed, it was thanks to the political and social prominence of his father that Bishop Juan was launched on his ecclesiastical career. In 1461, the year before the *contador* assured the survival of his line, and the obscuring of its Jewish origins, by founding the *mayorazgo* of Puñonrostro for his eldest son and heir, 'Pedrarias' Dávila, he played a large part in obtaining the bishopric of Segovia for his second son, Juan, who had been educated at the College of San Bartolomé in Salamanca, a university of which the affairs were to play an important part in the rise and fall of the *converso* prelate.[36] In the first place, it is necessary to return to the Bishop's record as a reformer, which concerned not only the Church but also the Castilian universities of Salamanca and Valladolid. The College of San Bartolomé was an ideal training ground for a reforming prelate. In Azcona's words, 'no existía . . . centro cultural más exigente', as it was 'decano y modelo de todos los otros colegios universitarios'.[37] After this education, Juan Arias became one of those pre-Tridentine Catholic reformers whose achievements are at last beginning to receive due acknowledgment. His activity is revealed, for example, in the acts of the Spanish Church councils of Aranda in 1473 and Seville in 1478. According to Azcona, his own diocesan synods, in 1472, 1478 and 1483, show great and unusual concern for his flock, and in particular for the raising of the cultural level of his clergy. He built a new cloister for his cathedral, and endowed its library with over a hundred manuscripts and incunabula, many of them from Renaissance Italy. In his will, he was generous to his old cathedral and to charitable work and foundations.[38] Bishop Juan also became actively involved in the Catholic Monarchs' efforts to secure the adoption of the severer 'observant' rule and discipline by the religious orders in Spain. One notable case, recounted by the admiring Colmenares, is that of the Franciscans in Segovia. In 1487-88, just at the time when the Inquisition was investigating him and his family, the Bishop, on the Queen's instructions, moved to 'rationalize' the two Franciscan houses and the two convents of Clares which then existed in the city, so as to strengthen the hold of the Observants at the expense of the Conventuals. The royal ambassador in Rome, the Count of Tendilla, obtained the necessary bull from Innocent VIII on 17 February 1486 and, on the feast of the Epiphany, 6 January 1488, it was presented at the Franciscan provincial chapter meeting in Arévalo. As a result, in April of that year, the Bishop evicted the Conventuals from San Antonio, which had been founded as recently as 1455, and replaced them with the Clares, whose previous accommodation was deemed to be cramped and uncomfortable. The inmates were thus forced to move to San Francisco, continuing under the Observant rule, and it is worth noting that the evicted friars came from the very house which had been the home of that inveterate enemy of Jews and conversos, Fray Alonso de Espina.[39] It will become clear in due course that this connection is of considerable relevance to the real causes of the Arias Dávila trial. At this stage, however, it is necessary to turn from Church matters to Bishop Juan's activities as a visitor and reformer of universities. As Fr Beltrán de Heredia's researches in the archives of the University of Salamanca have shown, in this same period 1486-87, the Bishop became a visitor of his own university, Valladolid, and also of Salamanca. In each case, he acted explicitly as the commissioner of the Crown as well as the representative of the Church. At Valladolid, he was accompanied by Dr Martín de Ávila, and in February 1488 the Crown instructed the *corregidor* of Valladolid, Juan de Ayala, to investigate the infractions of the university's statutes which had been discovered by the visitors. In the case of Salamanca, Bishop Juan Arias acted with Juan Arias de Villar, who was to succeed him in Segovia in 1498. Beltrán remarks that the fact that the Bishop was given these assignments, which were so important in the religious and academic policies of the Catholic Monarchs, indicates that, as late as 1487-88, he still 'gozaba de la plena confianza de los Reyes'.[40] Having been in trouble in Rome, as early as 1471, apparently over the administration of his diocese, Juan continued to receive concrete tokens of the Crown's trust in his abilities as a reformer and ecclesiastical judge at least up to 1485.[41] The lack of subsequent references to him in the royal archives is perhaps significant, however, and there are two aspects of Juan Arias's increasingly stormy career which may indicate some of the causes of his difficulties.

One such matter, which requires attention, is the relationship between the Bishop and Segovia's Franciscan communities, and in particular with their most famous, or notorious, member in this period, Fray Alonso de Espina. Here, the vital events do not concern a personal encounter between Juan Arias and the friar, but rather the supposed activities of Juan's father, Diego Arias, during the reign of his master Henry IV. Fray Alonso, who was the King's confessor, published his anti-Jewish compendium, *Fortalitium Fidei*, in 1460. When what were to prove to be the basic outlines of the programme of the Catholic Monarchs against Jews and *conversos* were being established, Espina was active in Segovia, in the Observant house of San Antonio. In 1459, Fray Alonso claimed to have discovered the attendance of *conversos* at the feast of Tabernacles (*Succoth*) in the city's Jewry, while in the *Fortalitium* itself, he accused Segovia's Jews of having desecrated a eucharistic host, or consecrated bread, in 1415, and claimed that Henry III's physician, Don Meir Alguadex, whose son and grandson were still enjoying tax concessions at the time of writing, in recompense for the doctor's services to the Crown, had in fact poisoned his master.[42] The charge of murder by poisoning may not be irrelevant to some of the denunciations against the *contador* Diego Arias which appear in the investigations of the Segovia Inquisition in the late 1480s. Two main accusations were made against Diego, concerning Alonso de Espina. One was that, during the friar's preaching campaign in favour of an Inquisition to detect 'judaizing' *conversos*, and also against homosexuals, the *contador* showed disrespect for the preacher's proposal that, if the King refused to enforce the wearing of a badge by Jews, then Christians should sew a badge of their own, bearing the name of Jesus, on to their hats. According to a public notary in Segovia, Diego refused to pay out money to claimants on the royal funds, if they presented themselves before him wearing such a badge.[43] However, the more serious charge, made by four witnesses, was that the *contador* was responsible for bringing about Espina's death, by the instrument of a Jewish doctor, Maestre Xamaya, in the convent of the nuns of Santo Domingo, outside the walls of Madrid. According to the Segovian Jew, Mosén Zaragoza, the murder was explicitly connected with *converso* opposition to the idea of an Inquisition, while the lawyer Juan de Nurueña, from the same city, accused the *contador* of having intervened in the affairs of the Franciscan order, in support of the *claustrales* (Conventuals), who opposed a new Inquisition in Spain, and against the Observants, who were zealous in their hostility to Jews and 'judaizing' *conversos*.[44] The similarity between these charges and those made before the Segovia tribunal in the late 1480s against Diego's son, the Bishop, is unlikely to have been coincidental. However, at this point it is necessary to return to the career of Bishop Juan himself, and in particular to his relations with one Juan de Castilla, professor and rector of Salamanca University and member of the Consejo Real.

Juan de Castilla seems to have been born at about the time that Juan Arias became Bishop of Segovia, in 1460 or 1461. His father, Sancho de Castilla, had been active for a number of years in the Palencia area as a supporter, first, of the rebel Prince Alfonso and then of Isabella herself, before she became queen. His mother, Beatriz Enríquez, was closely related to Ferdinand of Aragon. Not surprisingly, Juan's parents did well under the new regime after 1474, while their son went up to Salamanca in about 1475 at the age of fourteen or fifteen to read first arts and then canon law. By 1486 or 1487, he had risen to be rector of the university, and it was at this point that he came to the notice of the Catholic Monarchs. In 1486, they visited the university and, having apparently heard good reports of his academic and administrative abilities, immediately named him to be dean of the important cathedral of Seville. At the time, though, this office had not been vacated, and the incumbent, Juan Arias del Villar, had hastily to be transformed into a royal ambassador to the Roman Curia, to accompany the Count of Tendilla. To sweeten the pill, Ferdinand and Isabella secured the Dean's appointment as Bishop of Oviedo, in May 1487. At this point, Villar resigned his Seville post, which was immediately filled by Juan de Castilla, who nonetheless remained in Salamanca.

In view of this particular example of the royal manipulation of papal provisions, it is all the more interesting to note that the person appointed, by the Crown and also by the *maestrescuela* of Salamanca, Gutierre de Toledo, to visit and reform the city's university was none other than Juan Arias del Villar. One of the abuses that the visitors denounced was Juan de Castilla's acquisition of the 'Vespers' chair of canon law in Salamanca. Shortly before his nomination to the Consejo Real, as a legal, and no doubt political, adviser, the young academic and political rising star had applied for the vacant chair in his subject, which had previously been occupied by another politically active academic, Dr Pedro de Oropesa, who had himself become a member of the Consejo Real. However, Juan had a rival, in his colleague and friend Bachiller de Malpartida. This dispute might perhaps have been amicably resolved, had not a third candidate, Gonzalo de la Rúa, licentiate of Salamanca and canon of Ciudad Rodrigo, presented himself. According to Azcona, the canon's intervention was aimed at financial gain rather than the securing of the chair. In any case, as a condition of his withdrawal from the race, Gonzalo succeeded (thanks to threat of the complications which would be caused, under the university statutes, if there were three candidates) in obtaining a payment of 20,000 maravedís from Juan de Castilla. Gonzalo de la Rúa drove a hard bargain, insisting that the money should be handed over even if young Juan failed to secure the chair. He also insisted that his rival should provide guarantors. Juan did so, and those who obliged were two notable Salamanca Jews, Rabbi Judá, a physician, and his wife Doña Gracia. Other evidence indicates that this couple, and in particular Gracia, who seems to have contracted business on her own account, were in the habit of lending money to impecunious members of Salamanca University. In 1484, for example, a student of canon law, Juan Aranda, had fallen on hard times and owed money to Doña Gracia. When he found difficulty in paying, he suddenly discovered a conscience about having borrowed money with interest, and secured remission from the repayment of anything more than the principal on appeal to the Crown. In the case of Juan de Castilla, however, greater issues were involved.

Bishop Juan of Segovia and the dean of Seville were not impressed by Juan de Castilla's payment to Gonzalo de la Rúa, or by the manner in which he had secured financial guarantees. In the words of the chancery clerks who drafted the royal instruction in July 1488 to the *corregidor* of Salamanca to resecure the money from the canon, the deal was a 'pacto ilícito y torpe, no pudiendo vender lo que no tenía seguro ni en ello adquirido derecho alguno eso habiendo tenido tampoco efecto su ayuda; e syendo asi mismo contra derecho canónico e civil e contra las constituciones de dicho Estudio'. However, the visitors' judgment was quickly subverted by other parties. When Juan de Castilla was away from Salamanca, Rúa prevailed upon the *alcaldes* of the city to obtain the money to pay his fine from the unfortunate Rabbi Judá and his wife. The Jews complained to the Crown about this 'fuerza e manifiesta injusticia', and the Crown agreed that the guarantors should not have to pay. Nonetheless, a royal document of 9 August 1488 shows that the government was equally anxious that Juan de Castilla should be released from any ties, embarrassing as they were, to Gonzalo de la Rúa or Don Judá and Doña Gracia. By this time, the Monarchs and the Consejo Real were evidently looking after their own, and the loyal reformer in diocese and university, Bishop Juan Arias, was, like his companion the new Bishop of Oviedo, rapidly losing ground to his much younger rival, who now had reason to bear a grudge against him.[45]

Although it is not possible to make a direct connection, using the available documents, between Bishop Juan's conflict with Juan de Castilla and the investigation of the Arias Dávila family's Jewish proclivities, there can be no doubt that, by the beginning of 1490, the Bishop had lost faith in the ability of Castilian institutions, such as the Consejo Real and the Supreme Council of the Inquisition, to do justice to him and his relatives, both living and departed. However, his move to Rome, with papers concerning his trial, has caused fury in Spain, not only at the time but also among scholars in the twentieth century. The interest of the Catholic Monarchs' government was clearly to keep the investigations and trial within their realm. Thus, when their ambassadors reported, in May 1490, that the Bishop's case was under discussion in the Roman Curia, the monarchs ordered them to demand the return of the case to Spain, to be decided by four royally-appointed judges. One of these was to be none other than the canon law professor whom the Bishop had exposed as corrupt, Juan de Castilla – now not only a royal councillor but also, if a document in Salamanca Cathedral Archive is to be believed, a member of the Suprema. By the time of Bishop Juan's death, in Rome in 1497, his younger rival for the royal favour had left the Inquisition council, though the complaisant Alexander VI had, in 1494, appointed Ferdinand and Isabella's other three candidates as possible judges for the Arias Dávila case to the more significant role of joint Inquisitors-General of Spain, to replace Torquemada, who was then apparently in conspicuous physical and mental decline.[46] Juan Arias, though, seems in the 1490s to have moved ever further away from his earlier role as a faithful servant of the Catholic Monarchs. During this period, the royal ambassadors and agents in Rome supplied what purported to be details of the elderly Bishop's efforts to secure a favourable verdict in his case. The Pope himself, still at this time Innocent VIII, was offered and apparently accepted two elaborately embroidered rochets, fifty other cloths, a hundred pairs of Ocaña gloves and thirty or forty jewelled silver-gilt cups. Nine other cardinals were offered gifts, including cloth, rich clothing and mules, and nearly all accepted. Similar gifts were offered to the Pope's chamberlain, to the captain of his guard, and to other officials and witnesses in the case. These bribes, which must surely have been conventional in the Curia of the period, scandalized Fr Tarsicio de Azcona, who even suggests that Juan Arias's activities indicate a weakness on the part of the Spanish Inquisition, perhaps caused by the decline of Torquemada.[47] Such an explanation, however, if it contains any truth at all, can be no more than partial. More significant, perhaps, is a second Simancas document, published by Beltrán de Heredia.

This text also purports to be a despatch from a royal agent or ambassador in Rome to the Catholic Monarchs, though it does not appear in de la Torre's collection from the registers of the Aragonese Crown in Barcelona.[48] The anonymous author, who seems to have been trying to gauge the likely outcome of the Arias Dávila case in the court of Innocent VIII by talking to various cardinals, heard divided opinions. The Papal Datary apparently told the Spaniard that the Catholic Monarchs' cause was just, while the Cardinal of Alexandria thought that, if the Pope were to allow the proceedings to return to Spain, this would reflect adversely on his honour, though the ambassador added that the Cardinal insisted 'más como tiene la cabeza dura', that what he said should remain 'off the record' (which it clearly did not!), and 'no le imprime cosa que diga'. Even more interesting, though, is a statement by a servant of the Cardinal of Alexandria,

Licenciado Cieza, that his master had actually issued a sentence which absolved the *contador* Diego, Elvira González his wife, and the Bishop himself of all accusations, but that he refused to widen the sentence to include the other accused members of the Arias Dávila family. The level of distrust which existed in relations between Spain and the Papacy in the 1490s is indicated by the ambassador's observation, in the same despatch, that, although the Cardinal was an honest man, he gave sentence 'quizá contra la verdad', because many of the witnesses had been suborned. In order to block the corrupt actions which he anticipated from Bishop Juan, he was prepared to buy the trial documents with gold, if necessary, to help his employers.[49] It is highly questionable, however, whether the issue between the Catholic Monarchs and their former episcopal servant can be properly understood in terms of 'judaizing', by him or by his family – and it has already been noted that no such accusation was made against the Bishop himself – or of the level of morality of legal processes, whether in Spain or Rome, including the attempts of the accused to influence the verdict by procedural moves or bribes. Rather, it is surely the case that the attitude of Rome should be understood in terms of the Papacy's deep and long-standing reluctance to accept the growing control of Ferdinand and Isabella over the Spanish Church, and in particular over the Inquisition in their kingdoms.

When Bishop Juan arrived in Rome in May 1490, he had every reason to expect a friendly reception, both from Innocent VIII and from a large section of the Curia. Two years earlier, the Pope had, to the fury of the Spanish government, issued a bull which appeared to accept the truth of many of the complaints which Spanish *conversos* and others had made against the practices of the independent inquisitorial tribunals which had been working, with increasing comprehensiveness, since 1480. The Papacy, as an institution, clearly regarded Sixtus IV's bull of 1478, which founded the new Spanish Inquisition, as a dangerous concession of powers which rightly belonged to the Roman see, and so a counter-move was inevitable, once an individual pope was prepared to take on the might of Ferdinand and Isabella and their agents. Innocent's bull caused great anger in Spanish court circles, and the vindictiveness with which Juan Arias was pursued by their agents and in the Curia must surely reflect the bitterness of the conflict between the Catholic Monarchs and the Church over provisions to ecclesiastical posts, and the reform of the religious orders, of the secular clergy, and perhaps above all of the Inquisition. The Roman Curia was certainly not unwilling in principle to dispossess 'judaizing' *conversos* of their sees. Indeed, at the very time that Juan Arias was pleading his cause, one of his episcopal colleagues, Bishop Pedro Alonso of Calahorra, was in Rome under the same accusation. However, while the Bishop of Segovia died without any papal slur on his reputation, Pedro Alonso was removed for heresy and judaizing, even though Pope Alexander VI tried to protect him.[50] It appears that the Bishop of Calahorra was all too vulnerable to the kind of accusation which the Catholic Monarchs sought to bring against his colleague in Segovia. Juan Arias, on the other hand, seems to have suffered for having ceased to hear clearly enough his master's – and his mistress's – voice.

University of Birmingham

NOTES

1. Henry C. Lea, *A History of the Inquisition of Spain*, 4 vols (New York: Macmillan, 1922), II, 42.

2. Pablo Álvarez Rubiano, *Pedrarias Dávila. Contribución al estudio de la figura del 'Gran Justador', gobernador de Castilla del Oro y Nicaragua* (Madrid: CSIC, 1944), pp. 24-30, cited in Tarsicio de Azcona, *La elección y reforma del episcopado español de los Reyes Católicos* (Madrid: CSIC, 1960), p. 220.

3. The main sources are *Fontes Iudaeorum Regni Castellae (FIRC)*, edited by Carlos Carrete Parrondo, III, *Proceso inquisitorial contra los Arias Dávila segovianos: un enfrentamiento social entre judíos y conversos* (Salamanca: Universidad Pontificia, 1986); *Documentos sobre relaciones internacionales de los Reyes Católicos*, edited by Antonio de la Torre, III *(1488-1491)* (Barcelona: CSIC, 1951); *Registro General del Sello (RGS)*, Archivo General de Simancas (AGS), Catálogo 13, *1454-95* (Valladolid: CSIC, 1950-74); Bernardino Llorca, *Bulario pontificio de la Inquisición española en su período constitucional (1478-1525)* (Rome: Gregorian University, 1949).

4. *FIRC*, III, 19-120.

5. *Ibid.*, 123-46.

6. *Ibid.*, 146-48, 150-59.

7. De la Torre, *Documentos*, III, 299-305, 314, 381-85.

8. *FIRC*, III, 148-50.

9. AGS, Diversos de Castilla, 9-39, in Vicente Beltrán de Heredia, *Cartulario de la Universidad de Salamanca*, II, *La Universidad en el siglo de oro* (Salamanca: Universidad Pontificia, 1970), 100-02.

10. Azcona, *La elección*, pp. 219-20.

11. Yitzhak Baer, *A History of the Jews in Christian Spain*, 2 vols, 2nd edition (Philadelphia: Jewish Publication Society of America, 1971), II, 282-83.

12. Alonso de Palencia, *Crónica de Enrique IV*, BAE, CCLVII (Madrid: Atlas 1973), 40, 65, 84-85.

13. Biographical notes to Palencia's *Crónica*, BAE, CCLXVII (Madrid: Atlas, 1975), 251n; Robert Brian Tate, 'Political Allegory in Fifteenth-Century Spain: a study

of the *Batalla campal de los perros contra los lobos* by Alonso de Palencia (1423-92)', *Journal of Hispanic Philology*, I (1976-77), 169-86.

14. Palencia, *Crónica*, BAE, CCLXVII, 252n; Francisco Cantera Burgos, *Pedrarias Dávila y Cota, capitán general y gobernador de Castilla de Oro y Nicaragua: sus antecedentes judíos* (Madrid: CSIC, 1971), pp. 30-31n. The use of the phrase 'puto judío' to refer to Jesus himself appears in an accusation brought before the Inquisition of Soria-Burgo de Osma in *ca*. 1478 (John Edwards, 'Religious Faith and Doubt in Late Medieval Spain: Soria, *circa* 1450-1500', *P&P*, CXX (1988), 1-25, at 14) while by this period it was conventional to portray the Roman soldiers in the Passion story as Jews (Bernhard Blumenkranz, *Le Juif médiéval au miroir de l'art chrétien* (Paris: Études Augustiniennes, 1966), pp. 94-104).

15. Lea, *History*, II, 42-44; Juan Blázquez Miguel, *Inquisición y criptojudaísmo* (Toledo: Diputación Provincial, 1988), pp. 190-200.

16. Lea, *History*, II, 43; Azcona, *Elección*, p. 220; Diego de Colmenares, *Historia de la insigne ciudad de Segovia y compendio de las historias de Castilla*, new edition (Segovia: Academia de Historia y Arte de San Quirce, 1970), II, 131-32.

17. Azcona, *Elección*, p. 219 (text of bull in Llorca, *Bulario*, pp. 90-92).

18. Azcona, *Elección*, p. 219; G.A. Bergenroth, ed., *Calendar of Letters, Despatches and State Papers relating to the Negotiations between England and Spain*, I, *Henry VII, 1485-1509* (London: Longman, 1862), xlv.

19. Fidel Fita, 'La judería de Segovia – documentos inéditos', *Boletín de la Real Academia de la Historia*, IX (1886), 270-93, 353-54.

20. For an example of the use of these categories in the analysis of pre-trial inquisitorial material, see Edwards, 'Religious Faith and Doubt', 3-25.

21. *FIRC*, III, 19-33, 37-39, 42-54, 60-76, 78-81, 86-115, 117-20.

22. *Ibid.*, 19-24, 32-39, 41-44, 48, 50-58, 60-61, 63-64, 66-68, 71-77, 81, 83, 89, 93-94, 99-100, 103-05, 108-09, 113, 115-17.

23. *Ibid.*, 26-27, 57-58, 70-71, 78, 112, 114-15.

24. *Ibid.*, 20-21, 26, 28, 53-54, 80-81, 92-94, 101, 114, 116.

25. *Ibid.*, 23, 27, 29, 31-33, 36, 40-45, 59, 77, 88.

26. *Ibid.*, 30-31, 58, 61-62, 68, 89-92; Edwards, 'Religious Faith and Doubt', 13-16, 20-25.

27. *FIRC*, III, 41, 85-86.

28. *Ibid.*, 40-42, 46, 55, 63-64, 99-100.

29. Haim Beinart, *Records of the Trials of the Spanish Inquisition in Ciudad Real*, 4 vols (Jerusalem: Israel Academy of Sciences and Humanities, 1974-83); *Conversos on Trial. The Inquisition in Ciudad Real* (Jerusalem: Magnes, 1981); *Trujillo: a Jewish community in Extremadura on the eve of the expulsion from Spain* (Jerusalem: Magnes, 1980); Renée Levine, 'Women in Spanish crypto-Judaism, 1492-1520'

(unpublished Ph.D. dissertation, Brandeis University, 1982); Rafael Gracia Boix, *Colección de documentos para la historia de la Inquisición de Córdoba* (Córdoba: Caja de Ahorros, 1982); Edwards, 'Trial of an Inquisitor: the dismissal of Diego Rodríguez Lucero, inquisitor of Córdoba, in 1508', *Journal of Ecclesiastical History*, XXXVII (1986), 240-57; 'Religious Faith and Doubt', 6-11.

30.   *FIRC*, III, 31-32, 34, 55-56, 59, 100-01.

31.   *Ibid.*, 55-56; Beinart, 'Jewish Witnesses for the Prosecution of the Spanish Inquisition', in *Essays in Honour of Ben Beinart*, I, Acta Juridica, 1976 (Capetown: Juta, 1978), 37-46; *Trujillo*, pp. 93-94, 100-02, 304-05, 333-35; 'The Spanish Inquisition and a *converso* Community in Extremadura', *Medieval Studies*, XLIII (1981), 445-71; Edwards, 'Jewish Testimony to the Spanish Inquisition: Teruel, 1484-7', *Revue des Études Juives*, CXLIII (1984), 333-50; 'Religious Faith and Doubt', 7-8.

32.   Baer, *History of the Jews*, II, 282-83.

33.   Cantera, *Pedrarias*, p. 30n.

34.   Palencia, *Crónica*, BAE, CCLVII, 40, 84-85, 93.

35.   Eleazar Gutwirth, 'Elementos étnicos e históricos en las relaciones judeo-conversos en Segovia', in *Jews and Conversos. Studies in society and the Inquisition (Proceedings of the Eighth World Congress of Jewish Studies, held at the Hebrew University of Jerusalem, August 16-21, 1981)*, edited by Yosef Kaplan (Jerusalem: World Union of Jewish Studies, 1985), p. 86.

36.   Cantera, *Pedrarias*, p. 14.

37.   Azcona, *Isabel la Católica* (Madrid: Biblioteca de Autores Cristianos, 1964), p. 453.

38.   Azcona, *Elección*, p. 220; J.N. Hillgarth, *The Spanish Kingdoms, 1250-1516*, II, *1410-1516. Castilian Hegemony* (Oxford: Clarendon, 1978), 181; Colmenares, *Historia*, II, 138-39; Lea, *History*, II, 43.

39.   Edwards, 'Fifteenth-century Franciscan Reform and the Spanish *conversos*: the case of Fray Alonso de Espina', in *Monastic Studies: the continuity of tradition*, edited by Judith Loades (Bangor: Headstart History, 1990), pp. 203-210.

40.   Beltrán, *Cartulario*, II, 96-97: *RGS*, 10.2.1488.

41.   Beltrán, *Cartulario*, II, 95; *RGS*, 13.3.1478, 19.12.1480, 15.12.1483, 26.11.1484, 10.5.1485, 18.5.1485, 18.6.1485, 19.12.1485.

42.   Baer, *History*, II, 285-88 (*Fortalitium Fidei*, book III, Consideratio vii: *De crudelitatibus Iudaeorum*).

43.   *FIRC*, III, 33, 37-38, 79.

44.   *Ibid.*, 37-38, 43-44, 72, 79-80.

45.   Azcona, *Juan de Castilla, rector de Salamanca. Su doctrina sobre el derecho de los reyes de España a la presentación de obispos* (Salamanca: Universidad Pontificia,

1975), pp. 14-38; Beltrán, *Cartulario*, II, 97-99; Carrete, *FIRC*, I, *Provincia de Salamanca* (Salamanca: Universidad Pontificia, 1981), 124-25.

46. Azcona, *Juan de Castilla*, pp. 32-33.
47. Beltrán, *Cartulario*, II, 101-02; Azcona, *Isabel la Católica*, p. 453, referring to the documents which Beltrán, unlike Azcona, was able to publish.
48. Beltrán, *Cartulario*, II, 100.
49. Azcona, *Isabel la Católica*, pp. 410-11; *Elección*, pp. 220-22.
50. *Ibid.*, pp. 223-24.

THE DEATH OF ᶜANTAR :
AN ARABIC ANALOGUE FOR THE CID OF CARDEÑA

Brenda Fish

The rather bizarre account in the *Primera crónica general* of the Cid's activities shortly before and after his death has previously always been classed as pure invention by the monks of Cardeña to bolster the importance of their monastery and attract patronage and pilgrims. P.E. Russell considered that the legend was fabricated by the monks to account for pre-existing relics: 'It is easier to conceive of the peculiar tale of the Cid's auto-embalmment by means of Oriental unguents as an attempt to invent a history for pre-existing relics than as a result of the free exercise of monkish fantasy'.[1] This is still the generally accepted view, but it leaves open the question why the monks should have opted for that particular version of the death of the hero to explain their relic collection. Colin Smith has traced a Carolingian source for the embalming of the Cid; but as regards the fight against Búcar, the Cid's departure from Valencia strapped on his horse, and the re-occupation of the city by the Moors of Valencia, Smith has said: 'All is taken from the *Estoria*, which is repeatedly mentioned as the chronicle's source, and is purely Hispanic in inspiration'.[2]

This prevailing critical opinion in favour of a Christian, clerical source for this episode does not however shed light on why the chronicle account should repeatedly stress an Arabic source for these events. In the *Primera crónica general* the explicit source for the final siege of Valencia and death of the Cid is the '*Estoria del Cid*', which it says was written by Abenalfarax (p. 633a24-25), the nephew of Gil Díaz who before his conversion was Alhuacaxi, the 'moro alfaqui' who wrote the verses quoted in Arabic about the fall of Valencia to the Cid (p. 582a28). Moreover, we are told that the original *Estoria* was actually written in Arabic: 'Segunt cuenta Abenalfarax, que fizo esta estoria en aravigo ...' (p. 638a50-51).[3] I am not suggesting that we should take any of these statements at face value, merely pointing out that the compilers of the chronicle went to great pains to show their source for this episode, which they identified as Arabic. The strong Arabic element in the chronicle narrative at this point emboldens me to suggest an Arabic analogue for this episode for the death of the Cid. Some time ago I was struck by the parallels with the death of the Arabian pre-Islamic hero, ᶜAntar ibn Shaddād: in the epic account of his adventures, the *Sīrat ᶜAntar*, the dead body of the hero, in full armour and propped up on his horse, holds the enemy tribes at bay and allows his wife and followers to get back to the safety of their home territory. I hope to demonstrate in the present study that the similarities between the death of ᶜAntar and that of the Cid in the *Primera crónica general* are in several respects quite striking, and I would suggest that it may be worth bearing in mind the analogue of the death of ᶜAntar in any future analysis of the development of the Cid legend. The parallels between the two are especially interesting in view of the apparent absence of any other analogues in the deaths of heroes in other European epics; nor, indeed, does the motif 'dead hero on horseback' occur in Stith Thompson's *Motif-Index of Folk-Literature*.[4]

The adventures of ᶜAntar ibn Shaddād, the black knight of the ᶜAbs, have a long history in the Arabic oral tradition of story telling. ᶜAntar also has a place in the Islamic classical tradition by virtue of the autobiographical poems attributed to him – the *Muᶜallaka* which celebrate his valour and exploits, and extol the claim which these give him to the love of ᶜAbla. Collections of this poetry were already being made in the ninth and tenth centuries, with biographers adding accounts of the hero's life. Perhaps the most famous collector of these poems was al-Asmaᶜī, a noted grammarian at the court of Hārūn al-Rashīd and later at that of his son, al-Ma'mūn, in the late eighth to early ninth centuries. According to R. Blachère, there is a recension of this collection with commentary by the Spaniard al-Aᶜlam al-Shantamarī, who died in 1083, but unfortunately I have been unable to trace any translation of this.[5] At some time prior to the late fourteenth century these stories were gathered together in written form as the *Sīrat ᶜAntar* or the *Story of ᶜAntar*.[6] European translators frequently render the work as the *Romance of ᶜAntar*, which is not strictly correct. In Arabic the word 'sīra' means a biographical (implicitly historical) narrative, whereas a romantic (implicitly fictional) narrative would be called a 'ḥikāya'. It must be said, however, that 'history' for medieval Arabs, especially in the heroic tradition as we have here, was understood in much the same way as was 'history' for medieval Europeans: that is, it incorporated over time those legendary accounts or explanations of events that became sanctified by tradition. The *Sīrat ᶜAntar* is a mixture of both popular and learned elements and is considered by Arabs to be the model for all heroic narratives. There are in existence today various recensions of the *Sīrat ᶜAntar*. The generally accepted canonical version is the *Ḥijāzīya* (claiming to originate from the Hejaz, Saudi Arabia), which is very long, filling thirty-two volumes in the Bulaq edition of 1866-70. There are also shorter versions, denominated the *Sha'mīya* (claiming origin from Syria), the Beirut edition of 1865 having ten volumes. According to H.T. Norris (p. 220), both the *Ḥijāzīya* and the *Sha'mīya* versions recount the hero's death in similar narratives (I shall refer to the divergences later) but the poetic insertions are markedly different.

The date of these recensions is disputed. There is a tradition that the composition of a full-length *Sīrat ᶜAntar* began as a courtly pastime in Egypt at the end of the tenth century, but the earliest independent record of a written composition by Abū Mu'ayyad Muḥammad ibn al-Mujāllī ibn al-Sā'igh al-Jazarī appears in the first half of the twelfth century. The *Sīra* itself states it was the work of al-Asmaᶜī, i.e. written some time at the end of the eighth or early ninth century, but certain elements at least are obviously much more recent than this. Norris (p. 42), from a study of the internal evidence of the

Sīra, especially of the names of characters, suggests a final date of 1350, since the Frankish personalities mentioned would appear to come only from the First Crusade. But, for him, some parts would seem to date from an earlier period of Arab history, probably the tenth century.

Other recent critics have dated the Sīra as thirteenth-century Egyptian (Abel, again from internal evidence); early twelfth century (Dover, from what he sees as the earliest 'rédaction originale'); and pre-twelfth century (Marcos Marín, from his estimated dating of the poetry). Vernet, from the evidence of geographical names, suggests an early compilation in the tenth century and a later definitive version in the twelfth.[7]

cAntar is said to have lived in the late sixth century A.D., at a time when the Banū cAbs did indeed rise to pre-eminence over their neighbours. He is, therefore, theoretically a hero of pre-Islamic Arabia, but in the Sīra the coming of Muhammad is revealed to him and he acknowledges Islam, thus becoming the hero of the Islamic world too. Bernard Heller (p. 518) sums up the Sīra as follows : 'The Sīrat cAntar far transcends the unconscious development of a legend. By a bold stroke cAntar, the solitary hero, is raised to be the representative of all that is Arab, cAntar the pagan is made the champion of Islam.'

In the Sīra cAntar, the son of a North African Bedouin chief (himself a hero figure) and of a beautiful black slave, shows exceptional strength and skill as a leader of men in battle. Although originally of the same inferior status as his mother, he rises to become the greatest leader of his tribe, the Banū cAbs. He falls in love with and marries his beautiful cousin cAbla, after performing many Herculean tasks to win her hand. He establishes the superiority of his tribe over all the neighbouring ones, and then moves further afield, conquering peoples within Arabia and 'black' Africa, defeating the Franks, subjugating King Sancho (or it might be Santiago) of Spain and liberating the King of Rome.[8]

The account in the Sīra of the death of cAntar may be summarized briefly as follows:[9] cAntar, when camped overnight in enemy territory with his wife, cAbla, and all his men, is caught unawares and shot at by Wizr, an old adversary whom he had previously blinded in combat.[10] The wound itself is not serious, but the arrow is poisoned and cAntar realizes that within a few days he will die. Therefore he must devise a plan to get his wife and men and all the riches he has won in battle back to the safety of their home territory, because if the enemy sense that he is dead his people will be slaughtered and the caravan plundered. His first plan is to change roles with his wife. He will ride in her litter, and she will don his armour, carry his sword and spear and ride his horse, Abdjar, so that the enemy bands will believe he is still leading his men, and thus no-one will dare attack the caravan. This ruse is unsuccessful when a wily old enemy sheikh guesses the identity of the 'horseman'.[11] cAntar then changes back with his wife and, although in great pain, dons his armour, takes up his weapons and rides his horse at the head of his forces. This time the enemy keep their distance. When the caravan reaches a narrow defile, which leads to the security of their home territory, ^cAntar is in his death throes but he stands guard over the pass, keeping the marauding tribesmen at bay so that his people can pass through to safety. There death comes to him, unnoticed by the enemy, and all night the dead hero remains seated on his horse. In the morning he is still there, motionless, propped up by his spear, until suddenly the horse moves and his body crashes to the ground.

The following section of this study will summarize what I see as the parallels between the death of ^cAntar in the *Sīra* and the death of the Cid in the *Primera crónica general*, including also what are not strictly parallels but rather transformations, where similar structural elements appear in each story, albeit in an inverted form. In the first place I shall discuss parallels and transformations of the structural elements of each story, and then I shall compare some of the individual motifs.

1. ^cAntar learns that he will die when he is far from home and in a hostile land. Although when alive his reputation as a warrior is sufficient to ward off attack, he knows that once his enemies learn that he is dead his party will be overwhelmed. He has to devise a plan to get his wife and men back to safety amongst his own tribe before the news of his death becomes known to his enemies.

    The Cid is in a similar situation when he learns of his impending death, even though Valencia is a city he has held for five years, as opposed to the overnight camp of ^cAntar. The Cid explains to his wife and men that once he is dead they will be unable to defend Valencia, but he will show them what to do so that they can all get away to safety, taking with them all their wealth and his own embalmed body (p. 634b5-15).

2. Once ^cAntar has been hit by the poisoned arrow, he knows he will die. He accepts this with resignation, and tells his followers that no-one can avoid death, since all are subject to the same law. Because of the slow action of the poison, he has time to effect a plan of action. (In the *Ḥijāzīya* this takes five months and five days, whereas in the *Sha'mīya* the action all takes place within twenty-four hours.)

    St Peter gives the Cid thirty days' notice of death. Like ^cAntar, the Cid accepts the news calmly and stresses to his followers the inevitability of mortality. The Cid, therefore, has plenty of time to organize the action to be taken after his death (p. 634b30-39).

3. ^cAntar's first concern is to ensure a secure future for his wife ^cAbla. He arranges for her to go back to the safety of her homeland after his death and marry a 'man of valour' so that she may live out the rest of her life under the protection of one

who will console and look after her and see her to her grave (and, in the *Sha'mīya*, one 'who will defend your honour and your days').[12]
When the Cid reads out his will, after endowing a tomb for himself at Cardeña he sends Jimena to live out her days there 'bien et conplidamente a su onrra' with Gil Díaz to look after her (pp. 634b44-635a1).

4. The action by ᶜAntar to save his wife and men and all their wealth ends only with the discovery of his death by his enemies. The hero is directly in charge of events right up to the end; thus he is able to change his plan half-way through the account.
    The Cid, on the other hand, dies half-way through the action. But the plan he had decided on is carried out to the letter, right to the end of the episode; thus the Cid, too, is always in charge, even indirectly when he is dead (p. 635a20-b28).[13]

5. The tribesmen first decide to attack the caravan of ᶜAntar when they think he is dead and the caravan too weak to resist them. They run away terrified and perplexed when they realize he is still alive. In the *Sha'mīya* version most of them return to their own camps and only forty remain; in the *Hijāzīya* version 'they fled defeated into the wide deserts' but their reaction then is that ᶜAntar has tricked them and they return. At the end of the story, the tribesmen do not dare approach him, because they believe mistakenly that ᶜAntar is still alive and still suspect a trick. But the old sheikh is puzzled: ᶜAntar must be dead or he would fight. So this time they do not run away, but wait, and later plunder his body when they grasp the truth.
    In the siege of Valencia Búcar and his Moors arrive three days after the Cid's death, and after nine days they prepare to attack because they think the Cid does not dare to come out and fight; he is in fact dead (p. 636b25-30). The next day they are 'maravillados' and 'espantado(s)' by the attack of the mysterious white knight and the sixty thousand knights, and they run away 'et non tovieron rienda fasta en la mar' (pp. 637b25-638a4). Later on, the Moors of Valencia think the Cid is alive when they see him setting off for Castile, mounted on Bavieca, sword in hand, and 'fizieronse maravillados' when nobody comes back (p. 638b1-9). They do not dare to approach the tents of Búcar or enter the town, because they think the Cid is alive and they suspect a trick. When they realize the truth they and other Moors enter Valencia 'mas maravillados que antes' and the next day they all sack the tents of Búcar and get enough food to last them for ten years, let alone all the strange animals and rich treasures (pp. 639b1-640a19).

6. ᶜAntar's wife, ᶜAbla, is dressed (by him) in his armour, girds on his sword and holds his lance in her hand. She rides on his horse, Abdjar. ᶜAntar rides in her litter, and they set off at the head of all their men. The Syrian version translated by Caussin de Perceval specifies that ᶜAntar's brother, Jarīr, leads Abdjar while his

nephew Khadrouf guides the camel and litter carrying ᶜAntar. The enemy tribesmen recognize ᶜAntar's armour, weapons and horse, and think they see him leading the caravan. Only the old sheikh realizes that the person inside the armour is not ᶜAntar. Later, when the real ᶜAntar is mounted on Abdjar and wearing his armour, he rides by the side of ᶜAbla. Later still, the dead ᶜAntar is kept upright on his horse by leaning on his lance.

Perhaps we could combine these two personae of ᶜAntar and draw here a parallel with the dead Cid strapped on Bavieca to keep him upright, clad in mock armour, and with his sword tied to his hand, being led by Gil Díaz, with Don Jerónimo by his side and with Jimena 'a sus espaldas'. In this instance, the Cid is real, but his stance, his armour, etc. are not, except for his sword, and that is tied on (pp. 637a23-47). I would tentatively suggest that these two personae of ᶜAntar might be compared also to the appearance of the mysterious white knight, who arrives from nowhere and leads sixty thousand men into battle while the dead Cid, strapped on his horse, is being taken unobtrusively out of Valencia and back to Castile. This white knight with the fiery sword is presumably Santiago, since St Peter promised his help when he appeared to the Cid earlier on, and it is surprising, perhaps, that the *Primera crónica general* is not more explicit on this point.[14]

7. ᶜAntar leads ᶜAbla, the men and all the caravan until they reach the Gazelle Pass, where he stands guard while his wife and men continue through a narrow gorge into the safety of their homeland beyond. The narrowness of the gorge is stressed in the *Shámīya*, and is perfectly natural given the terrain of Northern Africa; in the *Ḥijāzīya* there is no mention of a valley or gorge, and we are told merely that the Banū ᶜAbs went deeper and deeper into the desert and the hills.

Jerónimo and Gil Díaz lead the Cid's body, Jimena and the baggage train out of the 'angostura' of the *huerta* into a 'llano' and towards Castile (p. 638a6-13). The word 'angostura' may refer to the restricted terrain around Valencia, where progress would be impeded by all the irrigation channels; or the 'angostura' may refer to the narrow strip of land between mountains and sea at Murviedro (modern Sagunto), which would appear to be their obvious route back to Osma. But the route described in the *Crónica* is to Siete Aguas that night, and eventually to Salva Cannete, which would appear to take them too far to the west.[15] In the ordinary course of events 'angosta' seems hardly the most apt description for the fertile *huerta* around Valencia, either in its usual meaning of 'narrow' or the older meaning of 'barren' given by Colin Smith in his edition of the *Poema de mio Cid*.[16]

8. Before his death ᶜAntar calls on ᶜAbla to mourn at his tomb 'when the dust rises in the deserts'. After death his body is first stripped of his armour and weapons by his enemies and then buried by them in the desert with the acclamation 'Oh noble

knight, in your life and after your death you guarded your herds and womenfolk'. But when the Banū ᶜAbs realize his fate they return, disinter his body, wrap him in shrouds, lay him on a camel and take him back through the hills and valleys to his homeland. There they bury him next to his father and friend, on a high peak where passing travellers and poets mourn him (according to the *Sha'mīya*): 'Glory to thee, brave warrior! During thy life thou hast been the defender and leader of thy tribe; and now, even in death, thou hast served thy brethren by the terror of thy corpse and of thy gallant name. May thy soul live forever! May the refreshing dews always moisten the ground of this thy last great exploit!'

Before his death the Cid orders his corpse to be taken to Cardeña so that his body shall not be 'aviltado nin desonrrado' after his death (p. 634b35-38). (Perhaps unnecessary stress is put on this point in the narrative.) After his death, the body is clad in the complicated mock armour and then placed on Bavieca and taken back to Cardeña, where many people come to honour his body and where his wife spends the remainder of her life in 'vegilias por onrra del Cid'. After ten years his body is buried next to his wife (pp. 636b36-643a22). (One is tempted at this point to refer also to the earlier version of the Cid's death, given in the *Historia Roderici*, where the hero is first buried in Valencia Cathedral and later disinterred by Jimena and taken back to Castile when Valencia is abandoned to the Moors.)[17]

Apart from the above parallels which may be traced in the structure of the two accounts, one can also see parallels in the motifs employed, which I will briefly enumerate:

a. Both heroes, when they realize death is imminent, are at pains to point out that death comes to all men and no-one can avoid it however great he may be.

b. ᶜAntar and the Cid both tell their wives and their followers that they will save them all and get them back to safety.

c. ᶜAntar distributes all his possessions when he knows he will die, with the largest share to his wife. The Cid does the same, with Jimena as the main legatee.

d. When he is dying ᶜAntar arranges for his great friend and companion, Amru, to kill every last man of his old enemy's tribe and then to return to his own people. The Cid on his deathbed arranges for Alvar Fáñez and Pedro Bermúdez to fight and defeat his old enemy Búcar, and to return to Castile afterwards.

e. Both heroes are given to weeping copiously at moments of great emotion. When ᶜAntar says his last farewell to his wife 'he gazed at ᶜAbla with the tears streaming from his eyes'. When the Cid tells his followers of his impending death he is 'llorando de los oios'; and later also on his deathbed he says a last goodbye to all his men 'llorando mucho de los oios'.

f.   Lastly, each hero has a famous horse which no-one will ever ride again after the death of its master (although in this they share a common element of medieval hero legends, as has been pointed out by Heller).[18]

Of course, the two accounts of the death of ᶜAntar and the death of the Cid, in spite of the many elements they appear to have in common, differ in certain fundamental and important ways; neither could be said to be a simple reflection of the other, and I do not intend to suggest this kind of relationship between them.

The most obvious difference, perhaps, is that the Cid's body is embalmed, and this is an important element of the Cid story which is quite missing from ᶜAntar. I wonder, would it be stretching it too far too argue that as far as the story of the Cid's death is concerned his auto-embalmment fills a similar structural role to that of the poisoning of ᶜAntar, albeit with opposite consequences? The poison is a foreign substance which is injected forcibly by an enemy into the hero's body and which eventually brings about his death and the decay of his body. The embalming balsam is a foreign substance which is taken willingly by the hero into his body, and which eventually brings about the lifelike appearance of his body which does not decay after death.

It does seem to me, however, almost perverse that the episode of the embalming, which makes the Cid's death so different from that of ᶜAntar, should contain so many Arabic or Oriental elements: the balsam and myrrh come from the Sultan of Persia; the 'escaño' is regarded generally as Moorish; the lifelike appearance of the Cid after embalming is constantly remarked on by the Christians as something strange and wonderful, and the practice of embalming is specifically attributed by Alfonso VI to the Egyptians (*PCG*, p. 640b4-14). Colin Smith has demonstrated clearly a Carolingian source for the cult in Cardeña of the embalmed body of the Cid and its related relics.[19] However, the chronicle narrative leading up to the Cid's death and final battle has other elements which are presented as solely Arabic in origin and which are not carried through to the later cult at Cardeña. A lot of space is given up to Nugeymath Turquia, the 'little star of Turkey', and her Amazon warriors (*PCG*, p. 637b24-38). L.P. Harvey has suggested that this is a mistaken identification of a band of Tuareg warriors.[20] Norris (p. 241), on the other hand, believes this may be a garbled reference to a legendary Yemenite female warrior, Zarqa (al) Yamama, stories of whom were popular amongst the Almoravids. If this is so, he says, it makes even more likely the borrowings of exploits of ᶜAntar in the same chronicle account. Another specifically Arabic element in the *Crónica* comes when the Moors of Valencia finally realize that the Cid is dead – they see written on the wall in Arabic the story of how he died and the subsequent events 'mas que lo levaran en aquella guisa por vencer al rey Búcar et porque non les contrallassen la yda ' (*PCG*, p. 638b31-35). As previously mentioned, the supposed source of the whole episode of the death of the Cid is Arabic, written by

Abenalfarax (the poet Ibn Faraj), and the man who takes the major role in the story after the Cid's death (not only in Valencia, but in Cardeña too) is the converted Moor, Gil Díaz, alias Alhuacaxi, 'el que fiziera los versos en razon de la cibdat de Valencia'. (Al-Waqqashī was in fact a well-known eleventh-century Andalusian scholar.) The prominence of these Arabic elements in the story of the Cid leads one to suggest that, whatever Carolingian sources may have existed for the actual embalming legend, there is at the same time a manifest arabization of the hero at this point in the *Primera crónica general*.

To turn to less controversial matters. There is another contrast between the two accounts, and this is the question of scale. Particularly in the *Sha'mīya* version, the account of the death of ᶜAntar is reasonable, rational and sparing in numbers. His original enemy, Wizr, has one slave, and the wily old sheikh has at first three hundred, later forty tribesmen. ᶜAntar himself has an unknown number of tribesmen plus close companions and family. (The *Sha'mīya* mentions only his friend, his nephew and ᶜAbla; in the *Hijāzīya* he has several companion knights plus uncles and other wives and slaves). Only Wizr and ᶜAntar are killed. There are no supernatural elements, nor complicated contrivances. In the *Sha'mīya* version of the *Sira* the whole action takes little more than thirty-six hours from start to finish, although in the *Hijāzīya* the same events take five months and five days. But even in the latter version the story of the death of ᶜAntar is striking, and indeed to the modern reader moving, in its sobriety and realism.

However, in the story of the Cid's death we have Búcar with thirty-six Moorish kings, three hundred Amazons and men camped in 15,000 tents. Many of the Amazons and Moors are killed in battle, and twenty kings and 10,000 men are drowned in the flight to the boats. In the Cid's party there are 1,500 knights and possibly more with Alvar Fáñez, not to mention the apparent host of 60,000 white knights led by Santiago. And, quite apart from the appearance of St Peter and the embalming process, there is all the complicated hardware and mock armour needed to fix the Cid on his horse. I should also include in this list of excesses the booty gathered by the Moors of Valencia (enough food to keep them for ten years and some left over to spare). Last of all there is the length of time the episode takes in the *Primera crónica general* – thirty days for the Cid to die, and another ten days of preparations before leaving Valencia.

Another facet of this contrast between the two accounts is that whilst the Cid episode is full of exotic elements, as already mentioned, the ᶜAntar episode seems consistently true to Bedouin behaviour and attitudes. Even amongst modern-day Bedouin there is still the practice of settling a blood feud between lineages which are related by marriage by binding the offender hand and foot so that he cannot move, tying him on his horse, and sending him over to the camp of the victim, accompanied by a holy-man, to offer his life in exchange for the life of the man he has killed. The anthropologist E.L. Peters adds that no Bedouin would agree for a moment to undertake this journey if he thought the offer would be accepted![21] I am not putting this forward as an example of some modern ritualization of ᶜAntar – which it is not – but as an example of Bedouin behaviour and attitudes in the present day. Moreover, the picture it conjures up is not so far from that of a dead hero on his horse.

I would suggest there is one last way in which the two accounts differ and that is in the extent of each hero's participation in his final battle after death. The dying ᶜAntar himself has to lead his people through enemy lands, and later his dead body mounted on Abdjar is still the only protector of the caravan. According to the *Sīra*, the dead ᶜAntar can indeed be seen to have actively participated in his last great victory over the enemy. Turning to the *Crónica*, however, we find that although St Peter promises the Cid that after his death he will defeat Búcar with the aid of Santiago (*PCG*, p. 633b41-42), in the event it is the Cid's men led by Alvar Fáñez and Pedro Bermúdez, together with Santiago, who defeat the Moors. In spite of all the elaborate preparation of the mock armour, which looks so real, and the ingenuity of the *tablas* to keep the Cid upright on Bavieca, we find that when the time comes to fight Búcar the dead hero on his horse is merely smuggled out of Valencia by a back way and led to safety by Bishop Jerónimo and Gil Díaz, together with Jimena and her attendants (*PCG*, p. 638a4-9). The dead Cid does not participate at all in the last battle of Valencia, and one wonders why the chroniclers put so much stress on all the mock armour and complicated apparatus to hold the hero on his horse, especially since these items did not feature in the relics at Cardeña later on and the chronicler tells us the armour was all taken off the Cid after the first day (*PCG*, p. 639a34-35). It seems such a fuss for nothing! Later popular ballad versions of the death of the Cid seem to follow a more logical conclusion, with the dead Cid himself leading his men into battle.

One final section remains of this present study, and that concerns whether the story of ᶜAntar was known in Spain, and if so when and in what form. Perhaps I should at this point make it clear that although we have been considering a written account of the *Sīra*, the story of ᶜAntar has since the Middle Ages and right down to the present day been part of a thriving and continuing oral tradition, recited by *rāwīs* (Arab minstrels) either telling stories learnt by heart or reading from the *Sīra*. In fact, the compiler of the *Sīrat ᶜAntar* frequently cites the scholar al-Asmaᶜī as the original *rāwī* who was the source of this written account. Thus: 'and al-Asmaᶜī, the *rāwī* of this collection, told us . . .'. Some *rāwīs* have always specialized in stories of ᶜAntar and are called *ᶜAntarīs*.[22] The genre was, and still is, essentially popular, and has consequently been frowned upon by classical and religious scholars of Islam, although an attempt was made within the ᶜAntar tradition to 'prove' the approval of Muḥammad for such stories. He is said to have exclaimed on one occasion that ᶜAntar was the only famous Bedouin warrior he could wish to have known. On another occasion it is said he told the Arabs to recount the story of ᶜAntar 'to make their children's hearts harder than stone'.[23]

It is certainly believed that Arab minstrels and story-tellers entertained at court in Christian Spain during the late Reconquest. Evidence of this is in the miniatures from the thirteenth-century *Cantigas* of Alfonso X showing Moorish and Christian *juglares* singing together, and also in the early twelfth-century record of the Arab historian Ibn Bassām who states, according to Menéndez Pidal, 'Cuéntase que en presencia del Campeador se estudiaban los libros; le leían los hechos y gestas de los antiguos valientes de la Arabia, y cuando llegó a oír la historia de Mohallab, se mostró extasiado, lleno de arrebato y admiración por tal héroe.'[24] Unfortunately, there is no specific mention of the stories or verses of ᶜAntar being told in this way in Christian Spain. We do know, however, that the stories and verses of ᶜAntar were recited in Moorish Spain. In a passage in Ibn al-Qūtiyya's *History of the Conquest of Spain* the Banū Qasī held hostage by the Caliph are ordered to stop reciting the verses of ᶜAntar, because 'no hacen más que enardecer y aumentar su afición a ser bravos guerreros'. The episode mentioned is said to have taken place in the reign of Emir Muhammad I (852-86), and according to Julián Ribera this history was written at the end of the tenth century.[25] The Banū Qasī were from the region of present-day Aragon, and were not in favour of the Omeya dynasty of the time. Ibn al-Qūtiyya describes them in another passage as being 'españoles islamizados' (p. xxvi). The Banū Qasī would appear to take their name from the Qays group of North Arabian Bedouin tribes, of whom the Banū ᶜAbs are a member. According to J.W. Fück, clans and families claiming (with perhaps uncertain justification) descent from these tribes were to be found in Spain.[26]

As for what exactly was recited in this oral tradition with regard to the death of ᶜAntar, we can of course only go by the written texts still extant. In the various biographies attached to his poems, ᶜAntar meets his death in differing ways. In the earliest versions (ninth and tenth centuries) he dies of old age in a dust storm, and in an eleventh-century version he is shot by Wizr the blind archer but manages to get back to his people before he dies. As already mentioned, the *Hijāzīya* probably dates from the mid-fourteenth century, so it may be reasonable to postulate a popular version of the story with the glorious finale to his death, on horseback defending his people, growing up between the eleventh and fourteenth centuries. Of course, with a culture as widespread as Islam, it is likely that different versions sprang up in different places. Norris (pp. 222-23) also suggests that variations in the *Sha'mīya* version indicate an earlier composition than the equivalent passages in the *Hijāzīya* version and that in particular certain components in the episode of the death of ᶜAntar were inserted in the *Sīra* in the tenth and eleventh centuries.

The **Estoria* was incorporated into the *Primera crónica general* some time in the mid fourteenth century (having been assembled previously by the chroniclers of Alfonso

X), if we accept Diego Catalán's dating, and was probably compiled between 1270 and 1283 according to Colin Smith.[27] On the basis of dates alone it might be argued, therefore, that the Cid could be the source for ᶜAntar in regard to the manner of their respective deaths, that is, if we accept there is a link between the two. What I think makes this supposition unlikely (although not, of course, impossible) is first of all the internal evidence that the account of the death of the Cid would appear to be a later reworking since it includes many exotic and fantastic elements, which the death of ᶜAntar does not.

Secondly, and I think more importantly, is the existence of yet another Arab Bedouin hero of pre-Islamic times, Rabīᶜa, whose death is remarkably similar to that of ᶜAntar. Rabīᶜa is a young man travelling with his sister and mother when they are attacked by a rival tribe exacting revenge for a blood feud. Rabīᶜa is mortally wounded in the fighting, but manages to ward off the enemy tribesmen, and stays sentinel on his horse at the head of the Gazelle Pass, even after death, to give the women time to get back through the valley to safety. The Arab chronicler who recounted this was apparently Abū Zakarīyā' (d. 1109), according to Lyall's *Translations of Ancient Arabian Poetry*. Lyall himself accuses the author of ᶜAntar of not scrupling 'to appropriate this heroic death for ᶜAntarah of ᶜAbs'. The chronicler, Zakarīyā', stresses several times that Rabīᶜa was the only hero to die this way, so it may be that by the early twelfth century there were already versions of ᶜAntar which had laid claim to this exploit.[28]

The parallels between Rabīᶜa and the Cid, however, are minimal, except for the dead hero on the horse motif, and defending his womenfolk in death as in life. ᶜAntar, on the other hand, has much in common with the Cid apart from the manner of their deaths. They were both depicted as heroes who had to overcome social obstacles in their early careers and who nevertheless gained for themselves positions of great power and wealth solely through their own exceptional skills of leadership in defeating their enemies in battle. It would seem logical, if we are to seek an explanation of the Arabic elements visible in the Cardeña legend, that ᶜAntar should provide the missing link.[29]

London

NOTES

1. P.E. Russell, 'San Pedro de Cardeña and the Heroic History of the Cid', *MAe*, XXVII (1958), 57-79, at p. 66.

2. Colin Smith, 'The Cid as Charlemagne in the *Leyenda de Cardeña*', *Ro*, XCVII (1976), 509-31, at p. 517.

3. All references to the *Primera crónica general* are taken from the edition of Ramón
    Menéndez Pidal, 2 vols (Madrid: Gredos, 1977).

4. Stith Thompson, *Motif-Index of Folk-Literature*, 2nd edition, 6 vols (Bloomington:
    Indiana University Press, 1966). The motif of the dead hero made to appear alive
    to frighten the enemy does occur (motif Z 292), but in every example it lacks the
    important element of the dead man on a horse. E.L. Ranelagh has suggested that
    the death of Cuchulainn is the closest to that of ᶜAntar (*The Past We Share*
    (London: Quartet, 1979), p. 151). H.T. Norris has said a part loan from the Old
    Testament kings Ahab or Josiah might be a possible source for the same episode
    in ᶜAntar (*The Adventures of Antar*, Approaches to Arabic Literature, III
    (Warminster: Aris & Phillips, 1980), p. 223). As I hope to demonstrate later in
    this study, there is no need to look so far afield for a source for the death of
    ᶜAntar.

5. R. Blachère, 'ᶜAntara', in *The Encyclopedia of Islam*, I (Leiden: E.J. Brill, and
    London: Luzac, 1960), 521-22, at p. 521. See also Bernard Heller, 'Sīrat ᶜAntar',
    ibid., pp. 518-21.

6. The most modern translation into English of episodes from the *Sīra* is that of H.T.
    Norris, *The Adventures of Antar* (see n. 4 above). Other so-called 'abridged'
    translations of the *Sīra* can be found in: Terrick Hamilton, *ᶜAntar, a Bedoueen
    Romance, translated from the Arabic* (London: John Murray, 1819-20); A. Caussin
    de Perceval, 'La Mort d'Antar' in *Journal Asiatique*, 2e série, XII (1833), 109-23; L.
    Marcel Devic, *Les Aventures d'Antar, fils de Cheddad. Roman arabe des temps anti-
    Islamiques*, edited by E. Leroux (Paris: Librairie de la Société Asiatique de l'École
    des Langues Orientales Vivantes, 1878); W.A. Clouston, *Arabian Poetry for English
    Readers* (Glasgow: privately printed, 1881), pp. 171-304 (a translation of Caussin
    de Perceval); Gustave Rouger, *Le Roman d'Antar d'après les anciens textes arabes*
    (Paris: H. Piazza, 1923) (this version based on Devic); E.L. Ranelagh, *The Past We
    Share* (an abridged version of Clouston). See also Diana Richmond, *ᶜAntar and
    ᶜAbla, A Bedouin Romance* (London: Quartet, 1978), for a reworking of the early
    episodes in the *Sīra*, based on translations made by Hamilton, Devic and Rouger.

7. Armand Abel, 'Formation et constitution du Roman d'Antar', *Atti del convegno
    internazionale sul tema: La poesia epica e la sua formazione. (Roma, 28 marzo-3
    aprile, 1969)* (Rome: Accademia Nazionale dei Lincei, 1970), pp. 717-30, at p. 729;
    Cedric Dover, 'The Black Knight', *Phylon (University of Atlanta Review of Race &
    Culture)*, XV (1954), Part II, 178; Francisco Marcos Marín, *Poesía narrativa árabe y
    épica hispánica: elementos árabes en los orígenes de la épica española* (Madrid:
    Gredos, 1971), p. 87; Juan Vernet, 'Antar y España', *BRABL*, XXXI (1965-66),
    345-50, at p. 347.

8. The Arabic 'Yuntā'īl' translates as 'Santiago', according to Heller, *op. cit.*); Norris (p. 206) argues that a better rendition might be 'she-elephant' or 'Santa Ella'.

9. For a full translation of the *Hijāzīya* text of the death of ᶜAntar in the *Sīrat ᶜAntar*, together with relevant extracts from the *Sha'mīya* texts, see Norris, pp. 207-22.

10. Norris (p. 219) has shown that the killing of a hero by a blind archer is a common motif in Oriental literature. In the *Sīra*, ᶜAntar is hit by the poisoned arrow when he has gone off by himself to urinate by the river bank. One is reminded here of a similar motif in the *PCG* when Sancho II is killed by Vellid Adolfo (*PCG*, p. 511a24-30).

11. His guess is confirmed when his men study the marks left in the sand after ᶜAbla has urinated. A hero's strength demonstrated in his manner of urinating was another popular motif in pre-Islamic stories, according to Norris (p. 226). Nineteenth-century translators of the *Sīra* either omit this episode, rewrite it, or give the details in Latin.

12. Caussin de Perceval, p. 115 (my translation).

13. This is an important consideration, which has been misunderstood by Bernard Heller, who suggests that whereas ᶜAntar knowingly defended his followers in this way, the dead Cid did so unknowingly, his body being merely used by others (*Die Bedeutung des arabischen ᶜAntar-Romans fuer die vergleichende Litteraturkunde* (Leipzig: H. Eichblatt, 1931), p. 144). In view of the explicit instructions given by the Cid in this respect, I feel that Heller's interpretation is mistaken.

14. The appearance of Santiago as a white knight fighting for the Christians against the Moors is, of course, a well-known motif in Spanish chronicles and follows his decisive intervention in the battle of Clavijo – a key victory in the early Reconquest. On the other hand, in the chronicle of the conquest of Mallorca the mysterious white knight who suddenly appears in the army of James I is said to be identified as St George: see Jaume I El Conqueridor, *Crònica o Llibre dels feits*, in *Les quatre grans cròniques*, edited by Ferran Soldevila, (Barcelona: Selecta, 1971), pp. 3-402, at p. 48. If we accept that it is indeed Santiago who appears at this point in the *Primera crónica general*, then he would appear to be acting as a 'proxy Cid': perhaps the nearest parallel in Spanish chronicles is when an angel takes a knight's place in battle so that he may fulfil his vow and remain in Church (*PCG*, pp. 426b25-427a14).

15. For the identification of Siete Aguas with modern Itiaguas see T.F. Glick, *Irrigation and Society in Medieval Valencia* (Cambridge, Mass.: Harvard University Press, 1970). I thank L.P. Harvey for his suggestion that 'angostura' here might refer to closed-in terrain or a dangerous situation (because of the danger arising from the siege), as opposed to the safety of the open land or 'llano', where the rest of the Cid's men catch up with them after defeating Búcar.

16. *Poema de mio Cid*, edited by Colin Smith (Oxford: Clarendon, 1972), p. 142

17. *Historia Roderici*, in Ramón Menéndez Pidal, *La España del Cid*, 7th edition, 2 vols (Madrid: Espasa-Calpe, 1947), II, 970-71.

18. Heller, in *Encyclopedia of Islam*, I, 520

19. Smith, 'The Cid as Charlemagne', pp. 518-31.

20. L.P. Harvey, 'Nugeymath Turquia: *Primera crónica general* Chapter 956', *JSemS*, XXIII (1968), 232-40.

21. E.L. Peters, 'Some Structural Aspects of the Feud amongst the Camel Herding Bedouin of Cyrenaica', *Africa*, XXXVII (1967), 261-80, at p. 270.

22. For an account of modern ^cAntarīs see Cedric Dover, 'The Black Knight', p. 41. For other accounts of earlier ^cAntarīs, see Norris, pp. 67-69.

23. Mentioned in A.P. Caussin de Perceval, *Essai sur l'histoire des Arabes avant l'Islamisme* (Paris: Firmin Didot, 1847-48), II, 514-27.

24. Menéndez Pidal, *La España del Cid*, p. 573.

25. Translated by Julián Ribera as 'Abenalcotía y su crónica' in *Disertaciones y opúsculos*, 2 vols (Madrid: Maestre, 1928), I, 79.

26. J.W. Fück, 'Ghaṭafān', in *Encyclopedia of Islam*, II (Leiden: E.J. Brill, and London: Luzac, 1965), 1023-24, at p. 1024.

27. Diego Catalán, 'El taller historiográfico alfonsí. Métodos y problemas en el trabajo compilatorio', *Ro*, LXXXIV (1963), 354-75; Colin Smith, 'The Cid as Charlemagne', p. 528.

28. Charles James Lyall, *Translations of Ancient Arabian Poetry, chiefly prae-Islamic* (London: Williams and Norgate, 1885), pp. 55-58.

29. A version of the present study was originally given as a paper at the Medieval Hispanic Research Seminar at Westfield College in May 1978 and I should like to take this opportunity to thank those present for their comments on my speculations. I should particularly like to express my thanks to Professor L.P. Harvey for reading an early draft of this paper at that time, and to Dr H.T. Norris who furnished me with various translations from the Arabic which were then unpublished.

BACK TO IBN QUZMĀN

T.J. Gorton

The debate over the metrical basis for Hispano-Arabic poetry is one which may be said without hesitation to have generated more heat than light.[1] This is doubtless attributable in part, at least, to the many related questions about which our knowledge is so very incomplete, and to the fact that to study the *zajals* of Ibn Quzmān or, to a lesser degree, the *muwaššaḥāt*, one ought simultaneously to be conversant with such disparate and relatively obscure subjects as a long-dead and still poorly documented dialect of medieval Arabic; the prosody and poetics of Classical Arabic poetry; medieval Hispanic linguistics; and various other more or less recondite fields. Suffice it to say that such breadth of knowledge is hardly encouraged in today's increasingly specialized academic environment.

Many years ago, I undertook a modest 'stock-taking' exercise of a polemic which once caused veritable torrents of ink to flow, and which is now (I believe) dormant if not outdated: the 'Arab Origins' theory of the genesis of medieval Romance lyric poetry.[2] My conclusion at that time was (to paraphrase) that, as no conclusive evidence one way or the other was likely ever to appear, interested scholars might just as well look at both Hispano-Arabic and medieval Romance lyrics as *poetry* rather than as an excuse for a good fight. One might be forgiven for making similar sententious remarks about the 'Metrical Debate', which one seasoned observer has described as suffering from the 'Emperor's New Clothes' syndrome.[3] Many of those who have investigated this problem have permitted themselves to indulge in intemperate descriptions of the motives, methodology, and manners of scholars whose ideas are opposed to theirs. This may be partly due to the variety of disciplines involved, national pride, even generational frictions.[4] As in the case of the delicate flowering of Provençal lyric or the best of Hispano-Arabic poetry, strophic or otherwise, the game is only worth the candle if it results in an advancement of our ability to understand and enjoy worthwhile works of art (an endeavour supported but not supplanted by the metrical, philological, or linguistic aspects), simplistic as that may sound in an atmosphere charged with invective.

Coming back to the question after several years of absence from the scene, I find that the battle-lines have blurred somewhat. As at least one of the first to expound systematically the idea that the basis of Ibn Quzmān's prosody was related to the quantitative rhythms of Classical Arabic metrics,[5] I have come in for a goodly share of criticism as an 'extreme' classicist. I came to the conclusion that, while many of his metres did not coincide with Khalilian *ᶜarūḍ*, they did display clear quantitative patterns behind which one could identify new juxtapositions of classical feet and other less readily classifiable, but clearly discernible, quantitative patterns. This was of course

103

anathema to the Spanish school of García Gómez, who had painstakingly assembled hundreds of Romance 'rhythmic parallels' to enable them to classify Ibn Quzmān's rhythms as, for example, 12-syllable anapaests. The evidence seemed to me, and still seems, to indicate that many of Ibn Quzmān's *zajals* were not isosyllabic and that the variations correspond to permitted quantitative equivalences familiar to Arabic prosody. Identical patterns are found in the Classical Arabic *muwaššaḥāt* Ibn Quzmān sometimes explicitly imitated.

I used the metrical patterns identified from the *zajals* and collated, usually with little difficulty, with Khalilian rhythms or variations thereof as a tool in preparing a complete critical edition of Ibn Quzmān's *Dīwān* in Arabic script.[6] Where the inadequate manuscript tradition was deficient, I found the metrical and expected linguistic forms to coincide in the overwhelming majority of cases.[7] In 1979, Federico Corriente published his *Gramática, métrica y texto del cancionero hispanoárabe de Aban Quzmān*, also containing a critical edition in Arabic script.[8] Sr Corriente refers to my work as an 'insistent defence' of a 'maximalist' classical theory,[9] but goes on to classify Ibn Quzmān's *Dīwān* according to Khalilian and neo-Khalilian patterns which govern the prosody of the songs even though the basic *force motrice* underlying them is held to be phonemic stress, not quantity. The patterns in Corriente's schemata are very often similar and in some cases identical to mine, which were identified taking quantity alone into account. The implication, not implausible but unfortunately very hard to prove, seems to be that Ibn Quzmān was writing as the boundaries blurred between vowel length and stress, with the two coinciding in some cases and not in others.

This approach is supported by impressive scholarship and I find it most appealing, if not entirely conclusive in view of the uncertainties still surrounding the genesis of Arab prosody;[10] the vexed relationship between quantity and stress in Arabic generally; and our imperfect knowledge of stress in medieval Spanish Arabic particularly.

That said, I do find myself concluding from Corriente's work that the most likely explanation for the very few of Ibn Quzmān's metres that defy convincing classification according to recognizable Khalilian feet is to be found in the grey areas between stress and pure quantity, and I applaud his efforts to increase our understanding of accent in Hispano-Arabic.[11] It remains to be seen how much further this enquiry can usefully be pursued as a tool for improving our understanding of Hispano-Arabic strophic poetry, however, given the various limitations mentioned above.

As to the *muwaššaḥāt*, neither Corriente nor anyone else has managed to show that their rhythms are other than classical, as defined to include new combinations of Arabic feet; their language, unlike that of the *zajal*, makes this eminently verifiable, so that the current vestigial debate on that subject is of limited relevance. As for the *zajal*, the identification of its metrical basis is still highly relevant given the obscurity of its origin as a poetic form, the intrinsic difficulty of the texts, and the poverty of the manuscript tradition. These same elements make the task as formidable as it is relevant, however, and I would like to conclude this retrospective with a critical edition and translation of one of Ibn Quzmān's 'atypical' *zajals*, which one might call 'The Ravens'.[12] It is indeed unusual in the totally non-*jongleuresque*,[13] wistful tone, its brevity, its unity of feeling, and especially its skilful blending of a ubiquitous classical *locus* (weeping over the campsite, *al-bukā' ᶜalā l-aṭlāl*) with personal pathos. García Gómez finds it characterized more by 'convencionalismo' than by the 'cierta fuerza lírica' he admits it displays;[14] I am reminded of the great Alfred Jeanroy's description of the poetry of the troubadours as 'un chapelet de lieux communs': Ibn Quzmān here is using subtle nuances to elicit poetry from the commonplace, just as classical writers did even when writing in strictly codified genres.[15] The Romance technique of formal poetics has been ably studied by Robert Guiette, who argues that the medieval reader was an initiate who instinctively separated the formula from its context in order to observe and appreciate the variations and nuances wherein 'formal' poetry resides.[16]

This is not to say that there were not hack poets in the Middle Ages who simply strung together *loci* in a conventional generic composition; nor even that Ibn Quzmān did not indulge in this at times, particularly in his long panegyrics. In 'The Ravens', however, the several registers on which he plays in turn are artfully juxtaposed in the style of true medieval 'formal' poetics, Arabic or Romance: the general *locus* (the Beloved's former dwelling) leading to the individualized suffering ('sooner could I reach the stars than bring him back'), and thence to the general misery afflicting Córdoba at the time ('laden with more spite than it can bear').

The text of 'The Ravens' which follows is edited from the Leningrad manuscript and newly translated. The rhyme being every bit as central to Ibn Quzmān's poetry as the much-discussed rhythm, I have not been able to resist rhyming at least the *asmāṭ* or second members of the refrain. For this and for any other departures from accurate literal translation I apologize; so far as I know, however, very few of Ibn Quzmān's poems have been translated into English, and those few with which I am familiar attempt a literal translation which at best conveys the prosaic meaning, but gives the reader unfamiliar with the original no idea of the poetry. García Gómez's translation in *Todo Ben Quzmān* succeeded admirably, in my opinion, in its avowed 'propósito de arte'. I therefore thought it worthwhile to attempt a translation which is other than literal: non-Arabist English-speaking readers ought to have a window on Ibn Quzmān, especially if the *Dīwān* is ever to be considered as poetry rather than as grist to the mill of arid polemics.

Zajal No. 147

1	dār al-ḥabīb muḏ bān	mahdūma lil-qāᶜ
2	ᶜalā ḥabār¹⁷ ad-dār	li-wuddi narjaᶜ

3		raḥal ᶜan al-mawṭin man hān¹⁸ raḥīlu
4		wad-dār qāᶜan ṣafṣaf¹⁹ kaḏā faṣīlu
5		yarthī fīh al-qumrī ᶜalā ṭibāᶜu

6	man fāraq al-khullān	b-ay khair hu yaṭmaᶜ
7	bal yandub al-āthār	mawḏaᶜ fī mawḏaᶜ

8		qad ḥirtu fi buᶜdu wa-nqiṭāᶜu
9		mass an-nujūm aqrab min irtijāᶜu
10		tarā fīh al-qumrī kamā ṭibāᶜu

11	. . . yā ban quzmān²⁰	(las bi-)llah (yanfaᶜ)
12	man dā(r) ᶜalā (d-diyār)	billāhi (yū)jaᶜ

13		ayn dar aban²¹ . . . w-ayn iḥtifālu
14		w-ayn ḥawmat al-jāmiᶜ wa-ayn jamālu
15		ḥummil min al-makrūh fawq iḥtimālu

16	uqrub tarāh faddān	yuḥrath wa yuzraᶜ
17	wal-bāqī istibbār²²	lil-qāma yaqṭaᶜ

18		ka'anni lam naḥḍar dhīk al-majālis
19		maᶜ kulli mustaṭraf malīḥ muwānis
20		yā fiyya ḥusn az-zay min malābis

21	wan-naqra fil-ᶜīdān	yafᶜal wa yaṣnaᶜ
22	wa ṣawlat al-mizmār	min barra tusmaᶜ

23		qad ṭāb aban quzmān ṭūbā lu in dam
24		qad kānat ayyāmu aᶜyād fil-ayyām
25		baᶜd at-tabal wad-duff wa fatl al-akmam

26	min ṣumᶜat al-ādhān	yahbuṭ wa yaṭlaᶜ
27	imām fi masjid ṣār	yasjud wa yarkaᶜ

28	ṣawt al-ghurāb makrūh min ajli qubḥu
29	ma awshaḥu miskīn ma -qalla milḥu
30	dāyim narā ḥuznu matā hu farḥu

| 31 | fa-lᶜanhum²³ min ghurbān | manẓar wa masmaᶜ |
| 32 | yā aswadan miṭyār | kam dhā tarawwaᶜ |

The Ravens

| 1 | A hollow wasteland is his Dwelling, since my lover left; |
| 2 | Amid its faint traces, I am drawn to seek him there. |

3	As one whose time has come, he left this land,
4	His home, its graceful hall – a plain of desolation.
5	The mourning-dove laments him with its cooing:

| 6 | Whose lover leaves him | No hope retains; |
| 7 | But only weeping | Love's remains. |

8	Abandoned, far from him, I lie bewildered –
9	Sooner could I reach the stars than bring him back!
10	See the mourning-dove, as is his wont, saying:

| 11 | Oh Ban Quzmān | You weep in vain: |
| 12 | Stirring through ruins | Brings nought but pain. |

13	Where is Ibn . . .'s Lane, with its bustle?
14	Where the Mosque Quarter, and its beauty?
15	Laden it is with more spite than it can bear –

| 16 | Come close! you'll see a | Field to plough and seed; |
| 17 | The rest infested | Head-high with weed. |

18	Those splendid parties – did I not attend them,
19	With so many refined, convivial beauties?
20	And me all robed in exquisite finery –

| 21 | Endlessly strumming, | Plucking of lutes; |
| 22 | Outside could be heard | Trilling of flutes. |

23	Aban Quzman has reformed – bravo! (if it lasts);
24	His every day was a feast among days,
25	'Midst drums and tambourines and dancing sleeves rolled up;

| 26 | Now it's to the minaret | Up and down, |
| 27 | Or genuflecting in his | Priestly gown. |

28	The raven's ugly caw is loathsome;
29	How wretched he is, how devoid of beauty!
30	We only see his sadness – has he no hour of joy?

| 31 | A curse upon ravens' | Foul sound and sight: |
| 32 | Birds of dire omen, | Black as the night. |

Georgetown University

NOTES

1. A reasonably complete recent bibliography on the subject may be found in James T. Monroe, 'Poetic Quotation in the *Muwaššaḥa* and Its Implications: Andalusian strophic poetry as song', *La Corónica*, XIV (1985-86), 230-50, at 243 n. 4.
2. 'Arabic Influence on the Troubadours: documents and directions', *JArabL*, V (1974), 11-16.
3. Alan Jones, 'Romance Scansion and the *Muwaššaḥāt*: an Emperor's New Clothes?', *JArabL*, XI (1980), 36-55.
4. See especially 'Jarchas, moaxajas, zéjeles (II)', signed Ángel Ramírez Calvente, *Al-Andalus*, XLI (1976), 159-74; or James T. Monroe, '*¿Pedir peras al olmo?*': on medieval Arabs and modern Arabists', *La Corónica*, X (1981-82), 121-47, at 129-30.
5. Inspired by the pathfinding work of S.M. Stern, who died tragically just before I came to study at Oxford. Besides his unpublished Oxford thesis on the *muwaššahāt*, his unfinished work on the subject is most easily consulted in *Hispano-Arabic Strophic Poetry*, posthumously edited by L.P. Harvey (Oxford: Clarendon, 1974).

6. 'The *Dīwān* of Ibn Quzmān of Córdoba: a metrical study and complete critical edition' (unpublished D. Phil. thesis, Oxford, 1976). I regret that time has still not permitted me to prepare it for publication, but it has been consulted by a number of scholars working on the subject; see most recently Gregor Schöler, 'Ibn Quzmān's Metrik', *Bibliotheca Orientalis*, XL (1983), col. 311-32.

7. As originally described in 'The Metre of Ibn Quzmān: a "classical" approach', *JArabL*, VI (1975), 1-29, and continued in '*Zajal* and *Muwaššaḥ*: the continuing metrical debate', *JArabL*, IX (1978), 32-40.

8. Madrid: Instituto Hispano-Árabe de Cultura, 1980.

9. *Ibid.*, pp. 70-71, nn. 1-5

10. Al-Khalīl was supposed to have been inspired to codify the rhythms of poetry while listening to the varied and (still) hypnotic rhythms of the *naḥḥāsūn* in the famous Aleppo copper-souk: obviously stress-based rather than quantitative!

11. Even the most unorthodox metres in Ibn Quzmān are constructed around at least *one* easily recognizable foot; thus *zajal* 100 ($\smile - - / \smile \smile - - //$) or its inverse found in *zajal* 14 ($\smile \smile - / \smile \smile - - //$).

12. No. 147, ff. 72b-73a; metre *basīṭ* Derivative III ($\smile \smile \smile - - - / \smile - \smile - - //$)

13. See J.T. Monroe, 'Prolegomena to the Study of Ibn Quzmān: the poet as *jongleur*', in *El Romancero hoy: 2do Coloquio Internacional (Davis, 1977)*, III (Madrid: Gredos, 1979), 77-129.

14. *Todo Ben Quzmān* (Madrid: Gredos, 1972), p. 726. (Hereafter, *TBQ*.)

15. See especially Francis Cairns, *Generic Composition in Greek and Latin Poetry* (Edinburgh: University Press, 1972).

16. 'D'une Poésie formelle en France au Moyen Âge', *Revue des Sciences Humaines*, LIV (1949), 61-68.

17. *ḥabār*: MS *jabra*; I emend tentatively using the metre.

18. *ḥān*: MS *ḥāl*; I follow *TBQ*.

19. cf. *TBQ*, II, 728, n. 1, and *Qur'ān* XX, 107.

20. These two lines, illegible in Gunzburg's reproduction (*Le Divan d'Ibn Guzman: texte, traduction, commentaire. Fascicule I: Le Texte d'après le manuscrit unique du Musée Asiatique Impérial de St. Petersbourg* [Berlin, 1896]), are marginally clearer in the manuscript. I tentatively restore the words and letters in parenthesis.

21. 'Aban Zaid', as *TBQ* and A.R. Nykl, *El cancionero de Aben Guzman* (Madrid: Imprenta de E. Maestre, 1933), before him, is metrically wrong and not supported by the manuscript, which is at best illegible and definitely has no *zā'*.

22. *istibbār*: place where *estepas* or rock-roses grow; see *TBQ*, III, 337-38.

23. *fa-ḥanhum min* ought to scan ($\smile - - \smile -$); perhaps the juxtaposition of two *mims* results in one of them being silent, rather than a geminate pronunciation as one might expect.

ARABIC PROPER NAMES IN THE BECERRO DE CELANOVA

Richard Hitchcock

The Becerro de Celanova is a collection of documents relating to the monastery of San Salvador de Celanova near Orense in Galicia. The documents date from the ninth century to the end of the eleventh, and are written in an apparently twelfth-century hand on parchment comprising 197 folios in all.[1] A later introduction refers to three 'Libri' for which there are internal indices, but the documents themselves are not copied in any semblance of chronological order.[2] The entire compilation is well-known as a source of information about the region of Galicia, the reigns of Leonese monarchs, the bishopric of San Rosendo, and the commercial activities of Cresconio.[3] The bequests of San Rosendo's mother Ilduara and his own will and testament, both in favour of the monastery, have also received much attention.[4] Since these documents, in particular, contain many Arabic words, they have been used as evidence of Mozarabic infiltration in the Christian territories in the north of the Peninsula.[5] They are by no means the only source for such words among the Latin monastic cartularies, but they occur in somewhat startling profusion at an early date and thus bear eloquent testimony to a substantial level of arabicization. The penchant of the Christian nobility for Arabic products in the first half of the tenth century is one thing; quite another is the multiplicity of foreign proper names.

The incidence of foreign, principally but not exclusively Arabic, proper names in the surviving records of many Leonese and Galician monasteries has not passed unnoticed. Scrupulous editors of monastic registers have indexed them, sometimes indicating variants, but mostly without any explanatory commentary.[6] They remain, however, a rather cryptic corpus, about which it is safest to say that they are agents of Mozarabism in Christian territories, notably in the tenth century.

It is of course a dangerous procedure to abstract the names from the documents in which they appear. In the majority of instances, however, the arabicized name occurs only in the lists of witnesses to a legal contract, so that there is only slight enlightenment to be gleaned from the context. For the most part the Arabic equivalent of the Latin form of these names is immediately recognizable. Once the original Arabic name has been reconstituted, there is an obvious point to be made: the names are everyday Arab names employed in al-Andalus. With some exceptions, they are Arab names and there is not a shred of evidence to connect them with converts from the indigenous population; they do not suggest conversion from Christianity such as do some Arabic names.[7] Furthermore, the bearers of these names made no attempt to conceal the origin of their names. In many instances one would have to believe that they themselves were the first bearers of those names in Christian territory. As the tenth century progresses, some of the Arabic names are retained as patronyms, but by and large one must presume that in most instances the names disappeared when the bearers died.

The most striking feature of these names, then, is that they are unambiguously Arabic. The bearers acquired them in al-Andalus at an indeterminate time. In other words these people, at a certain stage in their life, for reasons that the documents do not reveal, moved away from an arabicized environment to the confines of a Galician monastery or to a settlement in the surrounding area. The natural assumption that has been made is that these bearers of Arabic names were, in their majority, religious refugees fleeing for unspecified reasons from persecution in their place of origin. According to this line of argument, they were Christians or, following the traditional denomination, Mozarabs who achieved safety and a new life for themselves in the Christian-controlled territories of the Iberian Peninsula.[8] It is debated whether such allegedly Christian emigrés went north as a consequence of religious persecution, or as a consequence of the policy of repopulation actively encouraged by kings of León from the late ninth century onwards. What is generally accepted, however, is that they were Mozarabs. The evidence provided by the incidence of these Arabic names amongst the Celanova documents does not appear to lend weight to this argument. One does not have to postulate a Christian origin for the bearers of these Arabic names. It is as feasible, I think, to posit their Islamic origin, for these arabicized Andalusis could well have responded to the invitation to repopulate Christian lands in the same way as their Christian counterparts. However, it is not necessary to insist on a religious motivation at all. The evidence simply suggests that arabicized people settled in the north of the Iberian Peninsula for reasons which are largely unknown. With certain exceptions, there is nothing to indicate their religion of origin.

One area where these exceptions apply is that of slavery. Some documents specifically refer to the presence as slaves of 'moros' brought from beyond the confines of Christian dominions. Much can be deduced from an examination of the 'siervos sarracenos' attached to the monastery of Santa María de Sobrado, in the present-day province of La Coruña, towards the end of the eleventh century.[9] In an undated genealogical document, studied by Hinojosa, it can be seen that the monks went recruiting for slaves, that their slaves had particular skills, and that when they arrived at the monastery they converted to Christianity and subsequently adopted new names. Before conversion they were called 'pagani'. Some died unconverted but the general custom was a ceremony of baptism followed by the acquisition of a new name. Thus Gali (?Ghālib) became Thomas, *pelitario*, and Ali Muogu, *textor*, took the name of Laurentius after baptism.

In the Celanova corpus, there are references to 'servos de origine maurorum' and, more revealingly, to a 'Salvador Rudesindiz fuit maurus'.[10] This person, who had five sons all with Christian names, may have taken as his surname that of the bishop,

Rosendo, and may have been given Salvador as his baptismal name. In the eleventh century Count Rodericus made an endowment to Donna Toda, including 'mancipios et mancipellas quos fuerunt ex gentes mahelitarum [*sic*] et agareni'.[11] These may have been young Muslim slaves, male and female, brought into the household. Clearly the presence of slaves in Galician monasteries accounts for some of the Arabic names, but for a minority only.

The proper names presented here have been rearranged into chronological order, and proceed only from the Becerro de Celanova. Great care has been taken to reproduce the form of the name as it occurs in the documents, and checks have been made on three separate occasions. The only changes that have been made to the manuscript text are that upper case has been used for all proper names, and that the names of abbots have been italicized. Dates have been converted from Era dates to A.D. The folio references are given and where there are two columns on the page, this additional indication is provided for ease of reference. The list is not exhaustive, but proper names whose Arabic origin may reasonably be deduced have been included, and names whose Arabic provenance is uncertain have been omitted. Also left out are names whose form is so corrupt that the original name, whether Arabic or otherwise, cannot be reconstituted. Arabic equivalents are offered as aids, but not as definitive solutions. Notes are provided for the earlier incidences of Arabic names, principally to indicate trends. As in its heyday the monastery of San Salvador de Celanova was very much part of the Leonese political scene, analogous examples have been sought from contemporary documents pertaining to the monastery of Sahagún. In the documents it is clear that to possess an Arabic name attracted no opprobrium *per se*; indeed Arabic names were sometimes retained through various generations. The holders of such names formed an integral part of the new communities. Whether Arabs by origin or arabicized members of the indigenous population of al-Andalus, they emigrated north. Once in Leonese territory, they participated, wholeheartedly and without any shade of embarrassment or suspicion of inferiority, in the secular and ecclesiastical life that had as its centre the monastery of Celanova.

University of Exeter

SAN SALVADOR DE CELANOVA

LIST OF ARABIC PROPER NAMES

Ninth Century

Year A.D.	Name	Folio
879	Homar	f. 104 l. 3
	(ʿUmar)	
	Ceidone	
	(Zaydūn)	

Sayyidun and Saʿīdun are both possible, but Zaydūn is preferred because it is well known as the name of the leading Andalusi poet of the early eleventh century, Ibn Zaydūn. Ceidone, together with Abedon, Kazemon and Amedon, reflect the characteristic North African and Andalusi suffix *-ūn*. This unusual termination is a feature of Andalusi proper names. Ibn Ḥafsūn, the ninth-century rebel against the ʿUmayyad amirate is, perhaps, the most famous example.

879	*Hazme* abba confirmans	f. 104 l. 8
	(Ḥazm)	

This abbot is not included in the list of eighteen abbots with Arabic names culled from the cartularies by Gómez-Moreno;[12] although some of the names listed by Gómez-Moreno are doubtful, the Arabic provenance of this abbot seems undeniable.

Tenth Century

905	Homari presbiter	f. 42v
	(ʿUmar)	

This presbiter may not be the same 'Omar presbiter' who was witness to a document in Sahagún in A.D. 939.[13]

916	Abedon testis	f. 29
	(ʿAbdūn)	

926	Amira	f. 198 col. 2 l. 29
	(ʿAmīra)	

Amīra, a female name, was amongst the list of ten 'puellas', probably slaves, who, together with ten 'pueros', were given to the monastery by Gunterigus and Dulcissime. These may belong to the list of 'servos de origine maurorum' referred to in a separate document on the same folio. Stained and inexpert restoration makes the reading difficult. There is a Muza and a Ceti in the list of 'pueros' but most of the names in both lists are unequivocally of non-Arabic origin.

927   Muza Ibenabdella confirmans   f. 182v col. 2 l. 2

         (Mūsā ibn ᶜAbd Allah)

One of the few instances where both elements of the full name are Arabic, indicating a first generation immigrant. The unlikely alternative would be that there was a known family called ᶜAbd Allah who had settled in that area, when it is not possible to say, and that this and the following person, ᶜAbd Allah de Ventosa (conceivably the father of Mūsā), belong to the same family.

         Abdella de Ventosa

         (ᶜAbd Allah)

932   *Aila* abba testis   f. 173v col. 2 l. 8

         (? ᶜĀ'ila)

There must be a doubt attending this name which is taken to correspond to Arabic ᶜĀ'ila, not listed as one of the eighteen abbots with Arabic names by Gómez-Moreno. Aila is recorded elsewhere in the corpus of documents, although not in Celanova.[14]

934   Belella testis   f. 148v col. 1 l. 10

         (Abū al- ᶜAlā, Bilāl)

This seems likely to be a corrupt form of some familiar Arabic name, one of the two suggested perhaps. There is no doubt about the reading of this word in the manuscript. Bellela is to be differentiated from the Ballello and Bellello of the Sahagún documents of A.D. 930.

         Kazeme testis

         (Qāsimī)

Kazem, a relatively familiar name in the corpus of cartularies, is readily distinguished from Hazme; the original forms are quite different.

941   *Medoma* abba testis   f. 21
                            (Muḥammad)

It seems to be difficult to find an alternative to Muḥammad as the original form of this name. The fact that an abbot bore the name Muḥammad is surprising according to Gómez-Moreno, 'puesto que estos leoneses casi nunca se llamaron Mahómad, considerado tal nombre como una cierta filación espiritual del Profeta, impropia de cristianos'.[15] Gómez-Moreno does not list this abbot but, in a footnote, he refers to five instances of a form of Muḥammad, including ᶜAjuz Medomat (in an Astorgan document of A.D. 937).

                     Megitus Sarracini testis
                     (Mājid, Majīd)

                     Gualamirus Egani testis
                     (al- ᶜAmīr)

943   Muzalha liberte mee   f. 60v col. 2 l. 8
                     (?Musallam)

In an important document, reproduced by Gómez-Moreno,[16] Bishop Rosendo makes a solemn and lengthy restitution of rights to 'liberte mee Muzalha'. Gómez-Moreno hypothesizes that 'Muzalha, cuyo nombre hace sospechar que procediese de mercado musulmán, pudo ser su aya, su educadora'. Muzalha is absolved from all servitude, is accorded the privileges of Roman citizenship and receives generous gifts of territory. It may, however, not be wholly infeasible to consider Muzalha a male slave whose name was perhaps formerly Musallam, and now the beneficiary on account of faithful services rendered.

947   Sarracinus Iben Sila testis   f. 83 col. 2 l. 35
                     (Ibn Sahl, ?Ṣāliḥ)

950   Rapinatus Ybenconaza confirmans   f. 38

One of the purposes of drawing attention to these two names is to demonstrate the process of assimilation of a name formed entirely according to Arabic requisites, to one which, whilst retaining an Arabic element, conforms to the standard practice followed in the Christian north. These examples represent the initial stage in the process where one element of the name is ostensibly Arabic (Sila, less convincingly Conaza), and the patronymic is preceded by the Arabic 'ibn', 'son of'. This Rapinatus is quite a familiar figure in Leonese documents, being a witness, for example, to a donation made by Ramiro II in favour of the monastery of Sahagún in A.D. 945.[17]

950   [villa de] Abder Regaulfus   f. 39

            Kacemon
            (Quẓmān, ?Qāsimūn)

            Iohannis Marvaniz
            (Marwān)

The replacement of 'ibn' by the Castilian practice of using the genitive form '-iz' as a suffix to the patronym saw the virtual disappearance of the Arabic usage. Irrespective of the name of the father this Castilian practice became the norm, thus Iohannis Marvaniz, the son of Marwān.

            Karini Marvaniz confirmans
            (Marwān)

951   Gaudio Haceme   f. 149v col. 2 l. 24
            (Ḥazm)

952   *Alfidius* abbas confirmans   f. 192 col. 2 l. 34
            (Abu al-Fidā')

This abbot, not present in Gómez-Moreno's list, may correspond to Arabic al-Fidā' with the Latin nominative form appended. There may be an identification with Abol Feta.[18]

953   Zitoni confessus   f. 180v col. 2 l. 38
            (Sayyidūn, Zaydūn)

954	Maruane presbiter [donor] (Marwān)	f. 80 col. 2 l. 13
955	*Ziton* abba (Sayyidūn, Zaydūn)	f. 176v col. 2 l. 26
956	Ragiane testis (Rayyān, Rayḥān)	f. 140 col. 1 l. 23
959	Zalamma presbiter (Salāmā)	f. 133v col. 1 l. 7
961	Raian (Rayyān)	f. 142v col. 1 l. 6
962	Hazeme testis (Ḥazm)	f. 60 col. 2 l. 21
963	Servus Moysen cognomento Abdela una cum coniuge mea Trudildi (Muḥsin; ᶜAbd Allah)	f. 76v col. 1 l. 6

Gómez-Moreno speaks of the use of 'cognomento' for surnames.[19] It seems, however, that 'Moysen cognomento Abdela' is an unusual example, because both name and surname are Arabic. The examples he provides also postdate this one. The fact that the bearer of this name is described as 'servus' would seem to militate against a Mozarabic origin.[20]

967	Medoma testis (Muḥammad)	f. 141v col. 1 l. 38
968	Munnios Aiub confirmans (Ayyūb)	f. 37v
969	Homar testis (ᶜUmar)	f. 143 col. 1 l. 3

982   Zamarius Quiriaci   f. 160 col. 1 l. 17
                       (Zamar, ?Shamarī, ?Asmar)

                       Manni conversus confirmans
                       (Mānic)

                       Zakarias abba   col. 2 l. 5
                       (Zakarīyyā)

It may be understood that Zacharias is both a Jewish and Muslim proper name. It
is possible that the abbot adopted this name because of the biblical precedent.

983   Zeit diaconus   f. 149 l. 26
                       (Zayd, Sacīd)

                       Kazem presbiter
                       (Qāṣim)

                       Hodman testis
                       (cUthmān)

                       Abgalip testis
                       (Abū Ghālib)

                       Kazan testis   l. 30
                       (?Ghuṣn)

                       Zait testis
                       (Zayd)

                       Dominicus Zicri diaconus
                       (?Zakarīyyā, ?Dhikrī)

                       Zeit Abuibet testis
                       (Sayyid Abū cUbayd)

983   Abdimelki [vinea]   f. 150 col. 1 l. 22
                       (cAbd al-Malik)

983	Temam testis (Tamām)	f. 150 col. 2 l. 2
	Kazem testis (Qāsim)	
	Alaz testis (ᶜAlā)	
	Abdalla presbiter testis (ᶜAbd Allah)	
	Kazan presbiter testis (?Ghusn)	
986	Avelavel Gudesteoz confirmans (Abī al-?)	f. 7
	Harramel Alvariz (Ar-Ramal)	
	Guttiher Avolmondariz (Abū al-Mundhir)	
987	Habze [abze] (ᶜAbsī)	f. 38v col. 2
	Abdella (ᶜAbd Allah)	
	Timimi presbiter (Tamīm)	
	Melhe presbiter (Malīh)	
992	Abdella testis (ᶜAbd Allah)	f. 171 col. 2 l. 18

993	Mahamuti Alvariz (Muḥammad)	f. 104 l. 21
	Francolino Muzaz (Mūsā)	
	Menindo Zuleimaz (Sulaymān)	
999	Frater Abregon testis (?Abū Rayyūn)	f. 181v col. 1 l. 38

Eleventh Century

1000	frater Aiub presbiter confirmans (Ayyūb)	f. 28v
	Mauran de Legione (Marwān)	
1000	Zemal (Jamāl)	f. 55 col. 1 l. 13
	Amedon (Hamdūn)	
1003	frater Abaiube confirmans (Abū Ayyūbī)	f. 81v col. 1 l. 16
1005	Menindo Zuleimaz (Sulaymān)	f. 107 l. 20
	Magister Azla (Aslām)	
	Egita Mescitiz (?Masjid) (?Mashhad)	
1007	Kedisolo	f. 68 col. 1 l. 31

(?Qādi, ?Qadīs Allah)

Ysma presbiter
(Asma)

Zaman testis
(?Zaman)

1010   Aiub confessus confirmans   f. 127 col. 1 l. 35
(Ayyūb)

Confessus may simply indicate 'conversus', and may not necessarily point to Jewish origin. There is a 'Fafila confessus', testator of a document dated A.D. 952 (Becerro de Celanova, f. 191v, col. 2, l. 10 ff); 'Alvanus confessus', A.D. 950 (f. 180, col. 2, l. 37), and in the eleventh century 'Tekiloni confessa Sarracina', A.D. 1055 (f. 21v). In these instances what is being indicated is conversion to Christianity and abjuration of previous beliefs.[21]

1010   Domno *Zacarias* abba   f. 149 col. 1 l. 10
(Zakarīyyā)

     Abzaet testis   col. 1 l. 38
(Abū Saʿīd)

1012   Zemale testis   f. 188v col. 1 l. 3
(Jamāl)

     Vidiselo de Zetacon confirmans
(Sayyid + ?)

1016   Zeiti testis   f. 122 l. 32
(Saʿīdī)

1017   Zemal testis   f. 124
(Zamal)

1017   Menendo Medomaz testis   f. 135v col. 1 l. 6
(Muḥammad)

1018	Medoma Fafaliz testis (Muḥammad)	f. 134v col. 2 l. 14
1018	Medoma testis (Muḥammad)	f. 135 col. 1 l. 23
	Ysmael testis (Isma'īl)	
1021	Adanaricum cognomento Maruan (Marwān)	f. 134 col. 2 l. 30
1025	Medoma testis (Muḥammad)	f. 134 col. 1 l. 11
	alio Medoma testis	
1026	Gemal mater (Jamāl)	f. 55
1026	Jacob Zemaliz (Zamal)	f. 162v col. 2 l. 21
	Zemel mater de mulier de Sonimiro (Zamal)	l. 38
1029	Halephe (Khalīfa)	f. 157 col. 2 l. 24
	Alveidar	
	Semza	
	Zeida (Saʿīda)	
	Sunana	

Salamon
(Sulaymān)

Mabona

Cidi et quattuor suos filios
(Sayyidī)

| 1031 | Gatime testis | f. 45 |
| | (Khāṭim) | |

| 1037 | frater Maimoni confirmans | f. 96v l. 34 |
| | (Maymūn) | |

| 1037 | Sanbati[22] | f. 163v col. 1 l. 11 |

| 1054 | Cidi Aveizza | f. 102 l. 8 |
| | (Abū ᶜIzza) | |

| 1063 | Zemal Seginiz | f. 116v l. 18 |
| | (Zamal) | |

| 1095 | Almachius Romaniz confirmans | f. 13 |
| | (al-Makkī) | |

This Almachius also appears in a document of A.D. 1100 (f. 116, l. 28) as 'Almachius conversus', clearly signifying his conversion from Islam to Christianity. The lateness of the date suggests, however, that he may not belong to the same category as the 'confessos' of the mid tenth century.[23]

NOTES

1. Archivo Histórico Nacional, 986B. The label on the rather worn spine reads 'Monasterio de San Salvador de Celanova -- Siglo XII'. The thick binding of leather on wood with broken iron clasps may be early, but the clasps themselves have the appearance of being a more recent addition. Some folios have been abstracted and inserted again, somewhat inexpertly.

2. The index for 'Liber duo' is given on ff. 39r-40v, and the 'tabla liber 3' is to be found on f. 156rv.

3. Historical studies include Justiniano Rodríguez, *Ramiro II, rey de León*, Instituto Jerónimo Zurita, Estudios, XL (Madrid: CSIC, 1972), with some documents copied in the Appendices; Emilio Sáez, 'Los ascendientes de San Rosendo. Notas para el estudio de la monarquía astur-leonesa durante los siglos IX y X', *Hispania*, VIII (1948), 3-76, 179-233; Henrique Flórez, *España Sagrada*, XVIII (Madrid: Antonio Marín, 1764); María Inés Carzoglio de Rossi, '"Cresconio", preposito [*sic*] de Celanova. Un personaje gallego al filo del siglo XI', *Cuadernos de Historia de España*, LVII-LVIII (1973), 225-79; Manuel Gómez-Moreno, *Iglesias mozárabes. Arte español de los siglos IX y XI* (Madrid: Centro de Estudios Históricos, 1919; republished Granada: Patronato de la Alhambra, 1975), pp. 239-50. Cf. also C. J. Bishko, 'The Pactual Tradition in Hispanic Monasticism' in *Spanish and Portuguese Monastic History, 600-1300* (London: Variorum Reprints, 1984), I, 1-43; and for a view of the 'monacato mozárabe', Antonio Linage Conde, *Los orígenes del monacato benedictino en la Península Ibérica*, Colección Fuentes y Estudios de Historia Leonesa, IX-XI, 3 vols (León: Centro de Estudios e Investigación "San Isidoro" 1973), II, 442-68.

4. Becerro de Celanova, ff. 5v-6v and 3-4, and dated A.D. 938 and 942, respectively. These were copied, along with other documents from Celanova and elsewhere, in the eighteenth century (BNM, MS 18387).

5. Gómez-Moreno, *op. cit.*, pp. 122-29. Claudio Sánchez-Albornoz, *Una ciudad de la España cristiana hace mil anos*, 5th edition (Madrid: Rialp, 1966), Apéndices III y IV, pp. 184-206. Many of the words abstracted by Gómez-Moreno were utilized by Joan Corominas, as philological evidence, in his *Diccionario crítico etimológico de la lengua castellana*, 4 vols (Berne: Francke, 1954).

6. Notable examples are Francisco Fuentes, *Catálogo de los archivos eclesiásticos de Tudela* (Tudela: Institución Príncipe de Viana, 1944), pp. 427-48; Raimundo Rodríguez, *Catálogo de documentos del monasterio de Santa María de Otero de las Dueñas* (León: Centro de Estudios e Investigación de San Isidoro, 1948); José María Mínguez Fernández, *Colección diplomática del monasterio de Sahagún (Siglo IX y X)*, Colección Fuentes y Estudios de Historia Leonesa, XVII (León: Centro de Estudios e Investigación "San Isidoro", Archivo Histórico Diocesano, Caja de Ahorros y Monte de Piedad de León, 1976), pp. 439-83; and Antonio C. Floriano [Antonio Floriano Cumbreño], *El Libro Registro de Corias*, 2 vols, Colección de Fuentes para la Historia de Asturias, II (Oviedo: Diputación de Asturias, Instituto de Estudios Asturianos, 1950), Segunda Parte, pp. 13-312. This is a model *antroponímico*, but there are very few Arabic names.

7. Two examples may be quoted: Rabí Ibn Zaid al-ᶜUsquf (the Bishop), the name used for Bishop Recemundus in the caliphal court in Córdoba (A.D. *ca.* 961); and Muqaddam ibn Muᶜāfā (tenth century) one of the names given to the inventor of the *muwashshaha* genre, a possible translation of Latin 'Praefectus filius Salvati'; see Brian Dutton, 'Some New Evidence for the Romance Origins of the *Muwashshahas*', *BHS*, XLII (1965), 73-81, at 78-80.

8. The arguments are clearly expounded in Gómez-Moreno, *Iglesias mozárabes*, pp. 116-19.

9. Eduardo Hinojosa, *Documentos para la historia de las instituciones de León y de Castilla (Siglos X-XIII)* (Madrid: Centro de Estudios Históricos, 1919), p. 43; also F. Godoy Alcántara, *Ensayo histórico etimológico filológico sobre los apellidos castellanos* (Madrid: Real Academia Española, 1871; republished Barcelona: El Albir, 1975), pp. 244-48; now, see Pilar Loscertales de G[arcía] de Valdeavellano, *Tumbos del monasterio de Sobrado de los Monjes*, 2 vols (Madrid: Archivo Histórico Nacional, 1976), II, 129-31.

10. f. 198, col. 1, l. 31, a document whose date is obscured but which may date to the second decade of the tenth century; and f. 56, col. 1, l. 27, undated document.

11. Document dated A.D. 1029, f. 157, col. 2, l. 24. Gómez-Moreno makes a passing reference to this document, which he dates A.D. 1032 (*op. cit.*, p. 119).

12. *Op. cit.*, p. 108, n. 5.13.

13. Mínguez, *Colección . . . de Sahagún*, p. 105.

14. Mínguez, *op. cit.*, p. 127 (document of A.D. 950).

15. Gómez-Moreno, *op. cit.*, p. 111.

16. *Op. cit.*, pp. 242-43.

17. Mínguez, *op. cit.*, p. 132, where he adopts the less arabicized practice of signing his name Conanci, rather than Ybenconaza.

18. *Op. cit.*, p. 179 (document of A.D. 954), and elsewhere.

19. Gómez-Moreno, *op. cit.*, pp. 110-11, and n. 5.

20. For a contrary view and a discussion of opinions, see Juan Ignacio Ruiz de la Peña, 'Siervos moros en la Asturias medieval', *Asturiensia Medievalia*, III (1979), 139-61, at 144-45.

21. The theory has recently been expounded by Ramon Díaz, 'Judío y confeso', *BHi*, LXXIV (1972), 125-27: 'no creemos que "confeso" sea lo mismo que judío' (p. 127); 'confeso era quien se desdecía; se volvía por coerción ambiental o por libre albedrío también a veces, al cristianismo' (p. 125).

22. The forms of this name, and those without any suggested Arabic equivalent in the document dated A.D. 1029, are too corrupt to risk identification, but are thought to be sufficiently Arabic in appearance to justify inclusion in this list.

23. See note 21.

SOME PROBLEMS IN ROMANCE EPIC PHRASEOLOGY

David Hook

Since L.P. Harvey drew the attention of students of the medieval Spanish epic to the material encountered by Albert B. Lord in his investigation into the oral-formulaic epic songs of modern Yugoslavia, awareness of formulaic verse traditions in languages other than Spanish has become part of the stock-in-trade of scholarly commentary on the few surviving epic texts from Spain: the formulaic content of individual Spanish poems has been studied, and one poem compared with another in this respect, while the formulae of Old Spanish texts have been related to those found in medieval French.[1] This paper examines a number of fresh formulaic and verbal parallels between the Spanish and the French epics which may help to illuminate some of the various problems encountered in the examination of formulaic verse, and in the study of putative literary sources, which naturally arise in the study of relations between these two epic traditions.[2]

Definitions of 'formula' have occupied much space in the scholarly literature; those offered by Parry ('a group of words which is regularly employed under the same metrical conditions to express a given essential idea') and Rychner ('La formule exprime donc une idée simple dans les mots qui conviennent à certaines conditions métriques') seem to vary essentially in the degree of flexibility which they are prepared to accept within the confines of a single 'formula', and various attempts have been made to arrive at closer definitions.[3] For the purposes of the present study, a phrase is accepted as a 'formula' if it is repeated exactly elsewhere in the same metrical circumstances: in other words, if it has two identical occurrences. Repeated phrases which are stable in their basic structure and lexical associations, but which exhibit variation in their details, are regarded here as 'formulaic expressions'. Thus, the phrase 'Otro dia mañana' (*PMC* 394, 413, 645, 682, 2651, 2870, 2878) is a formula, but the structure /*pensar de* + (infinitive)/ studied by Adams is defined here as a formulaic expression because it accepts variants of tense and person in *pensar* and wide lexical variation in the infinitive, and because it may occur in isolation as a second-hemistich formulaic expression (e.g., *PMC* 394, 413, 537, 645, 949, 1489, 1680, 2870) or in association with other elements as a first-hemistich expression (*PMC* 10).[4] Similarly, the phrase 'tierra[s] estraña[s]' is here defined as a formulaic expression because its two occurrences in the *PMC* (1125, 1281) display variation from singular to plural. For the specific purposes of this paper, and without prejudice to other future studies, the minimum number of associated words which is taken to constitute a formula or formulaic expression is two, as in this example; such units may, therefore, constitute only part of a hemistich, as in the case of 'tierra[s] estraña[s]', for in both the *Roncesvalles* fragment and the *PMC*, this phrase is associated with other elements ('a tieras estraynajs morare', *Roncesvalles* 64).[5] Some definitions would not, of course, admit this phrase in *Roncesvalles* as formulaic since it is not repeated within that text; but, given the occurrences in the *PMC* and in French epic, it is clear that we are here faced with a noun-adjective association which is indeed formulaic within the Romance epic tradition. Accordingly, it is important to note that the repetition which characterizes formulae and formulaic expressions alike does not, for present purposes, mean repetition within a single text: a given verbal unit used only once in a particular work may occur frequently elsewhere in the Romance epic and may be repeated within other individual poems belonging to that corpus, and should, therefore, be regarded as part of the formulaic resources of the Romance epic. 'Adtores mudados' (*PMC* 5), 'mar salada' (*PMC* 1090) and 'traydor prouado' (*PMC* 2523), for which French parallels have been provided by Smith, are all examples of phrases encountered but once in the *PMC*, yet which are common in French epic, and which should be regarded, therefore, as formulaic material.[6] Another example is the cowardly exclamation of Diego González when fleeing from the lion:

diziendo de la boca: 'Non vere Carrion!' (*PMC* 2289)

This effectively conveys the panic of the fleeing Infante; it may be compared with the following utterances from various French epics:

Ne vairés mais de Nerbone la plaigne (*Cordres* 660)

Mais ne verrés les honors de Cambrai (*Raoul* 5021)

Ne ne verrai mes terres et mes fiés

ne mes effans; pregne vos en pitiés (*Raoul* 4708-09)

Jamés en France ne porrons reperier,

ne ne verrons ne anfant ne moillier! (*Aymeri* 1123-24)

Although these examples vary in grammatical person and in the details of precisely what will not be seen again, they share sufficient common ground for this group of examples to be accepted as constituting a single formulaic expression, the structure of which may be defined as /(negation) + (verb 'to see') + (object/placename)/, employed by Romance epic to indicate that a character is in dire straits.

Consideration of the Romance context of Spanish epic can enhance our understanding of it in a variety of ways. A case in point is the phrase 'a su[s] posada[s]', encountered twice in the *PMC*:

El Campeador adelino a su posada (*PMC* 31)

Todos essa noch fueron a sus posadas (*PMC* 2182)

This formulaic expression, part of a second-hemistich structure which could be defined, in its Spanish manifestation at least, as /(verb of motion) + *a su[s] posada[s]*/, finds abundant parallels in French epic:

Li castelains l'enmainne a son ostel (*Ogier* 44)

A Bertran vait el borc a son ostel (*Ogier* 4530)

Quant Bertran vint el borc a son hostel (*Ogier* 4462)
Ses en moine li gloz ou borc a son ostel (*Doon* 1697)
Fuant s'en va li gloz el borc, a son ostel (*Doon* 1702)
Cascuns le sien a son ostel (*Guillaume d'A* 1455)
Si me nouri a son ostel (*Guillaume d'A* 3146)

These instances all offer the second-hemistich-final position of the phrase which is
encountered in the *PMC*; some offer the association with a verb of motion. This
association is found even in cases where the phrase occupies the entire first hemistich,
with the verb of motion in the second:

A son hostel fu li Danois Ogier (*Ogier* 3179)
A son ostel s'en retorna Renier (*Girart de V* 548)
A son hostel se vait aparellier (*Ogier* 3694)
A son ostel ala descendre (*Violette* 2976)
A son hostel maintenant descendi (*Raoul* 7066)
A son hostal es vengut Olivier (*RollanS* 76)

Many other examples of the phrase, in first-hemistich-initial and first-hemistich-final
position, with other possessives such as *vostre* and *lur*, can be found in French epics:[7]

A lor ostelx en son cent repairet (*Ogier* 4650)
A lor ostel reperent li enfant (*Girart de V* 350)
A lor ostieus alerent herbergier (*Aymeri* 3407)
Vienent a lor ostels, prenent lor garnemenz (*Doon* 1084)
'Alez a vostre ostel', dit li dus, 'dame Olive' (*Doon* 811)

Returning to Spanish texts, we find the following in the *PFG*:

fueron a sus posadas, començaron a dormir (*PFG* 487a)

Given the frequency with which the phrase is encountered, there is clearly no prospect
whatsoever of identifying a specific French source for its use in Spanish epic; that is no
part of my approach. It is, however, possible to point to the sub-group of cases within
French epic which most closely approximates to the manner in which the formulaic
expression is used in the Spanish texts. To the possible objection that phrases like this
one and 'tierra[s] estraña[s]' are so minimal as to constitute semantic equivalents of, for
example, English 'home' (= directional adverb) and 'abroad' (= locational adverb), and
hence are scarcely capable of interpretation as formulaic material, it may be countered
that, given the other lexical alternatives available, questions of collocation, association,
and also metrical function do indeed endow them with formulaic qualities. It is, of
course, the case that a syntactically dependent unit like a noun-adjective combination
can, in some circumstances, constitute a formula in its own right.

Similar considerations are prompted by another phrase employed twice in the *PMC*,
and once in the *PFG*, in second-hemistich-final position:

de Castiella uos ydes pora las yentes estranas (*PMC* 176)

Moros de las fronteras & vnas yentes estranas (*PMC* 840)

Asy yvan foyendo de las gentes estrañas (*PFG* 94a)

Common to all the Spanish examples cited is the use of the plural. French examples of the unit encountered to date employ the singular:

Fil a putain, malvaisse gent estrange (*Cordres* 667)

Per guerriar paianz, la jent estraigne (*Girart de R* 117)

pour pris conquerre entre l'estrange gent (*Renier* 3465)

Qu'il n'i ait traïson ne nulle estrange gent (*Aye* 393)

The inverted order of noun and adjective which marks two of these French cases is encountered in other French examples where the phrase is used in other positions in the line:

Estrange gent tant le loent tut dis (*ChGuillaume* 76)

par povrete d'estrange gent ledis (*Renier* 1928)

A full examination of usage in French epic would be required before it could be determined which word-order and metrical location represents the commonest occurrence of this unit; for the present, the closest parallel to the Spanish cases is that in *Girart de Roussillon*. The Romance context may, however, be helpful in discussing the meaning of the phrase in the *PMC*. In the case of *PMC* 840, it has been suggested that a distinction is conveyed between the local Moors of the frontier region referred to in the first hemistich, and other Moors, perhaps 'patrols of the army from Valencia', in the second.[8] In the light of the new French parallels, however, it is necessary for us to confront the possibility that we may be dealing with a formulaic expression, a general cliché for 'pagans, Muslims, foreigners' inherited from Romance tradition, rather than with an original phrase used to create a significant semantic distinction between *PMC* 176 and 840. On balance, however, I incline to the view that Smith's conjecture is likely to be correct. When a phrase seems to be formulaic, special circumstances are required in order to justify investing it with a meaning other than its traditional formulaic meaning; but it seems that *PMC* 840 exhibits just such a special context, for most of the French examples encountered use the term in order to differentiate foreign population groups from the French, while this example in the *PMC* appears to distinguish separate groups among the Cid's Moorish adversaries.[9]

A clearer evaluation of the artistry of the poet of the *PMC* may be obtained from the relation of his formulaic material to its Romance context in other ways too. Let us consider the question of *verismo*, long hailed as a characteristic of the *PMC* and, in the words of one scholar, 'in considerable contrast to the *CR* and other French epics'.[10] One aspect of that *verismo* which has often attracted attention is the question of feeding the horses; there is an undeniable down-to-earth quality about lines such as the following:

'¡Temprano dat çeuada, si el Criador uos salue!' (*PMC* 420) fizo Myo Çid posar & çeuada dar (*PMC* 428)

Agora dauan çeuada, ya la noch era entrada (*PMC* 827)

This quality is in no way diminished by noting that 'dar çevada' finds abundant parallels in French epics, but the *verismo* certainly becomes less the exclusive preserve of the *PMC* poet in this detail at least:

De l'avaine et del feure se li don[e]rent (*Aiol* 780)

Et laise le ceval bien ostelé,

del feure et de l'avaine li done assés (*Aiol* 2141-42)

D'une part en la sale son ceval establer,

de fain et de l'avaine a grant plenté doner (*Aiol* 1759-60)

De feure et de l'avaine a vo[s] corans destriers (*Aiol* 6599)

Mais pensés del ceval c'ait a me[n]gier;

del feure et de l'avaine ne soit dangier (*Aiol* 227-28)

De l'avaine li done c'ot aporté (*Aiol* 4934)

Il a trové del feure, si lor en met devant (*Aiol* 5803)

Que lor face la fors grant liurason

pan e vin e cibade, prou a fuison (*Girart de R* 1173-74)

Molt me dona a boivre et a mengier,

fain et avaine a l'auferrant corsier (*Charroi* 551-52)

Et li vallet i vont l'erbe soier,

a lor cevals en donent a mengier (*Ogier* 8092-93)

Fuerre et avainne a son corant destrier (*Ogier* 6027)

Je t'ai soef nori et le crupe coverte,

et doné a mangier et del fain et de l'erbe (*Elie* 2256-57)

En une croute a vaute ont le destrier mené,

del feure et de l'avaine li donent a plenté (*Elie* 2415-16)

Li ont son cheval establé,

Si li donnent avainne et blé (*Violette* 5088-89)

So common indeed is the motif of stabling and/or feeding the horse that an indication of poverty or straitened circumstances may be given by a negative version of this in which the absence of due provision for the horse is noted:

Trois jors ne mange avainne ne fraage (*Ogier* 5958)

Ses chevals ne gousta de feure ne de blé (*Elie* 1044)

Si li donnent un poi de fain,

qu'il n'i ot orge ne avainne (*Violette* 1560-61)

Clearly, there is great variation in the literary expression of providing fodder in these (and other) examples, but a frequently-encountered element is the association of *donner* with nouns such as *feure* and *avaine*, so that this may be seen, with the parallel expressions in the *PMC*, as constituting the formulaic nucleus of this narrative motif in many of its applications.

Closely related to the fodder motif is that of shoeing the horse, another of the mundane details found in the *PMC*:[11]

> avn las ferraduras quitar gelas mandaua (*PMC* 1553)

Abengalbón's attention to his visitors' mounts should, however, be set against similar details in French epic rather than viewed as peculiar to the *PMC*:

> Garder li fait les piés s'il sont feré,
>
> et on le trova bien encore clavé (*Aiol* 2138-39)
>
> E si fist Marchegai bien establer,
>
> trestous les .IIII. piés li fist ferer (*Aiol* 1121-22)
>
> A Broiefort est venus son destrier,
>
> si li leva trestos les quatre piés;
>
> la ou n'ot clau, li bers li a fichié,
>
> si l'a defors rivé et reploié (*Ogier* 8498-8501)

Sometimes an account combines feeding or watering the horse with attention to its shoes:

> A Broiefort s'en revint son destrier,
>
> fuerre et avainne li done volentier,
>
> pus li souslieve trestous les .IIII. piés;
>
> ou il n'a fer, li bers si li asiet,
>
> si l'a defors ben rivé et ploié (*Ogier* 8313-17)
>
> Ces chevax ferrent et moinent abuvrer (*Aymeri* 3911)

Again, the occurrence of negative renderings of the motif should be noted:

> A clos chevals, a destriers desferrez (*Couronnement* 2256)

Unlike the fodder motif, that of the horse-shoes does not suggest an underlying formulaic nucleus, although it is possible that a more extensive survey of French epic texts would alter this initial impression. Here, then, we appear to be faced not with a single, identifiable formulaic expression of Romance epic, but with a narrative motif which is common to both French and Spanish traditions. The French parallels for the Spanish poet's expression of Abengalbón's generous loyalty to the Cid do, however, provide us with a wider context for evaluating it than has hitherto been considered.

The wider Romance context may also enable us to reach a better understanding of the Spanish epic exploitation of elements in the vast body of binary expressions encompassing synonymous and inclusive pairs. To Smith's pioneering study of this material may be added a footnote concerning the pair represented in the *PMC* by the following line from the poet's description of the plight of the besieged Moors of Valencia:[12]

> Nin da cosseio padre a fijo, nin fijo a padre (*PMC* 1176)

French parallels can be offered for the entire line rather than simply for the pair of nouns involved:

N'i atendi li pere son enfant (*Aspremont* 10407)

Ja ne garrat li petit pur le grant,

ne n'i pot garir le pere sun enfant (*ChGuillaume* 247-48)

Ja ne poura li peres a son anfant aidier (*Orson* 2184)

Et tant espés i sont li mort chaü

li pere i a son fil desconeü (*Aspremont* 10059-60)

Here it is not simply a question of the presence of the pair *pere/enfant*, but, despite the diversity of expression, of the context in which this pair is employed: in all these instances, the situation described is so dire that the normal father/son relationship of support and protection collapses, with fathers unable to succour their sons, or even to recognize them among the dead. This is clearly a powerful device for expressing the extremity of the situation in which these characters find themselves, and this is precisely the context in which the same expression occurs in the *PMC*, where, however, it is intensified by repetition of the paired nouns, making the inability to help mutual. Although the four French examples cited exhibit widely varied verbal expression, a common formulaic element in addition to the paired nouns may be discerned in the three of them in which all the characters involved are living; this is the presence of a negative and a verb relating to the semantic field of providing succour and company. These elements are present, too, in the *PMC*, and suggest that it may be profitable to view paired nouns not merely in isolation, but also in their context. A later Spanish variant of this formulaic expression may be traced in the *PFG*, with the substitution of one pair of nouns by another:

matavan a las madres en braços a los sus fyjos

non se podien dar consejo mugeres nin marydos (*PFG* 95bc)

The use of *mugeres/marydos* obscures the relationship of these lines to the formulaic expression found in *PMC* 1176, but the parallel between the first hemistichs of that line and *PFG* 95c is clear, and the existence of *madres/fyjos* in 95b suggests that this stark depiction of atrocities produced by the *clerecía* poet represents an adaptation of the already striking formulaic expression found in *PMC* 1176 and French epic.

Family relationships in the *PMC* form the basis of the next case to be examined too. On three separate occasions, the hero expresses the pious hope that he may continue to live long enough to benefit his family or to repay a debt of gratitude:

¡Plega a Dios & a Santa Maria

que aun con mis manos case estas mis fijas,

o que de ventura & algunos dias vida,

e uos, mugier ondrada, de my seades seruida! (*PMC* 282-84)

Si yo algun dia visquier seruos han doblados (*PMC* 251)

Si les yo visquier seran dueñas rricas (*PMC* 825)

A common formulaic expression may be traced in lines 251 and 825; for this,
abundant parallels occur in French epics in a variety of situations:

Se je vif longes, mout gran prou i areiz (*EnfGuillaume* 1390)

Se je vif longuement, merveilleus preus t'en iert (*Aye* 1918)

Se jo vif alques, mult grand prod i avreiz (*RolandO* 3459)

'Ermanjars, danme', dit li cuens Ainmeris,

'Se Deus m'aïst, veeis ici vos fiz.

Se Deus se donne, li rois de paradis,

que je tant soie et sains et saus et vis,

que je les voie chivelier devenir,

mout an seroit li miens cuers esjoiys' (*EnfGuillame* 46-51)

Car proié m'a Karles, li rois jentis,

que foi portaisse son fil qui est petis.

Si ferai jou, se Dieu plaist et jou vif (*EnfGuillaume*,

Appendix, MS C, p. 148, 12-14)

Seu vairés vos, se Deu plaist et je vi (*EnfGuillaume* 2363)

Other examples are encountered in which the same formulaic materials are related to
concepts such as revenge, justice, and retribution, rather than the future prospects of
children, or hopes of future status, but the underlying formulaic patterns are clearly
visible here too:

Mais se je vif, cier lor sera merie (*Ogier* 11847)

Se je vif tant que veingne a l'esclairier (*Ami* 2019)

Mais se vif longes, encor estra vengiés (*Ogier* 4268)

Se je vif tant ke je soie adoubeiz,

desoz Oranges le ramoinrai an preiz (*EnfGuillaume* 1056-57)

Se je vif tant que puise porter arme

au branc d'acier te cuit movoir tel chaple,

trancherai toi le chief sor la mamele (*EnfGuillaume* 1101-03)

Mais se vif longes, il en perdra la vie (*Ogier* 4180)

Se ge vif tant que ge soie adoubé (*Girart de V* 2848)

Se je puis vivre longement par aé

de l'un de nos iert l'orguel avalé (*Aspremont* 11354-55)

Se je vif tant ke j'aie armes novelles,

ne voz lairai une toise de terre (*EnfGuillaume* 1031-32)

Se je peüse vivre, de ce fusiez toz fiz,

la teste vous coupasse ains deus ans acomplis (*Orson* 1000-01)

Je la ravrai, se je puis vivre tant

qe je port armes desor mon auferant (*Raoul* 354-55)

134

Ma mere as arce, dont j'ai le quer irié.
Dex me laist vivre tant q'en soie vengiés! (*Raoul* 1696-97)
Or me doint Dex, par son digne conmant,
tant de santé et que je vive tant
que de cest cop vos ailliez repentant (*Girbert* 322-24)
Mais se vif tant qu'il soit ajorné
lors l'irai je l'empereor conter (*Ami* 711-12)
Je l'en prandra encor, se je vif, a ma lance (*Aye* 1827)
Se je vif tant ke soie chevaliers
je li vorai per mon cors chalongier (*EnfGuillaume* 1125-26)
Se je vi longes, je l'ai ben en pensé (*Ogier* 1556)
Droit en avrez se ge vif longuement (*Renier* 6531)
Se je ja tant puis vivre qu'armes puisse reçoivre,
je vos torrai les vies, les membres et les testes (*Doon* 1315-16)
Se je puis vivre tant qu'armes puisse baillir,
ce est .j. mariages qui durera petit (*Doon* 766-67)
Se Dieus me laisse vivre jusqu'as armes portant,
j'en penrai la venjance au mien commandement (*Doon* 1002-03)

Despite the variety of situations and verbal expression, we may distinguish two elements which offer parallels for the *PMC*: (a) those which invoke the agency of the deity in procuring future survival for the speaker, and (b) the simpler cases where survival is a condition of future action but is not linked to the divine volition. In the latter group there is a further division into (i) those which add a temporal indication (*longes, tant, longement,* etc.) to the hope for survival, and (ii) those which merely express that hope without further qualification. Group b(i) provides a good parallel for *PMC* 825, and b(ii) furnishes one for *PMC* 251, while *PMC* 282-84 find their French counterpart in Group (a).

Again, there is no question of my here suggesting specific French sources for the separate occurrences of this concept in the *PMC*. What the Romance context offers is, rather, evidence to suggest that it is probable that the Spanish material was ultimately inspired by French antecedents, rather than resulting from polygenesis or a common non-Romance ancestor, given the precise verbal equivalences between the Spanish and French epics in so many points of detail. It remains open whether the distinct manifestations of the basic concept in the *PMC* are the result of independent variation by the Spanish poet working within an established Spanish tradition itself based on French models, or arise from his own direct imitation of the separate modes of expression employed in French epic; but either way the French origin of the pattern seems clear enough.

Similar reflections are prompted by consideration of another formulaic expression encountered twice in the *PMC*, for which I have previously suggested French parallels:[13]

En su conpaña .lx. pendones [leuaua] (*PMC* 16)

E dozientos omnes lieuan en su conpaña (*PMC* 1817)

Neither of the French parallels I was able to point out on earlier occasions provided a precise equivalent for the use of the phrase *en su conpaña*, which, for reasons which will soon be apparent, could be better defined as a formulaic expression or even considered as a whole-line formulaic entity despite the difference between *.lx. pendones* and *dozientos omnes*; but the subsequent collection of around eight dozen instances of this formulaic pattern from French epics provides a corpus of variants which permits the two Spanish examples to be placed in a much clearer Romance formulaic context. The formulaic expression encountered in these lines from the *PMC* is an extremely common device in Romance epic narrative, and its application ranges from the extremely simple to the more involved; in analysing the formulaic structure of the French examples in the catalogue which follows, the component elements of the lines concerned are identified by these conventions:

C: copulative

F: formulaic nucleus (i.e., *en (sa/lor) compaigne*)

N: numerical indicator (i.e., adjective, numeral, or clause indicating number; occasionally the numerical function is performed by what is syntactically a qualifier, e.g., *maint*, but since this is a formulaic, not a syntactic, analysis, formulaic function rather than grammatical category is the determining factor here)

P: partitive (*en, de*)

Q: qualifier (adjective, adverb, noun in apposition, etc.)

R: relative pronoun

S: substantive (common or proper noun)

V: verb

The formulaic structure of *PMC* 16 would thus be FNSV, while *PMC* 1817 would be CNSVF. As the following catalogue (which is by no means exhaustive, and lists merely those French examples which I have encountered) makes plain, there are many more possible arrangements of the elements which constitute these formulaic lines.

I. First-Hemistich-Initial Position

A. Without Verb

1.   F + one element

     a) FN

       En sa compaign .ij. cens et .iiij. vins (*Garin* 8096)

b) FS

En sa conpangne Elinant et Gautier (*Girart de V* 4846)

En sa conpaigne Mansiaus e Beruier (*Ogier* 4126)[14]

2.   F + two elements

a) FNS

En sa conpaingne .iiij.c. chevallier (*Raoul* 7175)

En sa conpaigne .LX. chevalier (*Garin* 2451)

En sa compaigne quarante bacheler (*Charroi* 23)

En sa conpaigne .iiii.c. fervestis (*Garin* 6939)

En lor conpagne .CCCC. fervestis (*Ogier* 7333)

En sa conpangne .II. mile fervestiz (*Girart de V* 2333)

En sa conpangne .II. mile chevalier (*Girart de V* 4017)

En sa compagne cent mile chevaliers (*Aspremont* 8197)

An sa compaigne quarante bacheleirs (*EnfGuillaume* 796)

En sa conpaigne doi mile chevalier (*Ogier* 5972)

En sa compaigne vint mile combatant (*EnfGuillaume* 3097)

b) FSN

En sa conpaigne chevaliers .XXVI. (*Garin* 5794)

En sa compaigne chevaliers .IIIJ. vins (*Garin* 2791)

En sa conpaigne chevaliers .XXXVI. (*Garin* 6903)

En lor conpagne chevaliers .IIII. vins (*Garin* 1327)

En sa compaigne chevaliers .IIII.XX (*Garin* 7254)

En sa conpaingne chevaliers .IIII.XX (*Garin* 7925)

3.   F + three elements

a) FQNS

En sa conpangne bien .II. mile François (*Girart de V* 2381)

En lor conpagne plus de .II. miles Frans (*Ogier* 5473)

An sa conpaigne juc'ai mil chivelier (*EnfGuillaume* 624)

b) FSQN

En sa conpaingne chevaliers dusqu'a .X. (*Garin* 2719)

c) FPSN

En sa conpaigne de chevaliers .VII.XX (*Garin* 8929)

En sa conpaingne de chevaliers .VII.XX (*Garin* 7987)

En sa conpaigne de chevaliers .III.M. (*Garin* 7100)

En sa compaigne de Sarrasins dis mile (*EnfGuillaume* 1616)

d) FNSQ

En sa conpangne .C. demoisel legier (*Girart de V* 4758)

En sa conpaigne .C. damoisel proisié (*Ogier* 8806)

En lor conpaigne .M. chevaliers hardiz (*Garin* 3996)

En lor conpaigne .C. chevaliers baron (*Ogier* 10175)

En sa conpaigne maint chevalier vaillant (*Ogier* 5885)

En sa conpangne .M. chevaliers de pris (*Girart de V* 3993)

En sa conpangne .VII.M. home a escu (*Girart de V* 2040)

En lor conpagne mile ome conbatant (*Aspremont* 5345)

En sa compaingne mil chevaliers arméz (*Ami* 348)

En sa compaigne trante rois sarrasins (*EnfGuillaume* 2148)

An sa compaigne cent Sarrasins armeiz (*EnfGuillaume* 2844)

An sa conpaigne quatre rois de paiens (*EnfGuillaume* 598)

En leur conpaigne maint chevalier vaillant (*Renier* 13744)

En sa compaigne maint chevalier menbré (*Orange* 137)

e) FNQS

En sa compagne maint vallant chevalier (*Ogier* 6038)

En sa compagne maint gentil chevalier (*Charroi* 685)

En lor compaigne mainz vaillanz chevaliers (*Couronnement* 1894)

En sa conpangne maint vaillant chevalier (*Aymeri* 3747)

B. With Verb

1. Verb in Second-Hemistich-Initial Position

    a) FVNS

    En sa compaigne avoit il maint princier (*Charroi* 762)

    En sa conpaigne avoit .XII. Berton (*Ogier* 4433)

    En sa conpaigne a vint mil adoubez (*Renier* 708)

    En sa conpaigne ot .VII.C. chevalier (*Ogier* 1297)

    En sa conpaigne sont doi .C. chevaliers (*Ogier* 6325)

    An lor compaigne furent .X.M. armé (*Girbert* 170)

    En sa conpaigne sont dix mil combatant (*Renier* 16970)

    b) FVSN

    En sa conpagne ot chevalier assés (*Ogier* 9126)

    c) FVQS

    An sa conpaigne moinne son fil Bernart (*EnfGuillaume* 336)

    d) FVQNS

    An sa conpaigne amoine ses trois filz (*EnfGuillaume* 2334)

    En sa compagne ot tels .C. chevalier (*Ogier* 684)

    En lor conpagne sont ben .XX. mil a elmes (*Ogier* 11178)

    e) FVNQS

    En sa conpaigne ot maint bon bacheler (*Garin* 421)

    f) FPVNPS

    En sa conpaigne en ot .XX.M d'esliz (*Garin* 466)

138

g) FVPSN

En sa conpaingne ot de chevaliers .X. (*Garin* 2638)

En sa conpagne a de gent .C. milliers (*Ogier* 8528)

2.   Verb in Second-Hemistich-Final Position

a) FNSV

An sa compaigne quinze rois amena (*EnfGuillaume* 2172)

En leur conpaigne trente mil homes a (*Renier* 7591)

b) FNPSV

En leur conpaigne moult de bele gent a (*Renier* 11619)

II. First-Hemistich-Final Position

A. Copulative in First-Hemistich-Initial Position

1.   CVFNS

E ont en lor conpaigne .iii.m. chevaliers (*Aye* 1293)

Et sont an sa conpaigne quatre cent conpaignon (*Orson* 2827)

Et a en sa compaigne .XX.M. chevaliers (*Doon* 2821)

2.   CVFNPS

Et ot en sa compaigne .X.M. de chevaliers (*Doon* 3071)

3.   CVFSQ

Et ot en sa compaigne Rainewart au tinel (*Elie* 2535)

4.   CVFNSQ

Et sont an sa conpaigne cinc cent baron de pris (*Orson* 2583)

Et sont an lor conpaignes cent chevalier vaillant (*Orson* 2091)

Et ot en sa compaigne .XX.M. Turs armés (*Elie* 2430)

5.   CVFQNS

E sont en lor conpaigne plus de .ii.m. masçons (*Aye* 2686)

E sont en sa conpaigne plus de .m. chevaliers (*Aye* 2775)

Et sunt en sa compaigne plus de .c. chevalier (*Aye*, Vuillafans 15)

6.   CVFSQN

Et ont an lor conpaigne hommes plus de vint mil (*Orson* 3227)

B. *Si* in First-Hemistich-Initial Position

1.   *Si* + VFNS

Si ot en sa compaigne .LX. chevaliers (*Aiol* 4659)

2.   *Si* + VFNSQ

S'ot en sa conpaignie .m. chevaliers armez (*Aye* 301)

Si ait en sa compaigne .iij. homes a espées (*Doon* 634)

3.   *Si* + VFQNS

S'averont en lor compaigne plus de .XX.M. escus (*Elie* 876)

C. Subject Pronoun in First-Hemistich Initial Position
1. Subject Pronoun + FVNS
   Chascuns en sa compagne oit tre milie schu (*GuiN-PM* 334)

III. Second-Hemistich-Final Position

1. SVF
   Contes et rois ot en sa conpangnie (*Girart de V* 6172)
2. SQVF/QSVF
   Ricars, li preus, fu en sa compagnie (*Aspremont* 7755)
   Le roy Grebuedes vient en sa conpaignie (*Renier* 7219)
   Renier son filz iert en sa compaignie (*Renier* 14608)
3. NSVF
   .XX. milie Francs unt en lur cumpaigne (*RolandO* 587)
   .XX. milie Frrancs unt en lur cumpaigne (*RolandO* 827)
   .XXX. Lonbarz ot en sa conpangnie (*Aymeri* 2297)
   .X. escuiers ont en lor conpagnie (*Aymeri* 2707)
4. NVPF
   Cent mile furent ens en sa compagnie (*Aspremont* 8137)
5. Vocative + QNSQVF
   Deus, quels seisante humes i ad en sa cumpaigne (*RolandO* 1849)
6. Preposition + NSRVF
   De .X. mil homes q'oi en ma conpagnie (*Ogier* 5426)
   A .V.C. homes q'a en sa conpagnie (*Ogier* 5431)

IV. Second-Hemistich-Initial Position

1. QNSFV
   Bien vint mil homes en sa conpaignie a (*Renier* 4260)
   Bien dix mil homes en leur compaignie a (*Renier* 16735)

V. Two-Line Distribution

A. First-Hemistich-Initial Position
   En la compagne Rollant, le nief Karlon,
   furent set cent et doi mil compagnon (*Aspremont* 9731-32)

B. Second-Hemistich-Final Position
   Bertran n'ot mes enz en sa conpaignie
   que deuz mil homes dont puist avoir aie (*Renier* 5621-22)

140

This exercise in taxonomy has no pretensions to definitive treatment of its subject; aspects of it are open to objection, such as the question of whether the qualifiers should be seen as an integral part of the numerical indicators or the substantive-phrases rather than being separately listed, and a range of quite distinct criteria could be used to classify this material. More cases undoubtedly exist, and further variants may be expected within French epic. The approach taken here is broadly formal in order to locate those sub-groups within French occurrences of this formulaic expression known to me which most closely approximate to the whole-line structure of the two Spanish examples, which this prolonged excursion north of the Pyrenees is intended to elucidate. For the CNSVF structure of *PMC* 1817, Group III offers the requisite positioning of the formulaic expression F, with III.3 (NSVF) providing the closest parallel, lacking only the initial copulative of the first hemistich. This missing feature is found in Group II.A.1-6, but not in any of the Group III examples. We therefore have a close, but not an exact, French parallel for this application of the formulaic expression in the *PMC*. The FNSV structure of *PMC* 16, however, finds an exact equivalent in Group I.B.2.a: a very infrequent variant in the corpus of French examples assembled here. There is, moreover, a most notable similarity between the line in the *PMC* and that in *Les Enfances Guillaume*: the use of the verbs *llevar* and *amener* respectively. The latter is rather rare in the French corpus, encountered only in *Les Enfances Guillaume* (336, 2172, 2334) among all the poems examined; the commonest verbs used in the eight dozen examples of this formulaic expression located in French epic texts are *être* and *avoir*. The Spanish equivalent of *amener*, *llevar*, is, of course, used in both the examples in the *PMC*. An unusual structural arrangement, and a rare verb, are a striking coincidence in a single line; but before succumbing to the temptation to add yet another work to the list of specific French poems which have been claimed as literary sources for the *PMC*, we would do well to recall that the *termini* for the composition of *Les Enfances Guillaume* have been placed at 1205 and 1250, the earlier of these dates being the *terminus a quo* for the composition of *Aymeri de Narbonne*, on which *Les Enfances Guillaume* depends.[15] If both dating and dependence are correct, then it would be a most striking instance of speedy transmission for the North-Eastern French poem to have influenced the Castilian poet, the latest date for whose work currently accepted anywhere is *ca.* 1207.[16] It is also necessary to bear in mind, of course, that the earliest extant manuscripts of *Les Enfances Guillaume* are of the second half of the thirteenth century, and that the form in which the poem is known to us in any of these witnesses does not necessarily reflect, in formulaic details like this, the form or forms in which its text may have circulated at an earlier phase in its existence. I have already drawn attention elsewhere to this problem in relation to this very formulaic expression by pointing out the different versions of *Aye d'Avignon* 1785, where the II.A.5 structure of this line in the Vuillafans fragment (line 15) is not found in the Paris manuscript:[17]

Et sunt en sa compaigne plus de .c. chevalier (Vuillafans 15)

En la chanpaingne furent [plus] de .c. chevalier (Paris 1785)

This variant cannot be dismissed simply as an obvious scribal error produced in manuscript transmission, for the first hemistich of the Paris text is in fact a recognizable formula in its own right (cf. 'An la chanpaigne ki est et grans et large', *EnfGuillaume* 2731), and the Paris reading may well therefore have to be viewed as acceptable. Even those versions of this line which faithfully transmit the formulaic expression which is our principal concern here do not agree on every detail of it; the Venice-2 version, for instance, lacks the initial copulative, so that the II.A.5 structure of Vuillafans becomes an example of I.B.1.d arrangement in Venice-2 (*Aye*, p. 312 [= f. 2v], 39):

En sa conpagna estoient plus de .c. chevalier.

The discrepancy between the tense of the verb in each version should also be noted. A similar situation is encountered in *Le Charroi de Nîmes*, in which the I.B.1.a structure of line 762 in branch (A) is not encountered in branch (B), which instead offers an example of I.A.3.e:[18]

A: En sa compaigne avoit il maint princier

B: En sa conpaigne maint gentil chevalier

With this degree of variability among the manuscript witnesses to a single line in each of two epics, it is obviously inadvisable to place excessive reliance upon texts which survive only in later manuscripts as a guide to the specific formulaic details of whatever versions were in circulation at an earlier period.

In the case of *PMC* 16, we encounter a classic illustration of the difficulties of formulaic material of this kind, and of the problems involved in this area of comparative literary study. Although *Les Enfances Guillaume* offers a unique parallel for both the structure and the detailed content of the Spanish line, in particular in its choice of verb, the likelihood of its having influenced the *PMC* in this respect lies somewhere in the range between the negligible and the non-existent.[19] Some other explanation of the parallel must therefore be sought. One may be that earlier French examples of the I.B.2.a formulaic structure exist, as yet undetected by Hispanists; another may be that this pattern existed at an earlier date in lost versions of French epics in the later manuscripts of which these formulaic lines have undergone the kind of variation seen in *Aye d'Avignon* 1785 and *Le Charroi de Nîmes* 762. A third possibility, that this specific parallel is the result of independent evolution in each country, must also be considered. By this I do not mean polygenesis in the strictest sense of creation *ex nihilo* in two separate locations, but rather that, given a common original starting point such as I.A.1, individual practitioners within a formulaic tradition which admitted independent improvisation and variation (such as inversion to produce a required assonance) could well in time produce, quite independently, identical lines, or equivalent lines in separate Romance languages. In this particular case, the number and range of the details involved (not only general arrangement of the component parts of the line, but also the combination of the presence of a verb, absence of any qualifiers and a copulative, and the particular choice of verb) might seem such as to call this possible explanation into question, but I do not think it can be entirely excluded. Other possible explanations, such as an influence of the *PMC* on *Les Enfances Guillaume* or a common origin in a non-Romance ancestor, can, on the other hand, be regarded as highly improbable.[20]

In the quarter-century which has elapsed since L.P. Harvey's seminal article of 1963, considerable progress has been made in elucidating the problems of the formulaic content of the medieval Spanish epic. Much remains to be done, of course, and this is especially true of the wider Romance dimension of the question, where a desirable future development would be the separate publication of each epic manuscript witness, rather than the critical editions with an apparatus of variants which (with important exceptions) have hitherto tended to be the norm, in French at least, for epics known in more than one copy. The publication of individual witnesses, coupled with the employment of recent developments in computer technology, would greatly facilitate the study of the distribution of formulae and formulaic expressions across all branches of the Romance epic family. Within the French epic tradition, it would, for instance, permit diachronic analysis of the treatment of formulaic material in the transmission of individual texts, and synchronic studies of formulae current in all texts of a particular date or region. On a wider front, it would offer some prospect of providing quantitative evidence, in a form more reliable statistically than that arising from incomplete manual surveys of a small part of the available material (such as that offered in the present paper), of the extent of verbal parallels between the French and Spanish epic traditions, from which conclusions might be drawn about the relative probability of the various possible explanations for these from direct imitation to polygenesis or a common ancestor. It would also, of course, be of considerable benefit to other aspects of the study of the Romance epic; an obvious instance is the identification of narrative motifs common to the various separate traditions. In the absence of such a comprehensive treatment, it is easy for individual scholars working on specific segments of the epic corpus both to overestimate the amount of direct verbal borrowing from specific literary sources, and to underestimate the extent to which certain features are common to the French and Spanish traditions. Pending the accessibility of the entire corpus in this form, however, even the relatively limited kind of survey offered in the present study has clear implications for our understanding both of the formulaic content of the Romance epic and of aspects of the artistry of its medieval Spanish branch.[21]

King's College London

NOTES

1. L.P. Harvey, 'The Metrical Irregularity of the *Cantar de Mio Cid*', *BHS*, XL (1963), 137-43, an article concerned as much with methodology as with metre. To the studies listed in my 'The *Poema de Mio Cid* and the Old French Epic: some reflections', in *The Medieval Alexander Legend and Romance Epic. Essays in Honour of David J.A. Ross*, edited by Peter Noble, Lucie Polak and Claire Isoz (Millwood, N.Y.: Kraus, 1982), pp. 107-18, should be added the following: Alan Deyermond and David Hook, 'The *Afrenta de Corpes* and Other Stories', *La Corónica*, X (1981-82), 12-37; Kenneth Adams, 'Possible French Influence on the Use of the Historic Present in the *Poema de Mio Cid*', *MLR*, LXXV (1980), 781-96; Colin Smith, *The Making of the 'Poema de Mio Cid'* (Cambridge: University Press, 1983), especially pp. 104-24, 155-66, 188-206, and Spanish translation, *La creación del 'Poema de Mio Cid'* (Barcelona: Crítica, 1985). In this book one may note (despite the comments of Alan Deyermond, 'A Monument for Per Abad: Colin Smith on the making of the *Poema de Mio Cid*', *BHS*, LXII (1985), 120-26, especially pp. 123-24) traces of a continuing tendency to think in terms of specific sources, of which a good example is Smith's treatment of *Doon de la Roche* (p. 159). The latest contribution by Smith known to me is his 'Some Thoughts on the Application of Oralist Principles to Medieval Spanish Epic', in *A Face Turned Not to the Wall: essays on Hispanic themes for Gareth Alban Davies* (Leeds: Department of Spanish and Portuguese, 1987), pp. 9-25. A recent work of fundamental importance here is Joseph J. Duggan's *The 'Cantar de Mio Cid': poetic creation in its economic and social contexts*, Cambridge Studies in Medieval Literature, 5 (Cambridge: Cambridge University Press, 1989), especially pp. 108-123, 124-142. On the formulae of individual Spanish poems, see Ruth House Webber, 'The Diction of the *Roncesvalles* Fragment', in *Homenaje a Rodríguez Moñino*, 2 vols (Madrid: Castalia, 1966), II, 311-21; John Steven Geary, *Formulaic Diction in the 'Poema de Fernán González' and the 'Mocedades de Rodrigo'. A Computer-aided Analysis* (Potomac, Maryland: Studia Humanitatis; Madrid: José Porrúa Turanzas, 1980); and Edmund de Chasca, *Registro de fórmulas verbales en el 'Cantar de Mio Cid'* (Iowa City: privately published, 1968) is still useful.

2. Texts used in this study are as follows:

   PMC: *Cantar de Mio Cid*, edited by Ramón Menéndez Pidal, 4th edition, 3 vols, Obras completas, III-V (Madrid: Espasa-Calpe, 1964-69), III, 909-1016, with capitals and word-division regularized, the Tironian sign for the copulative replaced by &, long ſ rendered as s and R rendered as rr.

   Roncesvalles: '*Roncesvalles*: un nuevo cantar de gesta español del siglo XIII', in R. Menéndez Pidal, *Textos medievales españoles. Ediciones críticas y estudios*,

144

Obras completas, XII (Madrid: Espasa-Calpe, 1976), 8-99, at pp. 13-17 (reprinted from *RFE*, IV (1917), 105-204).

PFG: *Poema de Fernán González*, palaeographic edition by Ramón Menéndez Pidal in *Reliquias de la poesía épica española* (Madrid: CSIC & Instituto de Cultura Hispánica, 1951), pp. 34-180. Despite inaccuracies, this edition is at least free of the obtrusive computer code symbols which characterize the transcription by John S. Geary, *Historia del conde Fernán González* (Madison: HSMS, 1987). Significant errors have been corrected in my quotations.

Aiol: *Aiol*, edited by Jacques Normand and Gaston Raynaud, SATF (Paris: Firmin Didot, 1877).

Ami: *Ami et Amile*, edited by Peter F. Dembowski, CFMA, XCVII (Paris: Honoré Champion, 1969).

Aspremont: *La Chanson d'Aspremont*, edited by Louis Brandin, 2nd edition, 2 vols, CFMA, XIX & XXV (Paris: Honoré Champion, 1923-24).

Aye: *Aye d'Avignon*, edited by S.J. Borg, TLF, CXXXIV (Geneva: Droz, 1967). (For discussion of different manuscripts of *Aye*, see pp. 141-42 and n. 17 below.)

Aymeri: *Aymeri de Narbonne*, edited by Louis Demaison, 2 vols, SATF (Paris: Firmin Didot, 1887).

ChGuillaume: *La Chanson de Guillaume*, edited by Duncan McMillan, 2 vols, SATF (Paris: A. & J. Picard, 1949-50).

Charroi: *Le Charroi de Nîmes*, edited by J.-L. Perrier, CFMA, LXVI (Paris: Honoré Champion, 1968).

Cordres: *La Prise de Cordres et de Sebille*, edited by Ovide Densusianu, SATF (Paris: Firmin Didot, 1896).

Couronnement: *Le Couronnement de Louis*, edited by E. Langlois, SATF (Paris: Firmin Didot, 1888).

Doon: *Doon de la Roche*, edited by Paul Meyer and Gédéon Huet, SATF (Paris: Édouard Champion, 1921).

Elie: *Elie de Saint Gille*, edited by Gaston Raynaud, SATF (Paris: Firmin Didot, 1879).

EnfGuillaume: *Les Enfances Guillaume*, edited by Patrice Henry, SATF (Paris: SATF, 1935).

Garin: *Garin le Loheren, according to Manuscript A (Bibliothèque de l'Arsenal 2983)*, edited by Josephine Elvira Vallerie (Ann Arbor: privately published, 1947).

Girbert: see *Raoul*.

Girart de R: *Girart de Roussillon*, edited by W. Mary Hackett, 3 vols, SATF (Paris: A. & J. Picard, 1953-55).

Girart de V: Bertrand de Bar-sur-Aube, *Girart de Vienne*, edited by Wolfgang van Emden, SATF (Paris: A. & J. Picard, 1977).

GuiN-PM: Alfredo Cavaliere, *Il prologo marciano del 'Gui de Nanteuil'* (Naples: Giannini, 1958).

Ogier: *La Chevalerie d'Ogier de Danemarche*, edited by Mario Eusebi, Testi e Documenti di Letteratura Moderna, VI (Milan: Istituto Editoriale Cisalpino, 1963).

Orange: *La Prise d'Orange*, edited by Claude Régnier, 5th edition (Paris: Klincksieck, 1977).

Orson: *Orson de Beauvais*, edited by Gaston Paris, SATF (Paris: Firmin Didot, 1899).

Raoul: *Raoul de Cambrai*, edited by P. Meyer and A. Longnon, SATF (Paris: Firmin Didot, 1882); includes parts of *Girbert de Metz* (= *Girbert*) in an Appendix.

Renier: *Enfances Renier*, edited by Carla Cremonesi (Milan: Istituto Editoriale Cisalpino, 1957).

RolandO: *La Chanson de Roland*, edited by F. Whitehead, 2nd edition (Oxford, Blackwell, 1946; rpt 1975).

RollanS: *Rollan a Saragossa*, in *Roldán en Zaragoza (poema épico provenzal)*, edited by Carlos Alvar (Saragossa: Diputación Provincial, 1978).

In addition, later romances have been cited where they provide a useful instance of the survival of epic formulae into later literature:

Guillaume d'A: Chrétien de Troyes (attrib.), *Guillaume d'Angleterre*, edited by Maurice Wilmotte, CFMA, LV (Paris: Honoré Champion, 1927).

Violette: Gerbert de Montreuil, *Le Roman de la Violette ou de Gerart de Nevers*, edited by Douglas Labaree Buffum, SATF (Paris: Honoré Champion, 1928).

3. For Parry's definition, see Albert B. Lord, *The Singer of Tales* (Cambridge, Mass.: Harvard University Press, 1960; rpt 1981), p. 4; Lord uses the term 'formulaic expression' to denote 'a line or half line constructed on the pattern of the formulas'. There seems to be no good reason, however, why it should not be extended to a phrase which forms a component part of a hemistich if such a phrase has formulaic characteristics. The definition by Jean Rychner is in *La Chanson de geste. Essai sur l'art épique des jongleurs*, Société de Publications Romanes et Françaises, LIII (Geneva: Droz; Lille: Giard, 1955), p. 147. John S. Miletich's important article, 'The Quest for the "Formula": a comparative reappraisal', *Modern Philology*, LXXIV (1976-77), 111-23, has further extensive bibliographical references. See also Colin Smith, 'Some Thoughts on the Application of Oralist Principles', and Duggan, *The 'Cantar de Mio Cid'*, pp. 136-37, with further references.

4. Kenneth Adams, '*Pensar de*: another Old French influence on the *PMC* and other Mediaeval Spanish Poems', *La Corónica*, VII (1978-79), 8-12.
5. On this phrase, see my 'The *PMC* and the Old French Epic', p. 111. To the single example of *terre estrange* quoted there among variants such as *estrange contrée* and *estrange regnez* may be added further cases encountered subsequently, e.g. *estrange terre* (*Renier* 2707, 3440, 10596), *terre estrange* (*Guillaume d'A* 2349). In setting two words as my minimum criterion for formulaic status in this paper, I do not thereby call into the question the validity of the concept of the single-word formula, convincingly identified in the *PMC*, for instance, by J.M. Aguirre ('*Poema de Mio Cid*: rima y oralidad', *La Corónica*, VII (1978-79), 107-08; 'El nombre propio como fórmula oral en el *Cantar de Mio Cid*', *La Corónica*, IX (1980-81), 107-19). In my present study of French epic parallels, space does not permit adequate treatment of the specific problems associated with this concept.
6. A similar approach is taken by Ruth House Webber in 'The Diction of the *Roncesvalles* Fragment', which, given the small size of the sample provided by the extant text, draws parallels between phrases in *Roncesvalles* and those in other texts such as the *PMC* and *romances* in order to identify formulae; see especially pp. 320-21. (I should perhaps add that whilst accepting Webber's methodology here, I do not necessarily accept all her conclusions.) Joseph J. Duggan, on the other hand, confines his study of the formulae of the *PMC* to 'those hemistichs which are repeated within the poem' since these constitute 'as sure a set of formulae as is feasible under the circumstances' ('Formulaic Diction in the *Cantar de Mio Cid* and the Old French Epic', in *Oral Literature: Seven Essays*, edited by Joseph J. Duggan (Edinburgh: Scottish Academic Press, 1975), pp. 74-83, at p. 76; reprinted from *FMLS*, X (1974), 260-69). Leaving aside the identification of 'formula' with 'hemistich' underlying this definition (and found also in Duggan's earlier work: for references and a justification of this approach for purely statistical purposes, see *The 'Cantar de Mio Cid'* p. 136), the problem noted by Duggan, that 'it is impossible to aspire to a complete list of the Cid's formulas, given the scarcity of *cantares de gesta* which serve as an adequate basis for comparison' (p. 76), implies that he views some material which is not repeated within the poem as formulaic. Whilst agreeing with Duggan that complete listing of the poem's formulae is unattainable, I feel that in practice, by utilizing the Old French epic as a corpus of comparative material, and by cautious use of later Spanish texts such as *clerecía* verse and *romances*, the amount of formulaic material which would be overlooked is likely to be small. (See also Smith, 'Some Thoughts upon the Application of Oralist Principles', p. 13.) There are other problems, of course, in using such a body of comparative material to establish the corpus of Old Spanish epic formulae: in the case of *adtores mudados*, for example,

it would be easy to identify this with the parallel phrase in French epic; but, as I have pointed out elsewhere, the occurrence of this phrase in the *PMC* forms only one part of the pair 'sin falcones & sin adtores mudados', and the whole pair *faucon/ostor* occurs in various French epics ('The *PMC* and the Old French Epic', p. 109). In my 1982 study I was able to cite only three examples of this pair from French texts, and none of these included the adjective *mues*. This deficiency may now be remedied by noting the following examples:

Crïer faucons et cez ostoirs müez (*Orange* 247, 410)

Faucons ne nus ostoir ne oiseus d'outre mer (*Elie* 1710)

Neither of these, of course, is being advanced as a literal source for the equivalent expression in the *PMC*; rather they indicate that *PMC* 5 should be considered as a whole-line formulaic expression and not broken into its constituent parts in the search for French parallels. Smith (*The Making of the 'PMC'*, p. 233, n. 11) defends his claim for *Roland* as a source for this phrase in the *PMC* in a passage which fails to take account of various problems raised in connection with this pair and the other elements associated with it in *PMC* 3-5 which in fact make it highly improbable that the detail was derived from *Roland*. It is also perhaps worth noting in passing that if the reference to *adtores mudados* is of formulaic origin (whatever its antecedents may have been), it cannot safely be used, without further evidence that the poet was aware of the niceties of falconry, as an indicator of the time of year at which the Cid leaves Vivar, contrary to the suggestion of Anthony R.D. Pagden, 'A Reference to Falconry in the *Poema de Mio Cid*', *RF*, XCIII (1981), 138-42. The same objection would apply if *adtor mudado* were simply a designation for any adult bird which had lost its juvenile plumage (see Duggan, *The 'Cantar de Mio Cid'*, p. 114). Pagden is on much firmer ground when he discusses the social significance of *PMC* 5 (on which see also my 'The Opening Laisse* of the *Poema de Mio Cid*', *RLC*, LIII (1979), 490-501).

7. Note also the related formulaic expression without the possessive, *a l'ostel*, in line-final position in *Doon* 1606, 1676, 2101, and *Violette* 694; in line-initial position in *Violette* 304, 6078, 6188, and *Renier* 1664, 4104, 7873; and in other positions in *Renier* 1694, 9760, *Doon* 1259, 1775, 1889, and *Guillaume d'A* 2894.

8. Smith, *Poema de Mio Cid* (Oxford: Clarendon, 1972), p. 123: 'Presumably "and other Moors not native to those parts", i.e. patrols of the army from Valencia' (cf. Spanish translation (Madrid: Cátedra, 1976), p. 287, note to line 840).

9. For another discussion of the problem of specific meaning in a formulaic expression, see my 'The Opening Laisse', 493-95.

10. Smith, *PMC* (1972), p. xxii; (1976), p. 27.

11. Whilst French epic parallels can be adduced for both this detail and the previous point, that of providing fodder for the horse, it should also be noted that both are

a matter of daily reality in any society in which the horse is a vital means of transport and war, and as such are provided for in very specific terms in contemporary legislation. I have drawn attention to such clauses in connection with the provision of fodder ('On Certain Correspondences Between the *Poema de Mio Cid* and Contemporary Legal Instruments', *Iberoromania*, new series, XI (1980), 31-53, at pp. 44-45). For a modern parallel, see Cyril Falls, *Military Operations in Egypt and Palestine: from June 1917 to the end of the War*, I (London: HMSO, 1930), 53: 'each man carried two days' rations for himself, one day's forage, and a two days' emergency ration of grain in a sand-bag'. On the question of horse-shoes, see the rather vague reference by Menéndez Pidal in the note to line 1553 in his critical edition of the *PMC*, Clásicos Castellanos, XXIV, 12th edition (Madrid: Espasa-Calpe, 1968). Epic cliché and social reality come together in these details. Abengalbón is, of course, bearing the cost of fresh horse-shoes rather than checking the condition of the old ones and effecting necessary repairs, as in the French examples, but the similarity is clear.

12. Smith, *Estudios cidianos* (Madrid: CUPSA, 1977), chapter VII: 'Realidad y retórica: el binomio en el estilo épico', offers an excellent account of binary expressions. See also his 'On the Distinctiveness of the *Poema de Mio Cid*', in *'Mio Cid' Studies*, edited by A.D. Deyermond (London: Tamesis, 1977), pp. 161-94, especially pp. 185-90.

13. 'The *PMC* and the Old French Epic', pp. 114-15; 'The *Afrenta de Corpes* and Other Stories', p. 36, n. 51. Note that the 'leuaua' of *PMC* 16 is an interlinear addition, 'con la tinta anaranjada del primer corrector' (Menéndez Pidal, *CMC*, III, 909, n. 2) and is rejected by Menéndez Pidal, who is, however, concerned in his critical edition to maintain regular *o/e* assonance in this *laisse*. *PMC* 15, however, ends in 'entraua'. Among other editors, Smith has accepted 'leuaua', while Michael has rejected it: see Ian Michael, *Poema de Mio Cid* (Madrid: Castalia, 1976), p. 15, line 16, and p. 314, note to line 16).

14. This case could reasonably be viewed as constituting a two-line application of the formulaic expression, since 4127 continues the list with 'Bertons, Normans, Flamenc et Pohihers'. The basic formulaic structure is, however, complete at the end of 4126.

15. For the date of *Aymeri de Narbonne* and its implications for *Les Enfances Guillaume*, see Henry, ed. cit., pp. xxx-xxxi.

16. See Derek W. Lomax, 'The Date of the *Poema de Mio Cid*', in *'Mio Cid' Studies*, pp. 73-81.

17. *Ed. cit.*, pp. 221 (Paris MS, 1785), 297 (Vuillafans fragment, line 15). Line 39 of the Venice-2 fragment (p. 312) is discussed below.

18. *Ed. cit.*, p. 25 (line 762): 'A' version; *Le Charroi de Nîmes. Chanson de geste du XIIe siècle editée d'après la rédaction AB*, edited by Duncan McMillan (Paris: Klincksieck, 1972), footnote to line 762 for the 'B' version.

19. The chronological problem is outlined above. Close formulaic parallels for the *PMC* are common in French epics later than the immediate period of the Spanish poem; compare the following from *Renier* (dated tentatively by Cremonesi, *ed. cit.*, p. 71, to the second half of the thirteenth century), line 698:

En mi la sale ot un paile getez

with *PMC* 182:

En medio del palacio tendieron un almofalla.

The value of such later French testimony for formulaic and metrical patterns which may have existed in earlier French texts which do not survive is clear.

20. From a common origin in a Germanic formula, separate renderings into French and Spanish would be unlikely to produce so striking a similarity of verbal expression, if the characteristics of separate translations of a single original which one encounters in later medieval texts (and in modern language teaching experience) are any guide. Perhaps curiously, given the Germanic origins of the concept underlying the Vulgar Latin etymon of *compañía*, the older Germanic epic texts which I have examined do not seem to have any close approximations to this formula; the best I have found is *Beowulf*, 205-08, which, in the close translation of John Porter, reads 'Had the good man from Geats' tribe's / champions chosen those whom he bravest / find was able; fifteen together / sea-timber sought . . .' (*Beowulf*, edited and translated by John Porter (London: Pirate Press, 1977), unnumbered p. 10). The point is that a situation in which a structure akin to our Romance formulation might conceivably have occurred in fact adopts a wholly distinct means of indicating the number of companions following Beowulf. For a Spanish translation of these lines, see Luis Lerate, *Beowulf y otros poemas épicos antiguo germánicos (s. VII-VIII)* (Barcelona: Seix Barral, 1974), pp. 36-37.

21. I am most grateful to Drs Barry Taylor and Geoffrey West for their helpful comments on an earlier version of this paper.

NOTAS AL AZAR: PARA SIMULTANEAR LO PAR Y LO IMPAR

Francisco Marcos Marín

Los números están en el origen de nuestras diversas civilizaciones; si, en el marco cultural desde el que se escriben estas páginas, volvemos los ojos a nuestros primeros libros religiosos nos será fácil notar, p. ej., que el cuarto libro del Pentateuco bíblico es el Libro de los Números.[1] En el mundo hebreo tenemos también otros fenómenos en los que los números representan un papel fundamental, como la cábala, y, si fijamos la vista en el mundo grecolatino, observaremos que los números son esenciales para los pitagóricos;[2] universales son, también, múltiples formas mágicas, que por su carácter especializado, no caben aquí.[3]

El uso simbólico, mágico, místico y literario se confunden en ocasiones, quizá por ese valor misterioso que los pueblos primitivos atribuían a los dominadores de la palabra, conservado en los poetas modernos, como testimonia la abundante bibliografía dedicada al estudio de la presencia y el valor de los números y sus combinaciones en las obras literarias.[4]

Es posible, en algún caso, intentar rastrear una relación apoyándose en elementos de carácter numérico, o en combinaciones numéricas, especialmente en el mundo de los juramentos y maldiciones, las prácticas mágicas y los juegos. En el caso de la Península Ibérica, con su entrecruzamiento de influencias, podemos aventurarnos a buscar este tipo de relaciones en algún ejemplo concreto.

La aleya tres de la azora 89 ('La Aurora') del *Alcorán* registra una fórmula de juramento, *wa-l-šafᶜi wa-l-watrⁱ*, que se traduce 'por lo par y lo impar' (*šafᶜ* es 'par' y *watr, witr* 'impar'). Mahoma está criticando una serie de juramentos de su época, señalando la inconsistencia de su referencia, el sinsentido, diríamos con mayor propiedad. La interpretación teológica hace de Dios lo impar y del hombre lo par, tal vez para transformar alguna relación mágica primitiva. No entraremos en ello, porque nos desvía de otra asociación mucho más inmediata; pero tampoco quedará sin indicar que una versión lúdica de la relación de lo par y lo impar está en el juego de la taba, antecedente de los dados, dos de cuyas caras son el par y el non. Este juego, que requiere el uso de un hueso, tiene también su versión mágica y forma parte de las prácticas universales de escapulomancia.

Volvamos, no obstante, a nuestro hilo conductor. En el siglo X d.J.C., un poeta árabe cordobés, Muḥammad Ibn ᶜAbd Rabbihi, escribió un libro en el que recoge una valiosa muestra de la literatura árabe que se considera clásica, así como una serie de composiciones propias, entre las que, por su relación con la etapa primitiva de la épica hispánica, destaca una urchuza (poema historial en metro rachaz) sobre Abderrahmán III.[5]

El verso 99 se refiere a una expedición de castigo y nos dice, en su segundo hemistiquio: *wa kāna ka-l-šaᶜi li-hâdâ-l-witrʲ*, según la edición de Ahmad Amín, o, según la edición de Boulaq, *wa-kāna ka-l-šafᶜ bi-hā wa-l-witrʲ*.

El contexto es el siguiente: el Sultán ha enviado a un general, Ishâq ibn Muhammad, al-Coraixí, contra un rebelde, al-Sawadí. En el primer hemistiquio del verso 99 nos informa de que 'Después intensificó su fuerza con Badr', y, a continuación, viene el texto que comentamos.

De aceptar la lectura de Amín, la traducción sería 'y fue como el šafᶜ para este witr', donde los dos términos árabes se refieren a oraciones. Según E. Fagnan, 'la prière witr, qui se fait à la fin de la nuit, est composée d'une double rek'a [*sic*, por rekᶜa], *šafᶜ*, et d'une rekᶜa unique, *witr*, et celle-ci lui a donné son nom, RAd. I, 210, 27; 322, 8; Calc. 1471'.[6] La traducción podría ser 'y fue como las lecturas para este evangelio', si queremos conservar el juego religioso de 'dos' (genuflexiones en árabe, lecturas en español) y 'uno' (el evangelio).

Otra posibilidad es la segunda interpretación, la variante editorial de Boulaq, que se traduciría 'y fue como lo par en ella y lo impar', construcción que no aparece aquí aisladamente, sino que podemos ver en relación con otro lugar de la obra (*ᶜIqd*, IV, p. 308), no perteneciente a la urchuza, donde Abd Rabbihi, a propósito de acontecimientos del s.VII d.J.C. toma un verso atribuido a al-Hutî'a, quien utiliza la expresión:

li-ǧamaᶜta bayna-l-šafᶜi wa-l-witrⁱ

'para simultanear (lit. para que tú reúnas conjuntamente) lo par y lo impar', sin excluir juegos semánticos posibles, pues *witr* significa tanto 'venganza' como 'non, impar, singular'. Hay en él una constante, con un valor preciso.

Estos ejemplos árabes aducidos son suficientes para mostrarnos la existencia de una constante léxica, la del par y el non, que, en su versión mágica, corresponde al dos y el punto, dos y as en la transformación lúdica posterior.

Los números, no lo olvidemos, desempeñan un papel esencial en los juegos, por lo que pueden servir para aclarar aspectos de los textos, como testimonia el ejemplo siguiente.

La estrofa 754 del *Libro de Alexandre* dice así:

Quando uidieron su ora los que yuan fuyendo
tornaron las cabeças fuerte los refiriendo
tornaron pora Troya los troyanos corriendo
mas fue-s'-les la entrada en dos e as poniendo.[7]

El intento de regreso a Troya de sus habitantes, engañados por la estratagema de la retirada precipitada de los griegos, se ha hecho verdaderamente difícil, porque entre los emboscados que los persiguen y los que han salido del caballo que los aguardan, no tendrán salvación. El sentido de 'dos e as' en consecuencia es, en principio, claro: ha de ser un lance desafortunado del juego.

Emilio Alarcos, en su edición del episodio de la guerra de Troya incluído en el *Alexandre*, remite, como es natural, a la obra de juegos del siglo XIII por excelencia, los *Libros de ajedrez, dados e tablas*, pero se trata de una referencia general, sin entrar en el detalle del sentido, que se convierte así en el primero de nuestros objetivos.[8]

Son numerosas las ocasiones en las que las palabras 'dos' y 'as' se combinan en los *Libros de ajedrez, dados e tablas* (treinta y una, si nuestro recuento es exacto).[9] Se refieren a veces a posiciones (f. 4v, 34-35), a cantidades que se deben tener en dos dados para igualar la puesta de otro (f. 66v, 28), a juegos de tres dados, como el 'par con as' (f. 68v) en el que el ganador debe tener 'par en los dos dados & as en ell otro', o el 'seys dos & as' (f. 75r), que es un juego de tablero en el que para ganar se deben tener las casillas del seis, dos y as. La expresión, sin embargo, parece exigir un juego de dos dados en el que justamente sea esa postura la perdedora.

Parece tratarse, por ello, de un juego 'que llaman guirguiesca', o una variedad parecida, que se describe en el f. 71r, 3-15:

Otra manera a y de iuego que llama*n* guirguiesca *que* se iuega con dos dados en esta guisa. Los *que* quisiere*n* iogar an de alançar *prime*ramientre batalla. E el *que* la uenciere lançara *prime*ro. & si lançare senas o seys çinco o la soçobra destos *que* son dos & as o amas as sera azar. E gana*r*a por el un tanto de qual quantia pusieren entressi *que* vala.

En este punto son precisas dos advertencias de índole semántica. La palabra *soçobra* (moderno *zozobra*) está utilizada en su sentido técnico de 'cara del dado opuesta a la que se trata', y éste sería el más antiguo ejemplo de su uso según el *DCECH* de Corominas y Pascual (s.v. *so*). El dos y el as ocupan las caras opuestas al seis y al cinco. La palabra *azar*, por su parte, cuya primera documentación citada por el *DCECH* se encuentra en el *Libro de Alexandre*, 697b, significa 'cara desfavorable del dado, lance desfavorable del juego de dados'. Si los puntos más altos son seis y cinco, es lógico que sus 'zozobras' respectivas, as y dos, sean los puntos más bajos. Es innecesario advertir que el 'por el' del párrafo final se refiere al juego, no al azar, que es la mala suerte, pérdida; el que gana se lleva la puesta que se ha acordado previamente.

En 1611 tenemos dos refuerzos de esta interpretación, gracias a la obra de Sebastián de Covarrubias. El *Tesoro* (que servirá de autoridad en 1726 al *Diccionario de Autoridades* en este punto, pues lo reproduce literalmente) define *azar* como estorvo, desvío, mala suerte; . . . Los más convienen en que es arábigo, y dizen que sinifica la hora de las tres, la qual para los árabes es hora menguada. Es uno de los quatro puntos que tienen sus dados, y es el desdichado que los latinos llaman canis y ellos azar, el punto.[10]

No entraremos aún en ese valor azaroso de 'tres' (la suma del par y del impar) para los árabes, porque todavía Covarrubias nos ilumina un aspecto de lo que acabamos de citar, cuando define *as*:

> En nuestro castellano vale tanto como un punto, assí en el juego de los naipes como en el de los dados; y este punto era la unidad, dicho canis, el qual no sólo no gana, pero avía de poner en la tabla la posta que se jugava, para el que echava el punto dichoso de Venus, que barría con todo. Suetonio *In Augusti: Talis enim iactis, ut quisque canem, aut seniorem miserat, in singulos tallos singulos denarios in medium conferebat, quos tollebat universos qui Venerem iecerat.* Por otro nombre le llaman el punto. Para dezir que son pocos los que otros reputan por muchos, dezimos que son tres, dos y as.

Si recogemos las notas que hasta aquí se han desperdigado a la ventura (que no al azar), podremos concluir que la expresión del *Alexandre* se aclara a partir de un juego de dados en el que dos y as perdían. A los troyanos se les pone la entrada en 'dos y as', o sea, en ese lance del juego tienen los puntos más desfavorables o, como decimos con una expresión sacada de otro juego, del de naipes, 'llevan las de perder'.

Tal vez sea posible anudar las notas referidas a los árabes, al número tres, y a la interpretación de tres como 'lo par y lo impar', que, en el caso de Abd Rabbihi, especialmente en la urchuza, podría tomar un sentido similar al de 'dos y as' en el *Libro de Alexandre*, con preferencia por la lectura de Boulaq. El orden de los elementos es también el mismo en las dos lenguas. Desgraciadamente, la imprescindible compulsa de los manuscritos, en las presentes circunstancias, es una utopía, por lo que hay que operar con un riesgo que no sería aceptable en otros textos. El califa habría sido, en esa campaña, 'como el dos y el as', es decir, habría llevado a la desgracia a sus enemigos, derrotados como aquellos a quienes sale esa suerte, ese azar, en los dados. De ser cierta esta interpretación, nos encontraríamos ante una doble posibilidad: o que el léxico del juego, actividad de tan clara influencia árabe, hubiera proporcionado un calco semántico, que, desde el texto del *Libro de Alexandre*, habría llegado, al menos en los diccionarios, hasta el primero de la Academia, el de 1726, o bien que una expresión popular del juego de los dados, digamos hispanoárabe, hubiera sido asociada, por un poeta que hace alarde de recursos cultos, con el juramento que se cita en el *Alcorán*. Habida cuenta de que no parece que *witr* se haya utilizado en el sentido de 'as', pues el

árabe toma esta última palabra en préstamo del latín (AS), la segunda posibilidad
resulta más plausible. Constituye un interesante indicio aparente de que una fórmula
que se plasmará en castellano, por escrito, a principios del siglo XIII, podía haber sido
empleada en la Córdoba hispanoárabe del siglo X. En cualquier caso, la interpretación
de *Alexandre* 754d, que no ofrece ahora dudas, se halla también ahora en un entorno
mucho más sugerente.

Universidad Autónoma de Madrid

NOTAS

1. Herbert H. Paper, 'The Vatican Judeo-Persian Pentateuch: Numbers', *Acta
    Orientalia*, XXIX (1965), 253-310.
2. Clarence Tracy, 'Johnson and the Pythagorean Scale of Numbers', *NQ*, N.S.,
    XXIV (1978), 252-54.
3. Vincent F. Hopper, *Medieval Number Symbolism: its sources, meaning, and
    influence on thought and expression*, Columbia University Studies in English and
    Comparative Literature, CXXXII (New York, 1938); Karl Menninger, *Number
    Words and Number Symbols: a cultural history of numbers* (Cambridge, Mass.: MIT
    Press, 1969); Max Hammer, 'The Symbolic Meaning of Numbers and Alphabet
    Letters to Adults', *International Journal of Symbology*, I (1961), 31-39.
4. Gunnar Quarnstrom, *Poetry and Numbers: on the structural use of symbolic
    numbers*, Series 2 in Studier utg. av Kungl. Humanistiska vetenskapssamfundet i
    Lund (Lund: Gleerup, 1966); James Neil Brown, 'A Note on Symbolic Numbers in
    Spenser's "Aprill"', *NQ*, N.S., XXVII (1980), 301-04; J.M. Richardson, 'More
    Symbolic Numbers in Spenser's "Aprill"', *NQ*, N.S., XXIX (1982), 411-12; María
    del Pilar Palomo y José Romera Castillo (eds), *La literatura como signo* (Madrid:
    Playor, 1981); Leland Guyer, 'Arcane Numbers and Fernando Pessoa's "Passos da
    Cruz"', *Selecta: Journal of the Pacific Northwest Council on Foreign Languages*, II
    (1981), 81-85; Henryk Ziomek, 'El uso de los números en el *Quijote*', en *Actas del
    Sexto Congreso Internacional de Hispanistas* (Toronto: University of Toronto,
    Department of Spanish and Portuguese, 1980), pp. 825-27. El valor de los
    números en *La Celestina* ha dado origen a dos versiones de un trabajo de Henk de
    Vries: 'Sobre el mensaje secreto de Calysto y Melybea', en *'La Celestina' y su
    contorno social: actas del I Congreso Internacional sobre 'La Celestina'* (Barcelona:
    Hispam, 1977), pp. 135-51 y *'La Celestina*, sátira encubierta: el acróstico es una
    cifra', *BRAE*, LIV (1974), 123-57; para la discusión de los aspectos literarios
    implicados, véase Nicasio Salvador Miguel, 'El presunto judaísmo de *La*

Notas al azar

Celestina', en *The Age of the Catholic Monarchs, 1474-1516: literary studies in memory of Keith Whinnom*, edited by Alan Deyermond and Ian Macpherson, *BHS*, Special Issue (Liverpool: University Press, 1989), 162-77.

5. Manejamos las ediciones de Al-ʿIqd al-Farîd por Boulaq (El Cairo: al-ʿUryân, sin fecha, pero s. XIX), II, 369-84 y por Ahmad Amín (El Cairo: Dār al-Miṣr, 1944), IV, 501-27. Traducción y comentario en nuestra *Poesía narrativa árabe y épica hispánica* (Madrid: Gredos, 1971), pp. 104-67. En esta versión utilizamos la acepción 'venganza' de *witr* y la lectura de Amín. Las observaciones de Sigifredo Repiso, quien prepara su tesis doctoral sobre esta urchuza, nos hacen ver que el texto es mucho más complejo.

6. *Additions aux dictionnaires arabes* (Beirut: Librairie du Liban, sin fecha), s.r. *WaTaRa*. Sus autoridades son las glosas de ʿAdewi a la *Risala* de Ibn Abu Zeyd y un *Diccionario técnico*, sin más datos (Calcutta: N. Lees). Los términos en cursiva están en grafía árabe en el original, su vocalización es nuestra. *Rekʿa* es 'genuflexión'. Al-witr es también el día que se dedica a las plegarias en el monte Arafat, durante la peregrinación a la Meca.

7. Citamos por nuestra edición (Madrid: Alianza, 1987), donde se describen los textos manuscritos e impresos. Variantes del MS *O*: 754b fueron torna[n]do cara & fueronl. refferiendo; c fueron los a priessa lo que auien tomado sacudiendo, que anticipa 755b; d fuesse les. [*Nota de los editores*: por razones tipográficas, hemos utilizado la bastardilla en la cita en vez de la negrita que emplea el Prof. Marcos en su edición, para las convenciones tipográficas de la cual, véase la p. 60 de la misma.]

8. *Investigaciones sobre el 'Libro de Alexandre'*, Anejos de la *RFE*, XLV (Madrid: 1948), nota a la estrofa 754.

9. Citamos según la microficha de la edición de Lloyd Kasten y John Nitti, *Concordances and Texts of the Royal Scriptorium Manuscripts of Alfonso X, el Sabio* (Madison: HSMS, 1978).

10. *Tesoro de la lengua castellana o española* (Madrid: Turner, 1977). El texto de Covarrubias que citamos a propósito de *azar* continúa refiriéndose a las otras tres caras del hueso: *chuca, carne, taba*, que son 'chuque', 'curru' y 'taba' en el *Tesoro*. Véase Reinhart Dozy y W.H. Engelmann, *Glossaire des mots espagnols et portugais dérivés de l'arabe*, 2e éd., (Leiden: 1869, reimpr. Beirut: Librairie du Liban, 1974), s. v. *Chuca* es la cara que tiene una hendidura, *carne* es la parte cóncava con figura de cuerno (árabe *qarn*), y *taba*, además de designar todo el hueso, es la cara convexa.

LABIODENTAL /f/, ASPIRATION AND /h/-DROPPING IN SPANISH: THE EVOLVING PHONEMIC VALUE OF THE GRAPHS *f* AND *h*

Ralph Penny

1. The present study examines the use of the graphs *f* and *h* in Spanish from the pre-literary stage to the early modern period, with the aim of elucidating the changing phonemic value of these graphs. In particular, it challenges the assumption that medieval *h* could indicate the aspirate /h/ and the (less frequent) assumption that medieval *f* indicated a labiodental. These assumptions are implicit in the treatment given to the spellings *f-* and *h-* in Spanish etymological dictionaries, and elsewhere. Thus Corominas & Pascual (1980-) systematically give the earliest attestation of *h-* spellings, whether or not a spelling with *f-* is recorded earlier; this suggests to the reader that early MSp. *hablar* (for example) is a different phonological word from OSp. *fablar* and, specifically, that the different initial graphs indicate different phonemes, while the reality is surely that *fablar* and *hablar* represent chronologically successive spellings of the same string of phonemes. Conversely, Corominas & Pascual (1980-), like others, treat MSp. *fe* and OSp. *fe* as if they were phonologically the same, whereas it would be more accurate to indicate that OSp. *f* normally reflected a different phoneme from that indicated by MSp. *f.* Similar views are implied by Menéndez Pidal (1964, pp. 198-233) in discussing the 9th- to 11th-century forms spelt *h-* which are considered in section 2.1 below, and by those who have considered the *h-* spellings of the *Libro de Buen Amor* (see section 2.3).[1]

The view espoused here will be that *h* was a phonologically void symbol until the Renaissance, when it acquired the value /h/, only to become phonologically void again in more recent times. Likewise it will be argued that, in medieval Castile, *f* exclusively indicated /h/, only acquiring the additional value /f/ in later Old Spanish (self-evidently, after the appearance of this phoneme in that period of the development of Old Spanish); *f* comes to be restricted to the value /f/ only from the 16th century.

In the light of discussion of the graphs and phonemes in question at various stages of the history of Spanish, consideration will be given to the adaptation undergone in Spanish by loan-words from various sources (Ar., Fr., etc.), with the aim of testing and applying the conclusions reached.

2.0. The value of the graphs *f* and *h* will now be examined, according to their use in five historical periods.

2.1. The pre-literary period. In the pre-literary period, the existence of aspiration is concealed by the overwhelming use of *f* in cases of words whose initial consonant descends from F-. Because spelling is essentially etymological, *f* corresponds both to /f/ (in those areas which had labiodentals) and to /h/ (in those areas where, for whatever reason, an aspirate was the reflex of F-). But in the system of any one writer, *f* had only one value. There is a single exception to this last statement: we cannot exclude the possibility that *f* also corresponded to /zero/, especially in the Centre-North.

In a now classical study, R. Menéndez Pidal (1964, pp. 209-12) unearthed a number of early cases of departure from the etymological norm. Whereas the vast majority of cases, in the Peninsular documents of the 9th to 11th centuries, show the graph *f* where the word concerned was a reflex of a Latin word in F-, a small number of instances show the graph *h* or *zero*. In the area of Castile/Rioja, Menéndez Pidal cites:

Ortiço (863 Santoña; pers. name < FORTICIUS)

Hortiço (927 Santoña; pers. name < *id.*)

Haeto (912 Arlanza; top. < FAGEA + -ETU)

Oce de Ero (923 Nájera; 'gorge' < VL FOX, -CIS, CL FAUX, -CIS)

Garrahe (1016 San Millán; top.; a name which appears elsewhere as *Garrafe*)

Oja (1082 San Millán; the river name which also appears in the toponym *Rioja*; < FOLIA?)

Olia Castro (1052), Ogga Castro (1087; < FOLIA; = Ojacastro)

Hayuela (1057 Oña; < FAGEA + -OLA)

Haças de Felguera (1085 Santoña; < FASCIA; = Hazas in Santander)

Ormaza (1042, 1082 Arlanza: 'Ormaza de Fornillos'; < FORMACEU; = Hormazuela, NE Burgos)

Rehoio, Reoio (1212 DL; top. < *FOVEU) (cf. *Refoio* 1188 DL)

Errant, Ferrant (legal document of 1100 from Burgos; < FERDINANDUS)

A small number of such anomalies are also found in Aragon:

Hortiz (1099, 1103 Mt. Aragon), Ortiz (1106 Sum Port), Hortiz (1113; all < FORTICIUS)

Oçe (1095 Boltaña), Oze (1099 Mt. Aragon; < VL FOX, -CIS; = Hoz de Barbastro)

honsata ('army', 1132 Fuero de Asín, N. Zaragoza, 50km SW of Jaca; < FOSSA + -ATA).

Most are personal or place names, cases in which the scribe is most likely to have been uncertain of etymology and therefore more likely to attempt a 'phonological' spelling. If the scribe pronounced these words with initial /h/, he would be likely to spell them with *f*, since he would be aware of the many cases of correspondence between vernacular /h/ and Lat. F-. If, on the other hand, the vernacular name had no initial consonant (and he was unaware of its etymology), there would be no alternative to writing an initial vowel, or its alternative, *h* + vowel. As later evidence makes clear (see 2.2-3), *h* was a symbol without phonological value, arbitrarily added or omitted from words whose Latin counterpart required H-, but also arbitrarily added to many words with vocalic onset whose etyma lacked H-. We are not therefore entitled (contrary to what Menéndez Pidal (1964) thinks) to interpret the orthographical alternation between, say, *Ortiço* and *Hortiço* as a case of phonological alternation between /zero/ and /h/; both spellings indicate absence of initial consonant. To summarize, in Cantabria the relationship between relevant phonemes and graphs was:

/zero/ (< H- or F-) spelt *zero* or *h*
/h/ (< F-) spelt *f*;
while elsewhere the system was:
/zero/ (< H-) spelt *zero* or *h*
/f/ (< F-) spelt *f*.

2.2. The Alfonsine period. From the Alfonsine corpus (see Kasten & Nitti 1978), we can deduce the following system, no doubt reflecting educated usage in 13th-century New Castile:

/zero/ (< H-) spelt *zero* (sometimes *h*)
/h/ (< F-) spelt *f*
/f/ (via borrowing, phonologization of certain allophones of /h/, etc.) spelt *f*.

2.2.1. Although the large majority of words which show popular descent from etyma in H- are spelt in the corpus without initial consonant, there are considerable numbers of such words, together with large numbers of learned words, which are spelt *h*-. Leaving aside proper names, there are some 7112 tokens of this spelling; the following types show more than a hundred tokens each: *ha* 618, *han* 398, *he* 112, *heredar* and derivatives 867, *herege/heregia* 128, *hombre/homne* 138, *hora* 2095, *huerta/-o* 129, *huest* 1802, *humido* and derivatives 228. There can be no doubt that in these thousands of cases *h* corresponds to no phoneme (i.e., it is void). There is equally little doubt that *h* is void where it appears in the Alfonsine corpus in words whose etyma had no initial consonant, or which began with a consonant other than H- or F-. The highest frequency of *h* in words of this category occurs in *hermano/hermana* (1771 tokens), but a certain number of other instances are observable: *habondancia*, etc. 19, *hedad* 4, *hedificios* 3, *helemento* 5, *henemigos* 1, *huniverssidad* 1, *hunna* 'uña' 5, *husar*, etc., 45, *huuas* 'uvas' 9. We must therefore conclude that the small number of instances in the Alfonsine corpus in which *h* corresponds to F- (see 2.2.2) are also cases in which *h* is void.

2.2.2. Almost all cases of words whose etyma contain F- are spelt in the Alfonsine corpus with *f*. We must interpret this *f* as representing /h/, since, after two centuries of castilianization of the speech of the capital, it is next to inconceivable that this Castilian feature alone should not have become normal in 13th-century Toledo. Furthermore, as anticipated in 2.2.1, there are a few Alfonsine examples of the spelling *h* in words whose etyma show F-. To my knowledge, these cases have hitherto passed unnoticed; they are the following: *hablado* (*Ajedr.* 72r11), *hambre* (*Cruz.* 18v46), *haz a* 'hacia' (8 tokens in *Astr.* and *Cruz.*), *heda* 'fea' (2 tokens in *EEII*), *hembras* (*Rycas Hembras*, *EEII* 320v9, 58), *hongos* (*GEIV* 229v77). To these we may add *Hannez* (65 tokens, vs. 77 of *Fannez*), *hardido* 4, *hardiment* 11, *hardit* 4 (vs. 4 tokens of *fardido*), *hasta* 5, *hata* 154 (vs. 2585 tokens of *fasta* and 198 of *fata*), and *honta* 2. Given the conclusion in 2.2.1 that in many thousands of cases *h* is a void symbol, the cases of *h* noted here (including those in which *h* corresponds to F-) can hardly be regarded differently. We must conclude that the occasional example of *hablado*, etc., indicates /abládo/, etc., which we must interpret as occasional early cases of loss of /h/ (perhaps due to copyists of northern origin who worked in the royal scriptorium).

2.2.3. It is possible (but perhaps unlikely) that 13th-century Toledan speech had some words, borrowed from Mozarabic or influenced by Mozarabic speech, in which /f/ occurred, perhaps alternating freely (more probably in sociolinguistic relationship) with /h/. Spelling cannot reveal such a diversity of pronunciation, since *f* is the only letter available in the Alfonsine system to indicate both /h/ and /f/.

On the other hand, it is much more likely that, already in 13th-century Spanish, the phoneme /f/ was being introduced to Castilian from other sources. These sources include the following three:

1. Phonologization of the initial unit of *fuerte*, *fuente*, etc., cases in which the initial phone was until this time arguably the voiceless labiovelar allophone [ʍ] (hitherto assignable to the phoneme /h/ and to this day widely preserved in rural Castilian of all areas), but in the later Middle Ages modified to [f] in urban Castilian. Similarly, it is likely that at this stage the initial [ɸ] of words like *fresno*, *fruente*, etc., was being changed, in urban Castilian, from bilabial to labiodental articulation (although again leaving rural Castilian unaffected down to the present). I have argued elsewhere (Penny 1972) that these modifications occurred as a result of contact with French and Provençal in the period of greatest Gallo-Romance influence on Spanish, namely, the late 12th and early 13th centuries.

2. Borrowing of learned words by the vernacular from the Latin of the Church and the law, a Latin by this time read aloud according to the system of 'litterae', brought to Spain by French clerics and in which it is highly likely that Latin words spelt F were read aloud using a labiodental articulation. (For 'litterae' and the introduction of this system to Spain, see Wright 1982; see here also 3.3).

3. Modification of certain orally-inherited vernacular words (ones whose meaning laid them open to influence from ecclesiastical or legal language), in such a way as to produce stylistic alternation between traditional /h/ and 'Latin-inspired' /f/. Thus it can be argued that FIDES gave vernacular /hé/, but that in the 12th to 13th centuries, this word came to have a high-register counterpart /fé/, because the vernacular word was inevitably associated with the pronunciation of FIDES, now heard in the Church as /fídes/, or the like. Similarly, it was probably at this period that traditional /hebréro/ 'February', still heard today in Northern Spain, usually now without the aspirate (see, e.g., Penny 1970, p. 75), came to have a competitor /febréro/. The label I would attach to such forms as /fé/ and /febréro/ is 'semi-learned', although the mechanism, just expounded, by which these forms came about does not correspond exactly to conventional notions of 'semi-learned' transmission.

The result of these three processes is a phonological split. Up to this period, Spanish had no /f/ phoneme, but at this stage traditional /h/ -- perhaps better symbolized as /φ/ -- was split into /h/ and /f/. Thus traditional

/hablár/ [haβlár] *fablar* 'to speak'
/huérte/ [ʍwérte] *fuerte* 'strong'
/hrío/ [φrío] *frío* 'cold',

by modification of [ʍ] and [φ] to [f], and by the acceptance of Latin and French loans in which a syllabic vowel was preceded by [f] (e.g., /fórma/ 'shape', /faisán/ 'pheasant'), were reallocated to two separate phonemes:

/h/	/f/
/hablár/ *fablar*	/fuérte/ *fuerte*
/hórma/ *forma*	/frío/ *frío*
etc.	/fórma/ *forma*
	/faisán/ *faisán*
	etc.

It will be noted that such a split is not reflected in contemporary spelling, since *f* is used both for the original phoneme /h/ and for both products, /h/ and /f/, of the split. Spelling evidence is available only from the 15th century (see 2.4).

2.2.4. It follows that it is necessary to reject the view of Lapesa (1980, p. 240) that Alfonsine Spanish avoided /h/ as 'too regional' in flavour; in the epicentre of the spread of /h/, namely, in Burgos, 13th-century (and later) spelling continued to impose *f* as the graph corresponding to this phoneme. In this regard, Burgos and Toledo follow exactly the same spelling norm, and since in Burgos *f* indicated /h/, there is no reason to think that the same was not true in Toledo, two centuries after the beginning of the castilianization of that city.

2.3. The 14th century. The *Libro de Buen Amor* reveals the continuation of the Toledan norm of the Alfonsine period (see Criado, Naylor & Antezana 1973). Its language is presumably based on the educated usage of New Castile, no doubt incorporating the 'new' /f/ (see 2.2.3). The relevant phonemes are written in the following ways:

/zero/ (< H-) spelt *zero* (sometimes *h*)

/h/ (< F-) spelt *f*

/f/ (in learned, 'semi-learned', and some popular forms) spelt *f*.

2.3.1. With regard to the spelling *h*, the same conclusion is in order as for the Alfonsine corpus (2.2.1), namely that in the *LBA* it is a void symbol. The vast majority of cases of *h* (see following section) correspond to Latin H-, or to G^{e,i}-, and can therefore be interpreted only as /zero/.

2.3.2. As in the 13th century, in the 14th-century *LBA f* is the spelling overwhelmingly used in cases of correspondence with Latin F-. Since it is not doubted that the aspirate /h/ (< F-) had long since been established in New Castile (see 2.2.2), it is uncontroversial, in the case of these words, to establish the equivalence *f* = /h/.

However, there is some evidence from the spellings of the *LBA* that dropping of /h/ is beginning to occur. The spelling, in the three manuscripts, of words whose etyma contain F- is as in Table 1:

Table 1: Spellings of words whose etyma contain F-

MS	S	T	G
a) no. of tokens with spelling *f-*	*c*1850	522	*c*1250
b) no. of tokens with spelling *h-*	15	4	32
c) *h* as % of total	0.8	0.8	2.5

It is well known that the cases of *h* are concentrated in (but not limited to) the *serrana* episodes. The words concerned are either place-names or belong to a totally unpretentious portion of the vocabulary. In MS *S* we find:

haça 'ploughed field' < FASCIA 'strip'

hacerio 'mockery', der. *faz ferir*

hadedura 'ill-fated, accursed' < *FATIDURA

hato (2), *hatos* 'clothes' < *FAT '*id.*' + Ar. *hazz* 'portion due to each person'

heda 'ugly' < FOEDA 'shameful, repugnant'

Henares (2), top., < FENUM 'hay' + suffix

heuilla 'buckle' < VL FIBELLA (CL FIBULA) '*id.*'

Hita, top., < VL FICTA (CL FIXA) 'planted upright'

horaña 'wild, uncouth' < FORANEA 'foreign'

hoscos 'grey' < FUSCOS 'dark-coloured'

Huron (2), personal name (= 'ferret'?) < LL FURO, -NIS '*id.*'

In MS *T* we find (information is added only if the word cited appears here for the first time):

hunda (2) 'bag' < FUNDA

hundo 'destroy' < FUNDO

Huron.

And in MS *G* the cases of *h* < F- are the following:

haça

hacina 'stook (of corn), bundle (of firewood)', der. FASCIS 'bundle of wood'

hacerio (2)

hadas 'fates' < FATA '*id.*'

hadeduro (4), *hadura, haduros*

hado 'fate' < FATUM '*id.*'

harnero (2) 'sieve' < FARINA 'flour' + suffix

harta (2), *hartas* 'fed up' < FARCTA 'full, stuffed'

harte (pres. subj. of *hartar*, derived from preceding)

hato (3)

haua (2), *hauas* 'broad bean' < FABA '*id.*'

heda (2)

Henares

herrada 'bound with iron' < FERRATA '*id.*'

heuilla

hiebre 'fever' < FEBRIS '*id.*'

hito 'boundary-marker' < FICTUS 'planted upright'

hogaças 'round loaves' < FOCACIA 'rolls baked in ashes'

hoz 'sickle' < FALX, -CIS '*id.*'

hoscos

huelgo 'breath', der. FOLLICARE.

Such spellings with 'h-' are often taken as early evidence of the pronunciation of /h/ in Northern New Castile, a conclusion that carries the implication that the spelling *f-* indicated a different phoneme (presumably /f/). Thus, Corominas (1967, p. 67) explicitly takes the view that *h* indicates /h/, although he mentions 'algún caso indudable de desaspiración,' and refers to stanzas 515a and 588d. Likewise, Cejador (1960, footnotes *passim*), considers *haça*, etc., to indicate an aspirate pronunciation.

If *f-*, as I think, was still in the 14th century the normal spelling of /h/, how are we to interpret the minority of spellings which employ *h-*? The answer can be gleaned from an examination of the use of *h* in words whose etyma do not show Lat. F. MSS *S*, *T* and *G* respectively contain 240, 83, and 121 tokens of words spelt *h-* which are descendants of Latin words spelt H-, G- or J-. The graph *h* here must simply stem from an awareness that the Latin spelling (the main arbiter in matters of medieval Romance spelling) showed an initial consonant, although in some cases, especially before *i* and *u*, the *h* probably played an important role, helping the reader by specifying that the following letter had vocalic rather than consonantal value (and, indeed, making clear that the following minim(s) was not (part of) some other letter, such as *n*, *m*, etc.). What is evident is that in these cases – not to mention cases like *S hedat* (3), *T herizaron*, *G hedat* (3), *herrados* (< ERRATOS), *herré* (pret. of *errar*), *herror*, *huas* (< UVAS), *huso* (< USUS), where the etymon has *no* initial consonant – *h* can be assigned no phonemic value, and, since this is the case in such a large number of tokens, it is surely also true in the small number of forms in the *LBA* whose *h-* corresponds to Lat. F-; Juan Ruiz's use of *hato*, etc., instead of *fato*, etc., must be intended to indicate an aspirate-less pronunciation /áto/, contrasting with the standard pronunciation of his time and place, namely, /háto/, spelt *fato*.

Confirmation of this view is available from the cases of words spelt with internal *h* in the *LBA*. The words *traer*, *caer*, *Juan* (i.e., words whose etyma contain intervocalic H or D) show alternation between *h* and *zero* spellings, in the proportions shown in Table 2:

Table 2: Words whose etyma contain -H-, -D-

MS	S	T	G
a) spelt *zero*	32	16	12
b) spelt *h*	21	1	2
c) *h* as % of total	65.5	6.2	16.6

Thus the spellings *traher*, *caher*, *Johan*, etc., again make it clear that *h* cannot be assigned any phonemic value. The *h* is merely a sign of the writer's awareness that the Latin words related to these (namely, TRAHERE, CADERE, JOHANNIS) had an intervocalic consonant.

Having concluded that spellings such as *hato* indicate a pronunciation /áto/, we may next ask what social facts underlie the spellings. Most of the cases of *h* for *f* occur in the *serrana* episodes (st. 950-1042), when the Archpriest is involved in a number of amorous encounters in the Sierra de Guadarrama (i.e. on the borders of New and Old Castile). Although by no means all the *h* spellings occur in dialogue (they are also

164

frequent in the narrative of these episodes),[2] it is reasonable to conclude that Juan Ruiz intends to indicate by this means a non-standard /h/-dropping pronunciation observable at that time in this region of central Spain. Loss of the aspirate had, probably for some centuries, been typical of all or most of Old Castile. The evidence from the *LBA* is that in the first half of the 14th century, aspirate-less pronunciation was beginning (perhaps at a humble social level) to encroach upon Northern New Castile.[3]

2.4. The Renaissance. Widespread medieval introduction of learned words spelt *f*- and pronounced /f/ (see 2.2) had, by the 15th century, created an unstable orthographic system: two phonemes were written using the same symbol. Thus, for example, both /hórma/ 'shoemaker's last' (the popular reflex of FORMA) and /fórma/ 'shape, form' (a learned borrowing of the same word) were written *forma*. This major orthographical ambiguity is resolved during the period under consideration (the most rapid period of change being the turn of the 16th century) by the systematic use *for the first time* of the letter *h* to indicate the aspirate /h/. This readjustment of spelling can in all probability be put down to the account of one man, Antonio de Nebrija.[4] In his *Repetitio secunda* of 1486, whose aim was to reform the pronunciation of Latin in Spain, Nebrija shows an awareness of the need to pronounce Latin H- as /h/,[5] and immediately applied this knowledge to Spanish, recommending and using the spelling *h* for Sp. /h/ in the *Gramática de la lengua castellana* (1492a, p. 118), in the two bilingual dictionaries (1492b and 1516), and in the *Orthographia* (1517). Nebrija (1492a, pp. 121-22) recognizes three uses for *h*: in addition to indicating /h/, it is to be used in cases like *huésped, huerto, huevo* (where it serves to specify the vocalic value of following *u*), and in 'diciones latinas', such as *humano, humilde*. A fourth value is later specifically listed (1517, pp. 139-40), namely its role in the digraph *ch*. However, it is noticeable that Nebrija by no means always writes *h* in the case of words whose etyma contain H-; he normally writes, as was the usual practice in earlier periods, *aver, vuo* (= *hubo*), *ombre*, *oi* (= *hoy*), etc. Clearly, Nebrija's concept of 'diciones latinas' was close to our concept of 'learned words'.

Nebrija's recommendations were followed by his contemporaries and successors (except for the lawyers, see 2.5), including even his most famous detractor, Juan de Valdés (1535, pp. 50, 54-55), so that the system in use from the beginning of the 16th century was the following:

/zero/ (< H-) spelt *zero* (*h* in learned words)
/h/ (< F-) spelt *h*
/f/ (via loan, etc.) spelt *f*.[6]

However, many speakers, educated and uneducated (especially those from the northern Meseta) had lost /h/ (see, e.g., Lapesa 1980, pp. 368-69), so that their use of *h* in *hazer*, etc., had become a matter of etymology, not pronunciation.

2.5. After 1550. Loss of /h/, which we have seen beginning to penetrate Northern New Castile in the 14th century (2.3), became increasingly general in this area after the establishment of Madrid as the capital in the 1560s, thereafter spreading to Toledo and the rest of New Castile, Eastern Andalusia, Murcia, etc. Dropping of /h/ was one of a number of features (the others were merger of /b/ and /β/ and the merger of the pairs of sibilants /ʃ/ and /ʒ/, /s/ and /z/, /ş/ and /ʐ/) which originated in Old Castile and became characteristic of educated Madrid usage in the second half of the 16th century, rapidly spreading southwards thereafter (see Lapesa 1980, pp. 372-73). This phonological loss, together with the increasing use of the spelling *h* in the case of popular words whose etymon showed H-, led to the following system of correspondences between phonemes and graphs:

/zero/ (< H-; popular and learned words) *h*

/zero/ (< F-; popular words) *h*

/f/ (< F-; learned words, loans, etc.) *f*.

Such a system does not imply that the 'same' word could *not* belong to more than one of its categories. Alternation between /zero/ and /f/ (represented at the graphical level by alternation between *h* and *f*) is observable in two classes of words.

On the one hand, Golden Age Spanish inherited from the previous period a number of instances like *hebrero ~ febrero*, where a semi-learned form with /f/ (now felt to be the only 'educated' form) competed with a popular alternant (and now increasingly felt to be 'rustic'), or like *horma ~ forma* where the distinction was semantic rather than one of register.[7]

On the other hand, it is likely that in this period a number of new cases of alternation came about. Among lawyers (unlike the rest of the community, who before the middle of the 16th century had abandoned the use of *f* in popular words such as *fazer, fijo*, etc., preferring *hazer, hijo*, etc.) the use of *f* in popular words continued perhaps a century longer (Lapesa 1980, pp. 368-69). However, we can be fairly certain that, in reading their documents aloud, such lawyers pronounced the written *f* using labio-dental /f/, and that it was by now lost from memory that *f* had once indicated the aspirate /h/. It is probably from the reading-aloud of such documents that a number of words, hitherto pronounced /h-/ (or /zero/ after aspirate-loss), passed into the general language with an /f/ pronunciation: *fallar, fecha, fallecer*, etc.

3.0. In the light of the foregoing discussion, an examination will now be made of a number of key groups of loan-words (including learned words) which appear in Spanish with the spellings *f, h* (sometimes *zero*), with the dual aim of testing the conclusions so far reached and giving a reasoned account of the processes of adaptation undergone by borrowings from the languages concerned.

3.1. Arabisms. Most arabisms which passed into Castilian were probably borrowed before the 13th century (and, therefore, before the establishment of /f/, which occurred from that time on). Since it is agreed that the language of the primitive Castile lacked a phoneme /f/ (although the reasons for this absence continue to be disputed; see Menéndez Pidal 1964, pp. 198-233, Penny 1972), the Arabic voiceless labiodental fricative was replaced by that Old Spanish phoneme which shared the maximum number of features with the Arabic phoneme, namely, OSp. /h/ spelt *f*. After the change of spelling practice in the Renaissance (see 2.4) and the widespread loss of /h/, those arabisms that survive appear in Modern Spanish with spelling *h* (= /zero/). Examples (with details from Corominas & Pascual 1980-, Kasten & Nitti 1978, and Nebrija 1516) are:

> *fúndaq > alfondiga* (1033), later *alhóndiga* (thus Nebrija) 'corn exchange'
> *fústaq > alfocigo (Cel.)* (beside *alfostigo*, Juan Manuel), later *alhocigo* (thus Nebrija, beside *alhostigo*) 'pistachio nut tree'
> *táfar > atafarra*, later *ataharre (Partidas)* 'crupper-strap'
> *tafúrma > atahorma* (1386) 'species of eagle'.

3.1.1. Similarly, the Arabic voiceless velar and laryngeal fricatives were open to interpretation as OSp. /h/ and therefore were often also spelt *f* in Old Spanish, with revised spelling *h* from the Renaissance. However, many of these borrowings (although ancient) are not attested until the modern period, and therefore are only found with the spelling *h*. E.g.,

> *hábra > hebra* (Sant.) 'cut of meat'
> *hadîda > alhadida* (Nebrija) 'copper oxide'
> *hâǧa > alhaja* (Nebrija) 'jewel, treasure, fine piece of furniture'
> *hálaq > falagar* (Berceo), *halagar* (Nebrija) 'to flatter'
> *hammâl > alhamel* (And.) (1585) 'casual labourer'
> *hanzal > alhandal (Aut.)* 'a certain insect'
> *hanîya > alhanía* (1406-12) 'cupboard, alcove'[8]
> *háqq > hoque* (1501) 'gratuity'
> *hárab > harbar* (Enzina) 'to botch (a job)'
> *haráka > alharaca* (A.Pal.) 'fuss'
> *hármal > harmaga* (Nebrija), *alharma* (1770) 'wild rue'
> *harûn > farón* (13c.; *LBA*), *harón* (Nebrija: *harona*), 'lazy' remodelled as *haragán*,
>   under the influence of *holgazán*
> *hasána* (?) *> fazaña* (1150), *hazaña* (Nebrija) 'courageous deed'
> *hazîn > fazinas (GEI), hazino* (1400, thus also Nebrija) 'wretched'
> *huwwârà > alhavara* (1527) 'kind of flour'

ḥairî > *alhelí* (1588) 'wallflower'

ḥílqa > *helga* (1585) '(metal) band'

ḥinna > *alheña* (Nebrija) 'privet, henna'[9]

ḥubs > *habiz* (1492, Granada) 'gift to Muslim religious institution'

ḥulba > OSp. *alfolva* (13c.), *alholva* (Villena, Nebrija) 'foenum graecum'

ḥurr > *alhorre* (1575) 'baby's rash'

ḥurr > *forro* (1074), *horro* (Nebrija) 'free (from serfdom)'

ḥuzâmà > *alhuzema* (1475, also Nebrija), later *alhucema* 'lavender'

ḥusaina > *alhuceña* (1780) 'kind of cabbage'

ḥurraiqa > *alhurreca* (Nebrija) 'kind of jellyfish (?)'

maḥássa > *almohaça* (Nebrija) 'currycomb'[10]

muḥádda > *almohada* (1400) 'pillow'

muḥárrab (?) > *moharra* (1728 *Aut.*) 'iron lance-point'

qáľa ḥurra > *calaforra* (*EEI, EEII*), now *calahorra*.

rahán > *rehén* (Nebrija) 'hostage'

saḥîna > *çahinas* (Nebrija) 'type of gruel'

ṣáḥri > *çahareño* (1385; Nebrija) '(falcon) difficult to tame'

taḥánnu > *taheño* (Nebrija) 'reddish (hair, beard)'

tahlîl > *tahelil* (1570), *tahalí* (1580) 'swordbelt'

zuharî > *zahorí* (Covarrubias) 'clairvoyant, water-diviner'.

By contrast with these cases, there is some evidence that the Arabic aspirate and voiceless velar and laryngeal fricatives were sometimes omitted in Castilian when words containing them were borrowed. The cases concerned are Spanish words with no letter corresponding to the Arabic phoneme (or, in Old Spanish before the 15th century, the letter *h*). Thus, in the Alfonsine corpus (see Kasten & Nitti 1978), we find *alhadida* (6 tokens, see 3.1.1) *alhaias* (1), *alhenna* (2), *calahorra* (10, beside *calaforra*, 2 tokens, see above). Other cases of omission of these Arabic phonemes are:

fahhar > *alfar* (18c.) 'potter's workshop' (see also 3.1.2)

hadúbba > *adruba* (1400) 'hump-back' (see also 3.1.6)

halûqi > *aloque* (1513) 'bright red'

háttà > *adta* (945) 'until' (see also 3.1.6)

háula > *ola* (1403) 'wave'

hazâna > *alacena* (1554) 'cupboard, pantry'

humra > *alombra* (late 14c.) 'carpet' (see also 3.1.5)

mahzén > *almacén* (1225) 'warehouse, store'.

3.1.2. Any case in which /f/ appears in the modern Spanish form of an arabism therefore requires a special explanation, of which the following are the most important:

An Arabic word containing /f/ was borrowed by a dialect (most frequently, no doubt, Mozarabic) which had retained labiodentals; this word was then passed on to Castilian after the latter had acquired /f/ (for this acquisition, see 2.2.3). It is often difficult to distinguish between such cases of indirect borrowing and those cases in which Castilian borrows directly from Arabic, but at a relatively late period (from the 13th century). No attempt will be made here to distinguish between these two possibilities. Words falling into this category of late or indirect borrowing are:

ᶜarîf > *alarife* (Nebrija) 'architect'

fâd > *fideos* (14c.) 'vermicelli'

fahhar > *alfahar* (1629), *alfar* (18c) 'potter's workshop' (whence *alfarero* (Lope) 'potter')

falûwa > *falúa* (1582) 'launch'

fanîd > *alfenique* (*LBA*), *alfeñique* (Nebrija) 'sugar icing'

fárza > *alferza* (*Ajedr.*) 'queen (in chess)'[11]

faqq (?) > *alfaque* (17c.) 'sandbank'

fārisîya (?) > *alferecía* (1555) 'epilepsy'

farás > *alfaraz* (1580) 'Moorish horse'

farḍa > *alfarda* (1575) 'a certain tax'

farda > *alfarda* (1303) 'Moorish woman's garment'

farš > *alfarje* (1633) 'carved wooden ceiling'

farrâs > *alferraz* (1884) 'kind of hawk'

fásfaṣa > *alfalfa* (1400) 'alfalfa'

fásha (?) > *alféizar* (*Aut.*) 'window-embrasure'

fassâs > *alfazaque* (1884) 'black beetle'

fîl > *alfil* (1283) 'rook (in chess)'[12]

fill > *alfil* (Nebrija) 'omen'

fitât > *alfitete* (1617) 'type of dough'

fulân > *fulano* (1155) 'so-and-so'

fuqqûs > *alficoz* (1423) 'kind of cucumber'

fustât (?) > *fustán* (1289; Nebrija) 'fustian'

fústaq > *fustete* (1552) 'a certain shrub (rhus cotinus)'

ǧufáina > *aljufaina* (1615-17), *jofaina* (1680) 'washbasin'

mafrâš > *almofrex* (Nebrija) 'bag for portable bed'

mukáffir > *almocafre* (1513) 'type of hoe'

múšrif > *almoxerif* (1081), *almoxarife* (1253; Nebrija), MSp. *almojarife* 'tax-collector'

qúffa > *cofa* (1745) 'crow's nest (of ship)'

raff > *rafe* (*Aut.*) (Arag., Murc.) 'eaves'

sanîfa > *cenefa* (*ca.* 1400) 'border, trimming (of clothes)'

Labiodental /f/, Aspiration and /h/-dropping in Spanish

táfah > *atafea* (1541) 'excessive meal'.

3.1.3. Similar to the previous cases are those in which the Arabic word contained an aspirate, or a voiceless velar or laryngeal fricative, interpreted as /f/ in dialects which lacked aspirates (e.g. Arag., Moz.):

hálhal (?) > *fárfara* (*Aut.*) 'membrane of egg'

habba (?) > *alfaba* (1272 Murc.) 'unit of dry measurement'

hǎgar > *alfarge* (Nebrija) 'nether mill-stone'

hallâba > *falleba* (1680) 'door-latch'

hardûn > *fardacho* (1817; Arag.) 'lizard'

hárnaq > *farnaca* (1836; Arag.) 'levret'

hárras > *alfarrazar* (1836; And., Murc.) 'to levy a tithe on crops'

harût > *farota* (*Aut*: Murc.) 'shameless woman'

hayyât > *alfayate* (1234, when *f* may indicate /h/ or /f/; thus also Nebrija, where *f* = /f/) 'tailor'

hurǧ > *alforja* (1400; Nebrija) 'saddlebag'

zâh > *zafarse* (1539) 'to escape, go off'.

3.1.4. A further explanation of the phoneme /f/ in the arabisms of Castilian is that such words do not have a continuous oral history in Spanish; an arabism written in Old Spanish with *f* (= /h/, whether derived from Ar. /f/ or from a velar or laryngeal fricative) falls out of use but is later reintroduced (e.g. as an historical term) with its *f* now interpreted as /f/. This case is therefore similar to that envisaged above (2.5) to account for the /f/ of certain Spanish legal terms. Probable examples are:

fáneq > *alfaneque* (1325) 'kind of hawk'

fakkâk > *alfaqueque* (*Partidas*) 'redeemer of captives' (Nebrija's spelling *alhaqueque* confirms this interpretation)

faqîh > *alfaquí* (1300) 'Muslim priest'

fasqîya > *fasquía* (1260) 'girth (?)'

hadîya > *alfadía* (1239) 'bribe'

haǧǧâm > *alfageme* (1250) 'barber' (confirmed by Nebrija's spelling *alhajeme*)

hánbal > *alfamar* (1179) 'tapestry, blanket', spelt *alhamar* in 1527 (Nebrija: *alfamar*, a possible misinterpretation of the Old Spanish spelling?)

hángal > *alfange* (*GE*) 'cutlass'

hakîm > *alfaquín* (*Astr.*) 'Muslim doctor'

harâm > *alfareme* (1406) 'Arab head-dress' (also spelt *alhareme* in 15c.)

hauz > *alfoz* (972) 'district'

hurí > *alfolí* (*Partidas*) 'granary' (Nebrija *alholí de trigo*)

kafal > *alcafar* (1300) 'crupper'.

3.1.5. Note that the same Arabic word may (at least in some instances) have entered Spanish by two separate channels, giving rise to competing forms. One type of alternation is that between OSp. /h/ (spelt *f*, later modified to *h*, and usually indicative of an early borrowing made directly from Arabic) and /f/ (spelt *f* both in late Old Spanish and Modern Spanish, usually indicative of late borrowing or that the word concerned was passed indirectly to Castilian via a dialect in which Ar. /f/ and the Arabic velar and laryngeal fricatives gave /f/; see 3.1.3). E.g. Ar. *hamra* directly enters Spanish as /alhómbra/ (Osp. spelling *alfombra*, Nebrija *alhombra*), and indirectly (via Mozarabic?) as the ultimately successful /alfómbra/ (also spelt *alfombra*). Similarly, I would argue that Ar. *faniqa* was borrowed by Spanish (in Old Castile) as /hanéga/ spelt *fanega*, but later /hanéga/ came into competition with /fanéga/, owing to reborrowing of the Arabic word (from a dialectal source such as Mozarabic) or to modification of /hanéga/ under the continuing influence of the Arabic word. In any case of alternation between competing forms of the same arabism, one of which had /f/ and the other /h/ (later /zero/), 16th-century Spanish would have shown a preference for the /f/-form, since in this period the phoneme /f/, where it alternated with /h/ or /zero/ in words of Romance origin, was, it seems, associated with more 'educated' register (see 2.5). Similar cases of possible double borrowing are the following:

> *fâris* > *alfiereç* (932), *alferez* (1171) 'standard-bearer, second lieutenant'. The form with /f/ which has passed into Modern Spanish is possibly not the descendant of the form first attested in 1171, but an independent form borrowed from another Hispanic dialect; Ptg. *alférez* is attested from 1112.
>
> *hilâl* > *alhilel* (Nebrija); beside *alfilel* (also Nebrija), later *alfiler* 'pin'
>
> *húzza* > *alfoza* (1438), later *alhorza* (1608), now *lorza*; beside *alforza* (Nebrija).

3.1.6. Another type of phonological alternation visible in Old Spanish arabisms is that between /h/ (spelt *f*, or, from the 15th century, *h*) and /zero/ (spelt *zero* or *h*). It is predictable that Ar. /f/, or an Arabic velar or laryngeal fricative, having been interpreted as Cast. /h/ during the borrowing process, should have been occasionally lost in Old Spanish, perhaps especially in Old Castile, since /h/-dropping in the northern Meseta dates at least from the 13th century, and probably earlier. It is probably this loss of /h/ which is reflected in the occasional Alfonsine spelling *h* (< Ar. /f/, /h/, etc.), alternating with more usual *f* (= /h/):

> *alhondiga* (1 token), beside *alfondiga* (also 1 token) (see 3.1)
> *alhaquim* (1), beside *alfaquim* (4) (see 3.1.4)
> *alhayat* (1), beside *alfaiat* (1), *alfayat* (1) (see 3.1.3)
> *alhoz* (2), beside *alfoz* (3) (see 3.1.4).

Other cases of Old Spanish alternation between /h/ and /zero/ are the following:

hadúbba > *adruba* (1400); beside *fadubrado* (13c.), *hadruba* (1475), *horoba
(whence *joroba* [*Aut.*]) 'hump-back'
háttà > *adta* (945), later *ata, hata, hasta*; beside *fata* (*CMC*), *fasta* (13c), *hasta*
(Nebrija) 'until'
hê > *he* (*ARM*); beside *fe* (*CMC*), *he* (Nebrija) 'behold'
hind > *alfin* (1270), *alfinde* (*Astr.*); beside *alhinde* (1278), *alinde* (1440) 'steel'
rahis > *rafez* (Berceo); beside *raez* (Nebrija) 'cheap, vile, easy'[13]
rihâla > *rafala* (13c), *rehala* 'flock'; beside *reyal* (*CMC*), *rehala* (*LBA*), *real* (1275;
Nebrija) 'domain'
sahr > *xafarron* (*Alex.*); beside *zaharron* (*Partidas*) 'person in ridiculous disguise'
tahûna > *atafona* (13c), *atahona* (Nebrija) 'mill(-stone)'; beside *tahona* (13c) '*id.*',
later 'bakery'
tahwila > *atafulla* (1272 Murc.), *tafulla* (1275 Murc.); beside *atahulla* (1272
Murc.), later *tahulla* 'unit of measurement (one sixth of a *fanega*)'.
One of the most complex cases of borrowing is that of Ar. *qáfᶜa*. The earliest Old
Spanish adaptation is represented by *gafo* (no doubt /gáho/), in the *Libre dels Tres Reys
d'Orient*, the 1219 *Fuero de Guadalajara, Alex.*, Berceo, Juan Manuel, Juan Ruiz. A
form with early loss of /h/ is represented by the form *gaho* in the *LBA*. However, both
these forms were later overtaken by /gáfo/ (newly borrowed from Arabic?), since the
forms recorded by Nebrija (*gafo, gafoso, gafedad*) are evidence of labiodental
pronunciation.

3.2. Borrowings from Gallo-Romance and Catalan. Consideration will be given here to
the adaptation undergone in Castilian by words of French, Provençal, and Catalan
provenance which in the language of origin present the phonemes /f/ or /h/. The
latter, of course, belongs exclusively to Old French, and is normally to be found in words
borrowed by Old French from Frankish.

3.2.1. Loans from the above sources are rare until the 13th century and therefore postdate, or are contemporary with, the appearance of the Castilian phoneme /f/ (see
2.2.3). Indeed, the incorporation into Castilian of loans from these sources may have
been one of the factors which led towards the establishment of Cast. /f/. Thus, French,
Provençal, and Catalan words containing /f/ show this phoneme being interpreted as a
labiodental, spelt *f* (although we must not lose sight of the fact that until the 15th
century *f* could also, and most usually did, indicate Cast. /h/). Among the medieval
loans which illustrate this process are:
faisán (*LBA*) 'pheasant' (with labiodental confirmed by Nebrija's spelling *faysan*)
fardel (1400) 'bundle' (whence *fardo* 1570)
flecha (1387) 'arrow'

flete (1478) 'charter-price' (Nebrija: *frete*)
flota (1260) 'fleet of ships'
folía (Berceo) 'foolishness'
fraile (1174) 'friar' (Nebrija: *frayle*)
franco (1102) 'free; generous; French;' etc.
fruncir (*CMC*: *fronzir*) 'to wrinkle'.

Words borrowed from the same sources since the Middle Ages naturally show the same process of adaptation, and include: *faca* (1884), *fachenda* (18c.), *faena* (1596), *fango* (18c.), *felpa* (1583), *flan* (1843), *flanco* (1700), *fonda* (18c.), *frambuesa* (18c.), *fresa* (Covarrubias).

However, one or two gallicisms evidently passed into Castilian before the establishment of the phoneme /f/, and therefore show replacement of 'foreign' /f/ by Cast. /h/, at first spelt *f*, later *h*. Thus Frankish *FALDA, via Provençal or Catalan (cf. Corominas & Pascual 1980-, s.v. *falda*), was borrowed as /hálda/ *falda* (Berceo) 'skirts of any garment'. This form was still in use in the Renaissance (Nebrija: *haldas*), and continues in rural use today, sometimes with changed sense (cf. Penny (1978, p. 61): /hálda/ 'meat from the ribs of the pig'). Its competitor, standard /fálda/ 'skirt', probably represents a re-borrowing of the same Provençal or Catalan word. It is similarly likely that the duality between standard *fieltro* (attested from the late 15th century: A.Pal.) 'felt', and the form with initial /h/ (*hieltro*, attested by Nebrija), is to be explained by early and late borrowing of the same form (Gmc FILT, via OFr., Prov., Cat. *feltre*), despite the difficulty of explaining the diphthong of the Castilian form.

3.2.2. OFr. /h/ (usually occurring in words of Germanic origin) posed no difficulty of adaptation to Old Castilian, which possessed a similar phoneme /h/ (< Lat. /f/, Ar. /h/, etc.), spelt *f*.[14] Thus, OFr. *honte* was borrowed by Old Spanish as /hónta/ (*CMC fonta* 'insult; shame'; but also /ónta/ *honta*, see 2.2.2) and OFr. *harpe* appears in Old Spanish as /hárpa/ (*Alex. farpa* 'harp'), and in the early 16th century was still articulated with initial /h/ (Nebrija: *la harpa*). Similarly, although the Spanish borrowing of Fr. *haler* appears relatively late (namely, *halar* (1573) 'to pull [by means of a rope]'), its adherence to the pattern of development here espoused is assured by the preservation of its initial aspirate in America, Andalusia, and Santander (cf. Penny 1970, p. 74 and 1978, p. 32); Sp. *hucha* (< OFr. *huche*) is attested even later (in Covarrubias, 1611), but its initial aspirate is assured by Sant. /hútʃa/ '(large) box for clothes, money, etc.' (see Penny 1978, pp. 190, 199). OFr. *hardi* appears to have reached Old Spanish by two distinct channels; on the one hand, direct borrowing produced /hardído/ *fardido* (*CMC*, etc.) 'bold', while transmission via an intermediary which lacked /h/ (i.e., Provençal or Catalan) produced /ardído/ *ardido* (also *CMC*; see also *hardido*, etc., 2.2.2). Only slightly different is the case of OFr. *héralt* (MFr. *héraut*), first adopted by

OSp. as /haráute/ *faraute* 'messenger; interpreter' and continued in this form until at least the 16th century (F. de Oviedo). However, before the disappearance of this word, it apparently had a competitor with /f-/ (witness Nebrija: *faraute de lenguas*), a form which may be similar to those arabisms noted in 3.1.4, which do not have a continuous oral history in Spanish. Nebrija (or another) may have culled this word from a medieval source (where *f* = /h/) and assigned it a pronunciation with /f/, a phoneme regularly written *f* by Nebrija.

3.3. Latinisms. The main problem in assessing the processes of adaptation undergone by Latin words when they were borrowed by the vernacular lies in our ignorance of how Latin was read aloud at various stages, and in various parts of Spain, during the Middle Ages. However, it is evident (see Wright 1982 for detailed discussion) that, whatever the manner of reading Latin aloud, the phonemes used were those of the vernacular of the place and time concerned. Since all evidence suggests (see Menéndez Pidal 1964, pp. 198-233) that the vernacular of Old Castile (and castilianized territories to the South) lacked labiodentals until at least the 12th century, it follows that in the reading aloud of liturgical or legal Latin up to that time the letter F cannot have been interpreted as /f/, but as some other phoneme (or none). The best guess must be that the various allophones of the phoneme /h/ were used (see 2.2.3 and Penny 1972):

[h] before syllabic vowels (and the glide [j]?; see 3.3.5) (Lat. FALSUS, FAMILIA, FUTURUS, like vernacular *fambre, fijo, fumo, fiel* 'hiel')

[ɸ] before /r/, /l/ (Lat. FRUCTUS, FLAGRARE, like vernacular *fresno, floxo*)

[ʍ] before the glide [w] (Lat. FUERUNT, like vernacular *fueron*).

The implication of this assumption is that Latin borrowings made at this stage by Castilian would thereafter be indistinguishable (with regard to their initial consonant) from orally-inherited words.

However, following the reform of the reading aloud of ecclesiastical Latin, and probably also of legal Latin, in the 12th century (see Wright 1982), which took place under French auspices, it is likely that Lat. F, before both syllabic vowels and glides/consonants, was equated (for the first time in Castile) with a labial articulation, a change no doubt initiated by the French-speaking reformers. It is reasonable to speculate that this labial pronunciation was either a labiodental [f], in the French manner, or a bilabial [ɸ], long used in Castilian words like *fresno, fruente*, but now extending its range of environments from pre-consonantal to pre-vocalic. Thus, after the reform, Lat. FAMILIA would be read aloud as /família/ or /ɸamília/, and as urban (including standard) Castilian increasingly abandoned bilabial [ɸ] (see Penny 1972), so Lat. F would increasingly be read aloud with exclusively labiodental [f].[15]

It is likely that the large majority of latinisms which have passed into Spanish have done so after the establishment of /f/ as a phoneme of Castilian and of [f] as the appropriate rendering of F in the Latin of Castile. The borrowing by Old Spanish of Latin terms containing F is therefore relatively uncontroversial. Such latinisms (= 'learned words') have always received the spelling *f* and have (except the very earliest) always been pronounced with /f/. The main cases of such borrowing by Old Spanish, with indication of first attestation (for which, see Corominas & Pascual 1980-, s.vv.) are the following:

> *fábrica* (A.Pal.) 'workshop, factory'
>
> *fallir* (*CMC*) 'fail, deceive', etc.
>
> *fama* (*Disputa del alma y el cuerpo*) 'fame, renown'
>
> *familia* (Berceo) 'family'
>
> *fantasía* (Berceo) 'fantasy'
>
> *fastidio* (*Calila*) 'vexation'
>
> *fatigar* (A.Pal.) 'to tire'
>
> *favor* (A.Pal.) 'favour'
>
> *feliz* (Berceo) 'happy'
>
> *feria* (1100) 'day of the week, feast day', later 'fair'
>
> *feroz* (A.Pal.: *feroce*) 'fierce'
>
> *feudo* (1260) 'feudal possession'
>
> *figura* (Berceo) 'form, figure'
>
> *fijo* (1283: *fixo*) 'fixed'
>
> *fingir* (A.Pal.) 'to pretend'
>
> *físico* (Berceo) 'doctor', later 'physical'
>
> *forma* (Berceo) 'form, shape'
>
> *fortuna* (13c.) 'fortune'
>
> *fraude* (A. Pal.) 'fraud'
>
> *funda* (*LBA*) 'cover'
>
> *fundar* (late 14c.) 'to found'
>
> *furia* (1449) 'fury'
>
> *futuro* (A.Pal.) 'future'.

3.3.1. More problematical are the so-called 'semi-learned' words which have /f/ in Modern Spanish. A sketch has been given above (2.2.3, para. 3) of the mechanism by which I believe certain orally-inherited vernacular words were modified in pronunciation under the influence of the Latin read aloud in the Church and the law-courts. In particular, certain words traditionally containing /h/ had this phoneme replaced by /f/. It is important to note that during the medieval period such a change is undetectable through spelling, since until the 15th century both /h/ and /f/ were spelt *f*. We are reliant upon 15th- and 16th-century spelling (particularly that of Nebrija, who is the first to distinguish consistently between the two phonemes), and upon the modern outcome

of a given word, in tracing this aspect of its phonological history. Leaving for later
discussion (3.3.5) those Modern Spanish words whose initial segment is /fie-/, it is
possible to detect the following cases of semi-learned substitution of /h/ by /f/:

> *falso* (Silos glosses) 'false'; the unmodified form /hálsu/ 'false hem' survives in
> Santander (cf. Penny 1978, p. 211)
>
> *falta* (Berceo) 'fault, lack'; indirectly modified (via OSp. *fallir*) by FALLERE
>
> *fe* (*CMC*) 'faith'; see 2.2.3
>
> *febrero* (1129) 'February'; see 2.2.3
>
> *feligrés* (1245) 'parishioner'; despite its etymon (FILI ECLESIAE), it is likely that this
> word was associated with *fe* 'faith' (see above), and was therefore
> phonologically remodelled along with the latter
>
> *fiar* (*CMC*) 'to trust', and its derivative *fianza* (1095: *fidanza*, Berceo: *fiança*) 'trust'
> were modified either directly by FIDERE/FIDENTIA[16] or by association with *fe*
>
> *fiel*[17] (*CMC*) 'faithful'; modified either directly by FIDELIS or indirectly by *fe*
>
> *fin* (*CMC*) 'end, limit'; modified by FINIS
>
> *firme* (*CMC*) 'firm'; modified by FIRMUS; earlier /hírme/ is indirectly attested by
> Santa Teresa's use of *ahirmar*
>
> *fondo* (Berceo) 'bottom (of sea, well, etc.)'; OSp. /hóndo/ functioned both as
> noun and as adj. ('deep'), the former alongside /hondón/ (cf. Nebrija *hondón*);
> the modification of the noun, under the influence of FUNDUS, PROFUNDUS,
> allowed a phonological distinction between noun and adjective
>
> *fundir* (1250) 'to melt, fuse'; rather than being a learned word (pace Corominas &
> Pascual 1980-, s.v.), and given its early attestation with the sense 'to melt',
> *fundir* is perhaps better regarded as a case of modification of /hundír/ 'to
> destroy', under the influence of Med. Lat. FUNDERE, the unmodified form
> surviving as *hundir* 'to sink'; in this case, as in that of *hondo/fondo*, alternation
> between traditional /h/ and Latin-influenced /f/ has been exploited to resolve
> phonologically an instance of polysemy.

Corominas & Pascual (1980-, s.vv. *falso, falta, fe, fiar, fiebre, fiero, firme*) envisage an
educated class in medieval Castilian society who continued to pronounce /f/ (directly
inherited from Vulgar Latin?), while the rest of society pronounced /h/; the legacy of
this 'educated vernacular' style is the survival into Modern Spanish of the consonant /f/
in the words under consideration here. I know of no independent evidence for this
view. This is not to say that I doubt that there were class-based differences of speech in
medieval Castile, since such differences are characteristic of all societies; and indeed,
Latin-influenced forms (with /f/) must have competed there with traditional forms
(with /h/), sometimes with total success of /f/, sometimes with total success of /h/,
sometimes with continuing competition (with or without semantic differentiation; see
fiebre vs. *hiebre* (3.3.2), *falso* vs. /hálsu/, *fondo* vs. *hondo*, above). What I find

impossible to accept is that one small segment (the educated class) of Castilian society should have preserved a feature (Lat. /f/) which centuries earlier had been replaced (by /h/) in the rest of society.

3.3.2. Turning now to those words of popular descent which show MSp. /f/, it still seems to me (cf. Penny 1972) that *fuego* 'fire', *fuelle* 'bellows', *fuente* 'spring, fountain', *fuera* 'outside', *fuerza* 'strength', *fuero* 'charter', *fuerte* 'strong', as well as the verb-forms *fue, fuese*, etc., are best explained as modifications (see 2.2.3) of earlier /huégo/, etc. (where the allophone of /h/ used was probably the voiceless labiovelar fricative [ʍ]).[18] The earlier, unmodified, forms are widely preserved today in non-standard (chiefly rural) Spanish, throughout Spain and America.[19]

3.3.3. Similarly, orally-inherited words which show *fr-* in Old Spanish and Modern Spanish (*fragua* (1210: *frauga*; 1400: *fragua*) 'forge', *frasco* (1570) 'bottle', *fregar* (1251) 'to scrub', *freír* (1400) 'to fry', *freno* (962) 'bit (of harness)', *frente* (1124: *fruente*; Nebrija: *frente*) 'forehead', *fresco* (*CMC*) 'new', later 'fresh', *fresno* (1210) 'ash tree', *frío* (1212) 'cold') probably followed the path outlined in 2.2.3 (see also Penny 1972): the allophone [ɸ] of the phoneme /h/, in use before /r/ from the earliest times in Castilian, was modified to [f] in the 12 to 13th centuries, as part of the process of phonological split by which /h/ and /f/ emerged from earlier /h/.[20]

3.3.4. Although with less certainty, it can also be argued that the popular Castilian descendants of Latin words in FL- (few apart from *llama* 'flame' < FLAMMA) show the same evolution: *flaco* (Berceo) 'thin', *fleco* (A.Pal., Nebrija: *flueco*; 1680: *fleco*) 'fringe, tassel', *flojo* (Berceo: *floxo*) 'weak', *flor* (San Millán glosses) 'flower'. Rather than describing the latter as 'semi-learned', a label which seems inappropriate to words with these senses, it would be preferable to seek an alternative explanation for the isolated form *llama*.

3.3.5. The most difficult group of *f*-words is undoubtedly that in which the consonant is followed by the diphthong /ie/. Of the Spanish descendants of words beginning FĔ- in Latin, only *hiel* 'gall, bile' (< FĔL) and *hierro* 'iron' (< FĔRRU) appear in the standard with /zero/ (following loss of /h/), while *fiebre* (Berceo) 'fever', *fieltro* (A.Pal.) 'felt', *fiero* (*CMC*) 'wild, fierce', all arguably uninfluenced by the pronunciation of medieval Latin, show /f/. However, the division of forms with /h/ and /f/ is not as clear as at first sight appears, since, on the one hand, *fierro* is widely used in American Spanish (especially rural varieties), and, on the other, both *hiebre* and *hieltro* are attested in Nebrija (see 3.2.1), solid evidence that in the early modern period these words could be articulated with /h/. This duality of forms probably goes back to the time of the phonological split (see 2.2.3) which brought about the contrast between /h/ and /f/. Whatever allophone of /h/ was used before the glide [j] (a voiceless mid-palatal fricative?), it was sometimes identified with the anterior allophones [ɸ] and [ʍ] (which occurred before consonants and the glide [w] and which ended up as /f/) and sometimes with the posterior allophone [h] (which occurred before syllabic vowels and which gave /h/, ultimately /zero/). Thus, I would argue that it is unneccessary to describe *fiebre, fieltro*, or *fiero* as 'semi-learned' (as they are usually described), but as fully popular forms. On the same grounds, and despite its religious associations, I similarly see no reason for categorizing *fiesta* (13c.) 'feast-day' as 'semi-learned'.

3.3.6. Two words, *feo* 'ugly', and *fino* 'perfect', later 'thin', remain for comment. They are clearly not learned, but neither can they be described as 'semi-learned'. Not only does their general register make Latin influence unlikely, but, in the case of *feo*, any pressure from FOEDUS could be expected to produce *fedo*, and, in the case of *fino*, there was no medieval Latin counterpart, since this word results from a Western Romance innovation (a derivative of FINIS). Corominas & Pascual's notion of a Leonese borrowing of *feo* (1980-, s.v.) seems unlikely in a word of this register, but their suggestion of avoidance of homonymic clash between */héda/ < FOEDA and *heda* < FETA '(woman) who has recently given birth' is astute. However, rather than resort to Leonese, it may be that in a linguistic environment (that of late medieval Castile) in which /h/ and /f/ alternated in a considerable number of forms, and in which /d/ alternated with /zero/ (cf. *crudo~crúo*), speakers resolved the collision by selection of the alternants which most distanced the reflex of FOEDA from that of FETA. In the case of *fino*, it may be that its semantic link with *fin* remained unsevered in Old Spanish. Continuing semantic affinity between 'perfect' and 'extreme' may have ensured that the /f/ of late Old Spanish *fin* (see 3.3.1) was extended to *fino*.

4. The aim of this paper has been to clear up what seem to me to be serious mis-apprehensions about one aspect of the phonological history of Castilian, and, in particular, to elucidate the successive phonemic values to be attached to the graphs *f* and *h*. It has been shown that it is impossible to interpret *h* as /h/ until the (second half of the) 15th century, and that between the 12th and the 15th centuries *f* was used with both the values /f/ and /h/. By applying these findings to lexical borrowings from Arabic, Gallo-Romance, and Latin, it is possible to refine the chronology of such borrowings and to support the general theory of development of Lat. F- espoused here. An important side-issue has been the drawing of more careful distinctions between 'learned', 'semi-learned', and 'popular' words containing the phoneme /f/.

Queen Mary and Westfield College, London

NOTES

1. Names of source-texts used in this study are abbreviated as follows: *Ajedr.* (*Libros de ajedrez, dados e tablas*), *Alex.* (*Libro de Alexandre*), *ARM* (*Auto de los Reyes Magos*), *Astr.* (*Libros del saber de astronomia*), *Cel.* (*Celestina*), *CMC* (*Cantar de mio Cid*), *Cruz* (*Libro de las cruzes*), *EEI* (*Estoria de Espanna*, part I), *EEII* (*Estoria de Espanna*, part II), *Form.* (*Libro de las formas e ymagenes*), *GEI* (*General Estoria*, part I), *GEIV* (*General Estoria*, part IV), *Jud.* (*Libro complido de los judizios de las estrellas*), *Lap.* (*Lapidario*), *Leyes* (*Libro de las leyes [Primera partida]*), *Pic.* (*Picatrix*), *Rab.* (*Libro del quadrante sennero [Rabizag]*), *Zar.* (*Tablas de Zarquiel*); Alonso de Palencia, *Universal vocabulario en latín y en romance*, is abbreviated thus: A.Pal.

2. There is similarly no distinction to be made between passages in *cuaderna vía* and those in lyric form; *h* forms are to be found in both metres.

3. A further, apparently promising, approach to the elucidation of Juan Ruiz's use of *h* lies in the question of syllable-count. Thus, lines like 1036b *De estaño e hartas* (6 syllables), or 1040a *Dixome la heda* (6 syllables), might potentially be exploited to show that *h* represents either a pronounced consonant (i.e. /h/) or that it is void. However, such an approach depends upon the metrical regularity (and upon the consistent use, or non-use, of synalepha) of the poetry concerned; neither syllable-count nor synalepha is consistent enough in the *LBA* to enable such an approach to succeed. See Arnold 1940, Le Gentil 1953.

4. Enrique de Villena is sometimes thought to have initiated the practice of writing *h* for /h/. However, we must not forget that his *Arte de trovar* (1433) reaches us via an extract made in the 16th century and that the process of extraction may have distorted the text. Certainly, the only direct reference Villena makes to the relationship between *f* and *h* (1433, p. 86: 'e porque la *h* en principio de diçion faze la espiraçion abundosa, en algunas diçiones, pusieron en su lugar *f*, por temprar aquel rigor, así como por dezir *hecho* ponen *fecho*, e por *herando*, *ferando*') is extremely obscure, seeming to imply that at a certain stage *h* was replaced by *f*, quite the reverse of the actual events.

5. See f. a6r: 'Circa vocales quoque aspiratas non nihil a nostris erratur, qui illas non aliter quam exiles pronuntiant, neque differt apud illos, quod ad sonum attinet, inter *ominis* qui est genitiuus ab *omen*, et *hominis* qui est ab eo quod est *homo*; atque inter *abeo* quod est discedo, et *habeo* quod est teneo.'

6. Some words showed alternation between these last two phonemes and spellings. In cases like *fuerte/huerte, febrero/hebrero*, the form with /f/ was no doubt already

perceived as more 'correct', and so spellings with *f* are much more frequent than those with *h*. While preferring *f* in such cases, Nebrija nevertheless reveals awareness of the alternation when he writes (1492a, p. 253), a propos of the formation of the past subjunctive: 'Pero los [verbos de segunda y tercera conjugación] que hizieron [su pretérito] en *e*, mudan aquella *e* final en *iesse*, como de *supe*, *supiesse*; de *dixe*, *dixiesse*, o *dixesse*, como de *fue* hezimos *fuesse*, quiçá por que no se encontrasse con el presente de optativo deste verbo *huio*, *huiesse*.' He clearly has in mind not the 'correct' form /fuése/, but the (already rustic?) form /huése/, a pronunciation still today heard in many rural areas of the Peninsula and Spanish America.

7. Villalón (1558, pp. 72-75) tries to come to grips with this alternation, but his inability (shared with many of his contemporaries) to separate discussion of spelling from discussion of pronunciation, together with his confused reference to different regional (and class?) styles, makes his account of little practical value.

8. The early spelling *h* in this word may indicate that Ar. *h* was in this case first interpreted as Sp. /zero/.

9. The spelling *alhenna* in *Partidas* probably indicates that this arabism was first borrowed as /aleɲa/.

10. The *LBA* spelling *almohaça* may indicate an alternative early borrowing with OSp. /zero/ representing Ar. *ḥ*.

11. The frequency in the Alfonsine corpus (Kasten & Nitti 1978) of the spelling *alfferza* (318 tokens, against 11 of *alferza*) provides a faint suggestion that the Alfonsine authors were moving towards a graphical distinction between /f/ and /h/, using *ff* for the former and *f* for the latter. A similar variation of spelling (and phonology?) is observable in the case of *alffil* (605 tokens, versus 10 of *alfil*). It is interesting to compare these cases with the spelling of the name *Alffons[s]o* (thus on 1159 occasions, against 296 tokens of *Alfons[s]o*). Does this variation of spelling, although ultimately rejected, reflect alternation between non-Castilian /alfónso/ and Castilian /alhónso/, the latter form giving way, after /h/-dropping, to *Alonso*? Since this article was finalized, Robert Blake (1987-88) has argued for precisely this correspondence between *ff* and [f].

12. This may be one of the earliest arabisms whose /f/ equated with the newly-acquired Castilian phoneme /f/ (see 2.2.3).

13. This alternation is well exemplified in the Alfonsine corpus: *rehez* (2), beside *rafez* (18) ~ *raffez* (1) ~ *refez* (3) ~ *reffez* (2).

14. I therefore cannot agree with Corominas & Pascual (1980-, s.v. *heraldo*) that OFr. aspirate *h-* was normally replaced by OSp. *f-*, with the implication that *f-* = /f/.

15. Since bilabial [ɸ] survives to this day in rural Castilian of the Peninsula and America, it is open to us to hypothesize that in rural settings Lat. F long continued (perhaps down to this century) to be read aloud by means of a bilabial.

16. Cl. Lat. FIDERE and FIDENTIA were replaced in all Western Romance by *FIDARE and *FIDANTIA.

17. Note that this word was bisyllabic until the Golden Age, and therefore is not to be grouped with *fiebre, fiesta*, etc.

18. Menéndez Pidal argues (1964, p. 221), unconvincingly, that dialect-mixing is responsible for the appearance of *fuerte*, etc., beside *hablar*, etc.; he does not specify from which dialect(s) *fuerte*, etc., are borrowed.

19. Only FOSSA > OSp. *fuessa*, late OSp./early MSp. *huessa/uessa*, 'grave', represents departure from normal development in the standard. In this case, OSp. /huésa/ must have undergone the influence of *[h]uesso* 'bone', to the extent of losing its initial /h/; pronunciation without aspirate is clearly attested by Nebrija's spelling without *h: uessa*.

20. On these grounds, I would argue that the /f/ of *fruto* (1192) 'fruit, product', and *fruta* (early 13c.) '(piece of) fruit', is the outcome of popular development (rather than Latin influence), although their /t/ clearly argues for such influence; cf. fully popular *frucho* (Berceo).

REFERENCES

Arnold, H.H. 1940. 'The Octosyllabic *Cuaderna vía* of Juan Ruiz', *HR*, VIII, 125-38.

Blake, Robert. 1987-88. '*Ffaro, Faro* or *Haro*?: F doubling as a source of linguistic information in the Early Middle Ages', *RPh*, XLI, 267-89.

Cejador y Frauca, Julio, ed. 1960. Arcipreste de Hita, *Libro de Buen Amor*, 8th edition, 2 vols (Madrid: Espasa-Calpe).

Corominas, Juan, and J. A. Pascual. 1980-. *Diccionario crítico etimológico castellano e hispánico*. 6 vols (5 so far published) (Madrid: Gredos).

Corominas, Joan, ed. 1967. Juan Ruiz, *Libro de Buen Amor* (Madrid: Gredos).

Criado de Val, Manuel, Eric W. Naylor, and Jorge García Antezana, eds. 1973. *Glossary to the critical edition of Arcipreste de Hita, Libro de Buen Amor* (Madrid: CSIC).

Kasten, Lloyd, and John Nitti, eds. 1978. *Concordances and Texts of the Royal Scriptorium Manuscripts of Alfonso X, el Sabio* (Madison: HSMS).

Lapesa, Rafael. 1980. *Historia de la lengua española*, 8th edition (Madrid: Gredos).

Le Gentil, Pierre. 1953. *La Poésie lyrique espagnole et portugaise à la fin du Moyen Age*, II: *Les formes* (Rennes: Plihon).

Menéndez Pidal, Ramón. 1964. *Orígenes del español*, 5th edition (= *Obras completas de R. Menéndez Pidal*, VIII) (Madrid: Espasa-Calpe; 1st edition, 1926).

Nebrija, Elio Antonio de. 1492a. *Gramática de la lengua castellana*, ed. Antonio Quilis (Madrid: Editora Nacional, 1980).

Nebrija, Elio Antonio de. 1492b. *Diccionario latino-español*, ed. G. Colón & A.-J. Soberanas (Barcelona: Puvill, 1979).

Nebrija, Elio Antonio de. 1516. *Vocabulario de romance en latín*, ed. Gerald J. Macdonald (Madrid: Castalia, 1973).

Nebrija, Elio Antonio de. 1517. *Reglas de orthographia en la lengua castellana*, ed. Antonio Quilis (Bogotá: Instituto Caro y Cuervo, 1977).

Penny, Ralph J. 1970. *El habla pasiega. Ensayo de dialectología montañesa* (London: Tamesis).

Penny, Ralph J. 1972. 'The Re-emergence of /f/ as a Phoneme of Spanish', *ZRPh*, LXXXVIII, 463-82.

Penny, Ralph. 1978. *Estudio estructural del habla de Tudanca*, Beihefte zur *ZRPh*, CLXXVIII (Tübingen: Niemeyer).

Valdés, Juan de. 1535. *Diálogo de la lengua*, ed. Juan M. Lope Blanch (Mexico: Porrúa, 1966). (The work was first published in the eighteenth century.)

Villalón, Cristobal de. 1558. *Gramática castellana. Arte breve y compendiosa para saber hablar y escrevir en la lengua Castellana congrua y decentemente, ed. Constantino García (Madrid: CSIC, 1971).*

Villena, Enrique de. 1433. *Arte de trovar*, ed. F.J. Sánchez Cantón, Biblioteca española de divulgación científica, III (Madrid: Victoriano Suárez, 1923).

Wright, Roger. 1982. *Late Latin and Early Romance in Spain and Carolingian France*, ARCA Classical and Medieval Texts, Papers and Monographs, VIII (Liverpool: Francis Cairns).

RAIMUNDUS DE BITERRIS'S *LIBER KALILE ET DIMNE*: NOTES ON THE WESTERN RECEPTION OF AN EASTERN *EXEMPLUM-BOOK*

Barry Taylor

When Menéndez Pidal called Spain 'eslabón entre la Cristiandad y el Islam', he referred to the significance, alongside that of the Hispano-Arabic lyric, of the translations of scientific and narrative works.[1] In one view, the history of translation in Spain is the history of the rise of the vernacular: a possible scenario might depict Spanish first limited to disposable oral intermediate versions, later promoted to written texts produced in tandem with the Latin, and finally supplanting Latin altogether. While the Hispanic philologist may possibly see the Latin versions as an archaic prelude to the capacitation of Romance, from a European viewpoint the vernacular translations may appear as side-roads if not dead-ends. As Alfonso X acknowledged in ordering parallel Latin and Romance versions of the *De judiciis astrologiae*, *Picatrix* and *Scala Mahometi*,[2] translations into Spanish could serve only a small community because, contrary to the modern perception, Spanish was difficult, Latin clear, as Raimundus explains: 'considerans ... librum Kalile et Dymne ... lingue hyspanice inexpertis non intelligibilem ... dictum *Librum* ... duxi in linguam latinam, que lingua communior est et intelligibilior ceteris' (pp. 384-85).[3] At least two other Arabic works translated into Spanish at the Alfonsine court, *Calila e Digna* and probably *Bocados de oro*,[4] were made available to the broader European community by means of Latin versions done outside Spain. The present study is concerned with one instance of the reception in the Latin world of an Oriental work in the transmission of which Spain, as so often, played a mediatory role.

By the end of the Middle Ages, three Latin versions of *Kalila* were in existence in Europe, although not all enjoyed equal diffusion. The sole Latin representative of the Syriac redaction was translated anonymously from the Greek of Simeon Seth and, following its exemplar, is entitled *Stephanites et Ichnelates*. From the fact that it is preserved in only two manuscripts, now in Vienna and Budapest, it seems that the Latin *Stephanites* was confined to an area of circulation in central-eastern Europe.[5]

Two Latin versions derive from the Arabic tradition. That of Johannes de Capua, the *Directorium humanae vitae* (*ca.* 1263-78), from the Hebrew of an unidentified Rabbi Joel, was by far the best known of the three Latin texts. Preserved in four manuscripts and four early printed editions, it was the basis for nearly all Western vernacular versions of the medieval and early modern periods.[6]

Largely dependent on Johannes is the main focus of this paper, the *Liber Kalile et Dimne* of Raimundus de Biterris, alias Raymond of Béziers, prepared for the French

183

court *ca.* 1303. Its interest lies not in any influence it may have had in the transmission of *Kalila* (it appears to have left no descendants) but in its handling of two received texts (one Latin and one vernacular); in the addition in one of its two extant manuscripts of a greater bulk of commentary than in any other *Kalila* version known to me; and in the curious way in which the translator/commentator's orientation of the text corresponds to approaches adopted in other versions of which he must have been ignorant.

By way of introduction, a brief description of the text is presented, expressed in necessarily broad terms in order not to prejudice the debate on certain controversial topics. More precise information will follow.

Raimundus's text is preserved in two manuscripts, both in the Bibliothèque Nationale, Paris. The relationship between them is unclear. The Longer version, Lat. 8504, is the earlier copy, dated by its editor, Hervieux, to the fourteenth century and adorned with illuminations, verses and authorities.[7] While the miniatures are distributed evenly throughout the text, the verses and authorities occur less consistently (there are seven on f. 12v and eleven on ff. 120r-135v) and vary greatly in extent from aphoristic comments to a transcription of several chapters of the *Liber consolationis et consilii*. Gnomic additions are in red, while other additions are embedded in the text in black. The Shorter version, Lat. 8505, with a colophon dated 4 July 1496, is not illuminated and lacks nearly all textual additions. The prologues differ in each manuscript, but in both Raimundus says that he began his translation for Jeanne of Navarre, suspended work at her death (2 April 1303), and resumed it for Philip the Fair (pp. 41-42, 380-85). Although he claims to have translated the book out of Spanish, broadly speaking this is true of only the first half of his work: the second half is a modification of Johannes.

Scholarship to date has been concerned with the priority of the two redactions, the question of Raimundus's plagiarism of Johannes and the authorship of the additions in the Longer Manuscript.

The manuscripts were first described by Silvestre de Sacy in 1818.[8] He thought that the additions of the Longer Manuscript were Raimundus's, that the Longer Manuscript was Raimundus's presentation copy for Philip, and that the Shorter Manuscript was a direct abbreviation of the Longer. In his edition of Johannes and Raimundus of 1899 (see n. 3), Hervieux argued vehemently against De Sacy that the Shorter Manuscript was a copy, albeit an inferior one, of the original text, that Raimundus's work 'a pillé celle de Jean de Capoue depuis le commencement jusqu'à la fin' (p. 54), because he was ignorant of Spanish (p. 57), taking only the names from the Spanish text (p. 52), and that the additions of the Longer Manuscript were so clumsily done that they had to be by another hand. The author of these additions, whether identical or not with Raimundus,

I term here the 'Pious Redactor' (henceforth, PR). Hervieux had also separately published the introductory essay to his edition in 1898.[9] In a review of this, Léopold Delisle sided with De Sacy on Raimundus's responsibility for the Longer Manuscript, which he maintained was a presentation copy, but thought it possible that the Shorter Manuscript preserved a primitive redaction (p. 166), because, he agreed with Hervieux, it did not derive directly from the Longer Manuscript.[10] Hervieux was then able to reply to Delisle by restating his position in the notes to his edition. In a study of 1906, Gaston Paris reaffirmed the identity of Raimundus and PR.[11] Most recently, Lacarra and Cacho Blecua have corroborated Raimundus's use of the Spanish text.[12]

The questions of the priority of the two redactions of Raimundus and the responsibility for the pictorial and gnomic complementary material of MS 8504 are best taken together. The following comments are offered as one possible answer, but do not claim to be conclusive.

The Longer Manuscript seems certainly to take priority in two cases. Firstly, the list of chapters in the Shorter Manuscript (ff. 4v-8r, at f. 5r) refers to the vision of Berosias, which is found only in the Longer (cf. pp. 434-39). Secondly, the Shorter Manuscript includes a number of rubrics for miniatures present in the Longer (f. 31r = p. 405; f. 38v = p. 441; f. 39r = p. 441; f. 42r = p. 448; f. 66r = p. 492), while the miniatures themselves are lacking in the Shorter Manuscript, nor are any spaces left for them.

A third case sheds little light on the priority of texts, but does suggest the authorship of the additions. Several authorities are present in the Shorter Manuscript.[13] They include four quotations of Walter the Englishman and one of the *Disticha Catonis*, which are quoted throughout the Longer version, and one Horatian maxim, 'Euolat emissum semel irreuocabile uerbum' (*Epistulae*, I, xviii, 71), which, I shall argue below, comes via Albertanus of Brescia, a major source of authorities in the Longer Manuscript (see nn. 25-27). This seems to indicate that these authorities are the contribution of the same person in both manuscripts, regardless of priority. In the light of the first two points above, it seems also to suggest that the Shorter text is an imperfect abbreviation of the Longer: the person responsible for MS 8505 set out to prune a copy of the Longer text of its maxims and commentary to highlight the tales themselves.[14] The coincidence of the Shorter text and Raimundus's original sources may be explained by the fact that departures from simple translation are clearly signposted by phrases such as 'Dixit philosophus' or 'iuxta illud' and sometimes written in red, and therefore easy to extract.

It should also be pointed out that the Shorter Manuscript could not have been abbreviated directly from the Longer Manuscript: it includes two rubrics for miniatures lacking in the Longer (f. 1v-2r = p. 42), preserves two lines of gnomic verse missing from the Longer (f. 2r9-10 = p. 42.22-23, cf. p. 380.12) and, although generally the inferior text, can be used to correct and supply readings, as Hervieux does throughout (e.g. p. 406, n. 1).

Thus, although it is not possible to draw firm conclusions, and although I shall continue in this paper to refer to Raimundus and PR as separate functions, the balance seems to me to suggest that they are one and the same person.

Before addressing the question of Raimundus's plagiarism of Johannes, it is necessary to delimit the use of the Spanish and Latin source-texts in his work. Furthermore, the inclusion of both redactions of the Spanish text in the comparison may cast some light on the nature of Raimundus's Spanish exemplar.

Up to p. 542.22 (approximately half-way through his work), Raimundus translates from the Spanish. However, five passages in this portion of the text are taken from Johannes.[15] In the latter section of the text, two passages are exceptionally taken from the Spanish.[16]

As a preface to some textual comparisons, it may be recalled that *SpA* and *SpB* are generally agreed to descend from a common Romance archetype, with *SpA* the earlier redaction, although a strong case for the priority of *SpB* has been put forward by Frida Weber de Kurlat.[17]

In the following cases, Raimundus is closer to *SpA*:

Raimundus 456.1-4	SpA 54.878-55.880	SpB 54.1016-55.1018
qui ponit in		
pedibus capitis		
ornamenta et . . .		
qui pedum orna-	quien pone en su	el que pone en su
menta nititur	cabeça el ornamiento	cabeça el orna-
in capite		mento
collocare,	de sus pies	de los pies
	en la cabeça [*sic*],	
et qui	e quien dagastona	e en sus pies
margaritas	las girgonças	el de la cabeça
coniungit	en el plomo	
plumbo		
et ipsas seminit		
(sic) inter porcos		

186

(Incidentally, Raimundus's interpolation here from Matt. 7. 6, present in both manuscripts (8504, f. 29r2; 8505, f. 46v17), is meaningless and seems to be an automatic response to the juxtaposition of 'folly' and 'pearls'.)

474.6-9	84.1262-65	84.1502-3
quamuis Cenceba esset	E sy Senseba fuese	Aun que Sençeba fuese
inimicus meus,	mi enemigo commo tu dizes,	mi enemigo, commo tu dizes,
non posset mihi	non me podria	non me podria
nocere,	mal fazer.	fazer mal
	¿E commo lo podria fazer?	
quia ego comedo	Ca el comme yerva	
carnes ct ipse	e yo commo carne,	
comedit herbas,		
et ipse est		
cibus meus,	e el es mio comer,	
et ego non sum	e yo non so	
cibus eius	lo suyo	

477.8	90.1363	90.1618
anati	anade	ome

479.10	96.1448	96.1714
damnam (sic for	abnue	lobo çerval
damam,		
according to Hervieux)		

(*Abnue*, 'jackal', is an Arabism, *ibn āwā*, not found outside *SpA*, which Raimundus understandably did not recognize.[18] *Dama* is a poor guess, as the creature is carnivorous in the story (Raimundus 481.24-482.2): the illuminator followed his text in painting a deer, but showed it as an onlooker in the massacre scene (482, n. 2). Raimundus normally renders *lobo çerval* as 'uulpis'. Elsewhere in this story *A* does use *lobo çerval* (95.1443): as *lobo çerval* can be seen as a standardization or modernization, it might be deduced that Raimundus's exemplar here was an earlier text than *A*, with *abnue* throughout the episode.)

508.5-6	137.2055	137.2336
in quadam ciuitate	una çibdat	en una çibdat
dicta Ouecii	que dizian Quertir	

(MS 8505: Ouetum)
(This hyper-hispanization of the source-text is parallelled by Raimundus's addition 'iuit ad quamdam patriam Maioricam' (448.11): cf. 'fuese . . . a una tierra' (*A* 43.683-84, *B* 43.816-17) and 'cum iret . . . in contractu que dicitur Mathor' (JC 112.20-21).)

518.5-6	155.2329	155.2614
quoddam animal	una bestia	un vestiglo
dictum Ziraba	que l' dezian Jauzava	que era gran amigo
(ll.22, 26 Zuraba;	(l.2345 Jausaba;	de Calilla
23 Durabe)	2357 Jauzaba)	

536.9-12	166.2489-92	166.2772-75
in quadam terra	en tierra de	en una tierra
que vocatur Dizilem	Duzat,	
prope quandam ciuitatem	çerca de una çibdat	çerca de una çibdat
que uocatur Morate . . .	que dezian Muzne . . .	. . .
coruus qui uocabatur	un cuervo que dezian	un cuervo que
Gebal	Geba	dezian Geba

The following passages are closer to *SpB*:

RB 417.1	*SpA* 11.219	*SpB* 11.217
Mugeren	Syrechuel	Nixhuen
(388.26 Nugerem)		(13.259 Nuyhuen)

442.7-8		34.608-9
Et similis est		E es atal commo
uasi pleno melle		la jarra de la miel,
et cuius profundo		que yaze en ella
		en su fondon
letalis pocio continetur		muerte supytaña

(The authenticity of the *SpB*-passage is corroborated by its use by Abū Bakr of Tortosa: see Lacarra and Cacho Blecua, p. 115, n. 32.)

473.18-21	83.1257-58	83.1498-1500
Et ille rex magis est	E el mas perezoso rrey	E el mas perezoso
paratus ad	es aquel que se da a	es aquel que se da a
perdicionem	vagares quando le viene	vagar;
qui magis est	la cuyta, e despreçiala	

occiosus,	
et est similis inueni	e el que mas semeja
(i.e. iuueni) elephanti	al elefante joven
qui non uertit captus	es aquel que non
(i.e. caput) propter	torna cabeça por
aliquod accidens	ninguna
et si facit (i.e. fiat)	cosa que aya
eis (i.e. ei) nocumentum,	de pesar, nin la
non curat	tiene en nada

507.15-16	136.2030-31	136.2313-14
ignis qui est in	El fuego que yace en	el fuego que yaze en
lapide et in ligno	la piedra e en el fierro	la piedra e en el
		fuste

(Pointed out by Lacarra and Cacho Blecua, p. 183, n. *h.*)

Raimundus also includes the introduction of Ibn al-Muqaffa[c] (pp. 405-16), found in *SpB* but not *SpA* (pp. 3-9), and the latter part of the lamentation of Berosias (pp. 443-44; *SpB* 38.697-40.777).

What little conclusions can be drawn from this comparison accord with the dates of the witnesses. Both Spanish manuscripts are of the fifteenth century: the older of the two Latin manuscripts, of the fourteenth century, presumably preserves the state of the Spanish text at the time of translation, *ca.* 1303. Because Raimundus reproduces readings unique both to *SpA* and to *SpB*, his exemplar was either a conflation (which seems unlikely), or a text closer to the archetype than either of the two extant Spanish witnesses.

There are two reasons why Raimundus's exemplar may have derived from a manuscript older than the common ancestor of *SpA* and *B*. Firstly, Raimundus (461-63) is free from the *carpintero/zapatero* confusion which Lacarra and Cacho Blecua (p. 56) pointed out in both Spanish manuscripts. Secondly, if the change *abnue > lobo çerval* is a modernization, this process is underway in *SpA* (which has both words) and complete in *SpB* (which has only *lobo çerval*). It may be argued that Raimundus could only have misunderstood *abnue* if his exemplar did not use *lobo çerval* elsewhere in the story. Hence the following possible stemma, where *x* is the Romance archetype, *y* the common ancestor of the two extant Spanish manuscripts, and *q* a copy with the two features just described:

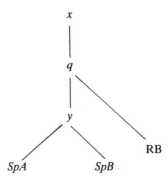

Such, then, is the quantity of Raimundus's debt to the Spanish *Calila* and to Johannes. The question of his plagiarism of Johannes is best approached in the context of a more general study of the qualitative changes which he makes to his two base-texts.

Raimundus's technique of translation from the Spanish is broadly abbreviatory, mirroring in this respect the amplification typical of translation into the vernacular.[19] As a token of this principle, I offer a brief examination of his treatment of vernacular doublets in the story of the camel who was tricked by the wolf, the jackal and the crow into giving himself to the lion as food (RB 479-82, *SpA* 96.1447-103.1548). The relevant portions of text are arranged in parallel columns below, and the transformation expressed as a ratio of Spanish to Latin: thus 2:1 denotes that two Spanish terms are rendered as one Latin term, 2:2 that the doublet is retained, and 2:0 that the Latin ignores the Spanish completely.

muy viçioso e muy seguro	2:2	faciam te securum et te preferam in aliqua dignitate
corriendo e rrastrando	2:1	ad sanguinis effusionem
en vuestra lealtad e en vuestro amor	2:0	-
non es de nuestro talle, nin de nuestra natura	2:0	-
pleito [e] omenaje	2:1	de fidelitate sibi prestitit iuramentum
fanbre que aviamos e cuita en que eramos	2:1	famem
diliçioso sin pro	2:1	non est nobis utilis

190

nin es de nuestra natura	2:1	nec in alico sequitur modum nostrum
nin de nuestro talle		
he atreguado al camello,	2:1	de omni fidelitate seruanda . . .
e que le he afiado		iuramentum
trayçion nin aleve	2:0	-
pleito e omenaje	2:0	-
commo e en qual guisa	2:0	-
lazrado e cuydado	2:0	-
por mal e por		
desconosçimiento	2:0	-
-	0:2	gratiam obtinebimus et fauorem
lazrado e enflaqueçido	2:0	-
por el bien e por la merced	2:0	-
los que fincaren de nos,	2:0	
e los que vinieren de nos		-
buena e alva e sana	3:2	delectabiles et salubres

The frequency of occurrence of each ratio is thus:

2:0	10 times
2:1	6
2:2	1
3:2	1
0:2	1

The comparison which follows will, I hope, suffice to show that the treatment of Johannes is quite different. The tale that teaches that man is more ungrateful than the beasts (RB XVI, 729-34; JC XIV, 316-19) shows a few substantive changes: as is commonplace in translations before the modern era, there are instances of Christianization and depaganization ('incantationes' (319.13) become 'remedia opportuna' (734.5)); the prayer 'Summe parens' is added (734.20); and direct speech turned to indirect (731.19 cf. JC 317.29). This passage is, however, typical:

JC	RB
Fertur quod,	Fertur quod,
cum ambularet quidam	cum ambularet quidam
heremita per viam,	heremita per uiam,
vidit foueam quam	uidit foueam quam
foderant venatores	foderant uenatores

ad capiendum animalia,	ad *animalia capienda*,
vt sua coria decoriarent.	ut sua coria excoriarent
	AD UTILITATEM PERSEQUENDAM,
Et, inspiciens ad fundum fouee,	et inspiciens in profundum fouee,
vidit ibi hominem	uidit hominem ibidem
qui erat aurifaber,	qui erat aurifex EXISTENTEM,
et cum eo erant symeus,	et erant ibi simius,
serpens et vipera,	serpens et uipera iuxta ipsum,
nec illum hominem	nec illum hominem
offenderant.	IN ALIQUO offendebant.
Et videns hec, heremita	Et uidens hoc, heremita
cogitauit dicens:	IN ANIMO cogitauit dicens:
'Aduenit nunc tempus	'Aduenit nunc tempus
quo magnam misericordiam	quo *magnam agam misericordiam*,
exhibeas,	DEO DANTE,
eruens hunc hominem	eruens hunc hominem
de dentibus aduersariorum	*de suorum aduersariorum*
suorum.'	*dentibus* PER HUNC MODUM.'

Here, as earlier scholars commented (e.g. Ward, p. 161), Raimundus contributes only slight changes in the word-order (italicized here) or meaningless additions (here in capitals). Paris (pp. 237-38) described those adjustments which fall at the end of a clause as examples of the *cursus*. In striking contrast to the treatment of the *Calila* passage, in the chapter as a whole, where Johannes has eleven doublets, Raimundus retains nine, rephrases two at equal length, and creates six of his own: 'humiliter et benigne' (731-32), 'loco et tempore' (732.2), 'habuit et voluit' (732.14), 'sermone et loquela' (734.7-8), 'sine causa uel culpa' (ll.10-11), 'ducat manum suam et palpitet' (l.11).

Is Raimundus then a plagiarist? Leaving aside the question whether literary copyright is a medieval concept, the fact remains that Raimundus reproduces Johannes's text without acknowledgement and generally with crude minimal adjustments which may be seen as attempts at disguising his original. However, these changes, clumsy as they undoubtedly are, may be explained by Raimundus's different attitudes towards vernacular and Latin texts.

De Sacy (p. 40) suggested that Raimundus began translating from the Spanish in ignorance of any other Latin version and that he became aware of Johannes at some time during the suspension of his work from 1303 onwards. This case is now reinforced by Blake's observation that multiple translations into English were fomented by mutual ignorance.[20] When Raimundus encountered Johannes, he may have found it a more authoritative text than the Spanish *Calila* firstly because it represented a version one step nearer the original than his own (Johannes claimed, probably correctly, to be working from a fourth-generation text (p. 80), Raimundus, less accurately, from a fifth (p. 386)), and secondly because it was in Latin. This linguistic discrimination, rather than translator's sloth or a defective Romance manuscript, seems to me to account for Raimundus's abandonment of the Spanish. (This abandonment was in any case not complete: as was noted earlier, Raimundus retrospectively supplies gaps in one version with the other.) Raimundus's respect for Johannes is suggested by his partial assimilation of his style, notably the doublets which he found unacceptable in the Spanish and the Hebraic pleonasm 'in animo cogitauit' (731.10 cf. JC 86.29, 159.2). When following a text in the vernacular (a language theoretically formless and without order),[21] Raimundus might treat it with a certain freedom. Having adopted a Latin source, he could hardly translate it, as he had done with the Spanish: for a Latin base-text, the counterpart to translation was glossing.

The original and best-known medieval glosses were of books of the Bible, although later on similar treatment was given to wisdom texts comparable with *Kalila*, such as the fables of Walter the Englishman and the *Disticha Catonis* (in both cases the base-texts were available to Raimundus).[22] The medieval gloss largely takes two forms: at a verbal level, the addition of more familiar synonyms (sometimes interlineally), and at a conceptual level, descanting on the meaning of the base-text, often with the citation of authorities. The following excerpt from a gloss on *DC* I, 4, 'Sperne repugnando tibi tu contrarius esse / conveniet nulli qui secum desidet ipse', is quoted as typical:

> Unde construe sic. *Sperne* (id est, noli) *esse contrarius tibi* (id est, contra teipsum) *repugnando* vel aliter *sperne repugnando* (id est, intendendo et contradicendo) inconstantie mentis tue *esse contrarius tibi* (id est, ne contradicas sententie a te prolate): itaque modo vis aliud et postea nolis e converso et supradictis modis: quia *conveniet nulli qui desidet* (id est, discordat) *secum*: qui enim discordat secum non potest convenire aliis quia 'Qui sibi nequam est, cui bonus est?' Quasi diceret: 'Nulli.' Unde: 'Qui sibi non parcit, tibi vel mihi quomodo parcet?' Et alibi: 'Qui sua divulgat, mea vel tua quomodo celat?' Et alibi: 'In tota vita discors tibi vivere vita.' 'Nil seiungit sua quia discordia pungit sperne' etcetera.[23]

Raimundus's uninspired doublets are, I suggest, due not to any attempt at the more rhetorical forms of synonymy such as *interpretatio* or the *stilus ysidorianus*, but to the same process that produced 'Sperne, id est, noli', etc.. Here too is found an analogue, if not a source, for Raimundus's pleonasms, which seem designed to clarify the text but in effect serve only to congest it.

The verbal gloss, then, affects only the portion of Raimundus's work derived from Johannes. Once his Spanish exemplar had been translated and his Latin source verbally glossed, the second stage of glossing could begin. (The continuity of these two processes seems to me to be further corroboration of the identity of Raimundus and PR.)

When commenting, PR adds little of his own. Many of his authorities, identified by Hervieux, are much what one would expect to find: the Bible, especially the wisdom books, and *Pamphilus* are cited throughout; Seneca, including the doubtful and supposititious works such as the *Sententiae* of Publilius Syrus, appears at least 24 times; Ovid is quoted ten times, Walter of Châtillon eight times and Cicero five times; there are also references to certain of the *Auctores octo*: the *Disticha Catonis* and Walter the Englishman (both *passim*), the *De contemptu mundi* (pp. 410, 549), and *Thobias* (p. 545). PR used a Cato glossed thus in leonines:

> *Mitte archana Dei celum[que] inquirere quid sit;*
> *Cum sis mortalis, que sunt mortalia cura.* (*DC*, II, 2)
> Quod secreta poli / fuerunt inquirere noli,
> Cum sis mortalis, / uolites mortalibus alis. (p. 635)[24]

(Ecclesiasticus 1.16 (= Ps 110. 10) receives the same treatment: 'Et inicium sapiencie est timor Domini. Iuxta illud: Principium menti/ timor est Domini sapienti', p. 664. See also 616.1-5.) In at least one case some leonines which stand alone can be identified as glosses on the *Disticha*:

> Consilium sanum / non dices spernere uanum;
> Vtile seruorum / uerbis non sperne tuorum. (p. 665)
> (Cf. Utile consilium dominus ne despice servi
> si prodest, sensum nullius tempseris umquam, III, 10).

The major source for PR, previously unidentified, is Albertanus of Brescia. His three works, the *De arte loquendi et tacendi, Liber consolationis et consilii* and *De amore et dilectione Dei et proximi* circulated both separately and as a group (they are found together in that order in at least three manuscripts: BL Royal 12.D.vii, Add. 6158, and Add. 19958), and all three are known to PR.[25] Albertanus seems to supply most of the rarer authorities: St Prosper (632.19-20=*Dil* 44ra30-31; 675.26-27=*Dil* 34ra37-38), Cassiodorus (560.20-21=*LCons* 120.18-19; 676.28-677.1=*Dil* 36rb29-35), 'Isidorus' (549.21-22: i.e. Cassiodorus=*LCons* 100.2-4), Ps-Martial (i.e. Godfrey of Winchester: 501.19-20=725.17-18=*Dil* 33rb7-8, 502.16-17=627.29-30=*Dil* 32va11-13; 565.19-20=*Dil* 37ra39-42), as well as some of the commoner -- Horace (632.5=*Dil* 44ra16-17) and Ovid (442.9=*Dil* 44ra17-18) -- and may possibly have transmitted the glossed Cato (cf. 473.10-14=588.1-2 and *ALT* 493.15-19).[26]

Longer sections of the *Liber consolationis* are utilized throughout by PR,[27] with by far the greatest contribution centred on chapter VII. The conflation here of the tale of the war between the crows and the starlings and the frame-story of the *Liber consolationis* is facilitated by the similarity between the two narratives: in the *Liber consolationis* enemies break into Meliboeus's house and assault his wife and daughter.

The bulk of the book is formed of the debate beween Meliboeus, who wishes hasty revenge, and his wife Prudentia, who urges patience and conciliation and is eventually successful. In *Kalila*, the starlings launch a night attack on the defenceless crows. The crows hold council, and a crow counsellor offers to infiltrate the starling defences disguised as a defector. The starlings hold council to debate what to do with him. Their king rules to admit the crow to his confidence, and the starlings are destroyed.

PR's longest single interpolation, in which topics such as the evils of war are debated, is misplaced in the second council, that of the starlings. As Hervieux points out (599n), this discussion is more suited to the first council, that of the crows. That the latter position was intended by PR is shown by the fact that Meliboeus has been transformed into *corvus* (*rex* is added interlineally), and Prudentia into *corvus* (*consiliarius*), and that at the end of this passage he is arguing for a just war:

> 'uolo cum predictis aduersariis pugnare et ita potero postea cum illis pacem habere.' Coruus \consiliarius/ autem non recipit ista uerba que dixerat rex coruorum (f. 96ra2-6; cf. *LCons* 112.10-14: 'volo cum praedictis meis adversariis pugnare; et ita potero cum illis postea pacem habere.' At Prudentia quasi irato animo ac vultu mutato dixit . . .)

A probable transition is made in some illegible marginalia and the *Kalila* text resumes with 'Volo, igitur, domine rex, quod coruum interficias' (598-99 = JC 235.14). Hervieux's conclusion that the interpolation could not be Raimundus's because it is out of place and tediously long-winded should be opposed on two counts: firstly, the misplacement of this section is scribal, and secondly, the discussions, although admittedly prolix, should be viewed as an extreme manifestation of an essential technique of *Kalila*, in which the characters regularly speak at length in maxims and *exempla*.

Two other sources are worthy of mention here because they relate to other aspects of the present study. Firstly, the verse prayer of Berosias (433-39) is taken from Book V of the *Anticlaudianus* of Alan of Lille and glossed in a smaller script in much the same way as the passage from the *Disticha Catonis* quoted above.[28] As the gloss (omitted by Hervieux) is written sometimes in the body of the text and sometimes in the margin, at least part of it must have been composed or incorporated by PR. Secondly, Paris (p. 251), pointed out PR's quotation in chapter XVIII of four *exempla* from the *Disciplina clericalis* of Petrus Alfonsi: XXIII, pp. 755-56; XIII, pp. 765-66; XIV, pp. 766-68; XV, pp. 769-71 (the beginning of this last is erroneously duplicated on p. 699). The first, being a story of guile, could be placed almost anywhere within the text without violence. The frame of this chapter concerns the bird Maziam who comes between his ostensible friends the bird Holgos and his wife and engineers their deaths. The fault lies undoubtedly with the Maziam, who is clearly referred to in the preamble: 'alter ipsorum [sociorum] est cordis seu animi fraudulenti, cupiens suum socium defraudare' (744.5-6). However, Raimundus/PR, taking his lead from the suggestion of adultery (745.10), threats this as a misogynistic tale, first commenting on woman's gullibility (762.18-30) and then on her cunning: 'Dic mihi si audiuisti vmquam tantam maliciam seu ingenia mulierum' (764-65), and finally adding two stories of the wiles of adulteresses and one of the cunning of the good woman. (These will be referred to again later.)

The final section of this paper is concerned with the place of Raimundus's work in the overall development of *Kalila*. The contents-list of the Longer Manuscript enumerates what it suggests are the three main components of an *exemplum*-collection: 'Nonum capitulum . . . Et sub illo capitulo continentur due fabule . . . Et sub isto capitulo xv versus continentur, figure iii' (398.7-10; throughout the contents-list Hervieux expands 'f[igure]' as 'fabule'). The use of verses and pictures to complement the fables is a constant in the history of *Kalila*: gnomic verses are found as early as the *Panchatantra*, and the earliest mention of miniatures seems to be a tenth-century reference to a Central Asian manuscript of the ninth.[29] Either of his base-texts might easily have inspired Raimundus to have his work illustrated: *SpA* has line-drawings, and although no manuscript of Johannes is illuminated, there are rubrics for miniatures in MS BL Add. 11437, as well as references to pictures in the introduction (reproducing the Hebrew, which in turn reproduces the Arabic): 'propter dulcedinem verborum ac sermonum delectationem figurarumque et imaginum intuitionem que in ipso [libro] sunt' (81.2-4).

The question of Raimundus/PR's use of verses points up a remarkable quality of his text: the way in which, independently of its predecessors, it conforms to certain standard features of the *Kalila* tradition. The origins of Raimundus/PR's verses are unproblematical: they come from a habit of mind, i.e. glossing and commentating, central to Latin culture but not exclusive to it. However, he could not have found any verses in the Spanish or Johannes, and Raimundus/PR might thus be seen to be returning the *Kalila* to a norm from which it had deviated in its sources.

This pattern can also be discerned in three other areas of Raimundus/PR's work: its presentation as a *speculum principis*, its Christianization, and its contamination with tales of the *Sindibad* tradition.

Raimundus explicitly identifies his text as a 'Liber regius' (385): 'Documenta igitur huius libri spectant ad secreta regalia pertractanda' (387). This claim is not consistently implemented. In some cases, Raimundus omits royal material from his original, in others he merely reproduces it and in others he expands it slightly with a single authority.[30] However, he once abbreviates a jaundiced view of kingship from his Spanish source (477.19-23: cf. *SpB* 92.1654-93.1663; although this may simply be in accordance with his usual trimming of his vernacular text) and on two occasions he presses large extracts from Albertanus into service: in chapter XVI (discussed above) and at the end of chapter IV. Here, after translating the Spanish account of the execution of Cenceba, Raimundus adds the conclusion from Johannes (RB 500.26-501.8; cf. JC 167.5-14) in which the audience of the story are called 'cupientibus intelligenciam' (501.3). PR then addresses mankind in general ('Debemus autem euitare socitatem et amorem praui'), intersperses two passages on the vices from *Dil* (33rb1- and 32va10-), and follows them with advice for kings ('Eligere debent reges et principes bonos et humiles', 502.1), thus ending the chapter on a theme dear to the *specula principum*, the choice of counsellors.

All versions of *Kalila* refer to kings, but the element of the *speculum principis* is to the fore in, for example, the Persian and Turkish versions of Husayn Va'iz Kashifi and Ali Çelebi and attenuated in the Hebrew and Spanish texts and their Arabic ancestors, grouped by Sprengling in his Class E.[31] Lacarra and Cacho Blecua's characterization of the Spanish *Calila* is, I think, applicable to all this Class:

> Sólo cuando la temática permita una conexión con los deberes regios, se extenderá el filósofo teorizando en su respuesta a modo de 'espejo de príncipes' ... Las ideas políticas incluidas en el *Calila* no difieren mucho de las expuestas en las colecciones de sentencias, aunque no puede afirmarse que la preocupación exclusiva del libro sea la conducta regia. (pp. 32, 46)

Of these texts, Johannes and his Hebrew source are, like medieval Jewish literature as a whole, the least interested in princely concerns.

Thus in discerning and expanding the latent qualities of his sources as works of royal instruction, Raimundus/PR is duplicating the choices made by his less immediate predecessors in the textual tradition.

The process of Christianization pervades Raimundus, but it is most explicit and concentrated in chapters III (the autobiography of Berosias) and V (the trial of Dimna, pp. 525-34). The latter chapter is the addition of al-Muqaffa[c], author of the Arabic translation, in response to the inherent tension between ethics and pragmatism in much wisdom literature.[32] Where al-Muqaffa[c] ensures that justice is done and Dimna executed, Raimundus/PR unknowingly continues this process by having Dimna make confession and receive Christian absolution.

The textual tradition of *Kalila* is bound up, in ways still unclear, with those of *Sindibad* and the *Disciplina clericalis*, written at some time after 1106 and the latest of the three. The coincidence of material among certain versions of these texts of Semitic origin is tabulated overleaf.

Disciplina clericalis	*Sindibad*	JC	Spanish *Calila*

Exemplum common to all texts

XXIV	Hebrew *Sendebar* p. 261-71, 372-73[33]	pp. 98-100	*A*23-26 = *B*24-27

Exempla common to *Sindibad* and both *Kalila* texts

Spanish *Sendebar*

	No. 2 (pp. 63-65)[34]	pp. 158-59	pp. 160-63
	No. 12 (pp. 117-18)	pp. 260-61	pp. 254-55
	No. 15 (pp. 133-34)	p. 289	pp. 289-90

Exempla common to *Sindibad* and *Disciplina clericalis*

XI	No. 5 (pp. 75-77)
XIII	No. 10 (pp. 105-08)
XIV	Most versions of the *Seven Sages of Rome*, 'Puteus'[35]

Therefore in incorporating four *exempla* from Petrus, Raimundus is unknowingly further strengthening the bonds within this group of texts. Moreover, as two of these stories probably originate in *Sindibad*, treat of the wiles of women and are presented as wonder-tales for entertainment rather than instruction ('Quod adhuc dicam [est] quoddam mirabile et s[t]upendum', Raimundus's addition, 765.2), he is endowing his text with characteristics central to the *Sindibad* tradition but alien to that of *Kalila*.

To conclude: some estimates date the *Panchatantra*, the ancestor of our text, to between 100 B.C. and A.D. 500 (see Edgerton, p. 11). In the West, editions of the fables of Bidpai designed for reading rather than literary research appeared up to the eighteenth century. These tales have proven so durable because each translator at once invests his text with his own concerns and conforms to models laid down by generations of his literary ancestors. Accordingly, I hope to have shown that Raimundus's version repays attention both in its own right and as one more link in a centuries-old chain binding East and West.

The British Library

NOTES

1. Ramón Menéndez Pidal, *España, eslabón entre la Cristiandad y el Islam*, Colección Austral, 1280 (Madrid: Austral, 1956).
2. Gonzalo Menéndez Pidal, 'Cómo trabajaron las escuelas alfonsíes', *NRFH*, V (1951), 363-80, at pp. 365-66, 367; R. Menéndez Pidal, pp. 59-60.
3. Raimundus de Biterris, *Liber Kalile et Dimne*, in Léopold Hervieux, *Les Fabulistes latins depuis le siècle d'Auguste jusqu'à la fin du Moyen Age*, V, *Jean de Capoue et ses dérivés* (Paris: Firmin Didot, 1899), pp. 379-775. I have also worked from microfilms of the two manuscripts of this text. The conventions used throughout this paper are as follows: RB = Raimundus de Biterris, *Liber Kalile et Dimne*; PR ('Pious Redactor') = the author of the interpolations in the Longer Manuscript of Raimundus; JC = Johannes de Capua, *Directorium humanae vitae* (see n. 6); *SpA* = the Spanish *Calila e Digna* from MS Escorial h-III-9, *SpB* = the Spanish *Calila e Digna* from MS Escorial x-III-4 (see n. 16); *Kalila* refers to this text in any manifestation, *Calila* to the Castilian text (*SpA* or *SpB*); *ALT* = *De arte loquendi et tacendi* of Albertanus of Brescia, *LCons* = his *Liber consolationis et consilii*, *Dil* his *De amore et dilectione Dei et proximi* (see n. 25); *DC* = *Disticha Catonis* (see n. 24).
4. On Giovanni da Procida's translation of *Bocados*, the *Liber philosophorum moralium antiquorum*, see the bibliography cited in Barry Taylor, 'Don Jaime de Jérica y el público de *El conde Lucanor*', *RFE*, LXVI (1986), 39-58, at p. 57, and C.F. Bühler, 'The *Liber de Dictis Philosophorum* and Common Proverbs in George Ashby's Poems', *PMLA*, LXV (1950), 282-89.
5. Alfons Hilka, *Beiträge zur lateinischen Erzählungsliteratur des Mittelalters, I. Der 'Novus Aesopus' des Baldo. II. Eine lateinische Übersetzung der griechischen Version des Kalila-Buchs*, Abhandlungen der Gesellschaft der Wissenschaften zu Göttingen, Philologisch-Historische Klasse, Neue Folge, XXI:3 (Berlin: Weidmannsche Büchhandlung, 1928), pp. 59-166.
6. References are to Hervieux's edition (see n. 3), pp. 77-337. See also Friedmar Geissler, 'Handschriften und Drucke des *Directorium vitae humanae* und des *Buches der Beispiele der alten Weisen*', *Mitteilungen des Instituts für Orientforschung*, IX (1963), 433-61.
7. On the miniatures of MS 8504, see Camille Couderc, *Album de portraits d'après les collections du Département des Manuscrits* (Paris: Impr. Berthaud frères, [1908]), p.

4 and pl. IX (1), and *Les Enluminures des manuscrits du Moyen Age (du VIe au XVe siècle) de la Bibliothèque Nationale* (Paris: Editions de la Gazette des Beaux-Arts, 1927), pp. 65-66 and pl. XXXV; Carl Nordenfalk, 'Maître Honoré and Maître Pucelle', *Apollo*, LXXIX (1964), 356-64, at p. 358; M. Alison Stones, 'Secular Manuscript Illumination in France', in *Medieval Manuscripts and Textual Criticism*, edited by Christopher Kleinhenz, North Carolina Studies in the Romance Languages and Literatures, Symposia, IV (Chapel Hill: UNC Department of Romance Languages, 1976), pp. 83-102, at p. 88, pl. [V]; Maurice Smeyers, *La Miniature*, Typologie des sources du Moyen Age Occidental, VIII (Turnhout, 1974), p. 56, n. 77. None of these studies, however, is concerned with the fable-illustrations. I am grateful to François Avril for all these references.

8. 'Notice de l'ouvrage intitulé *Liber de Dina et Kalila*, manuscrits Latins de la Bibliothèque du Roi, nos 8504 et 8505', *Notices et Extraits des Manuscrits de la Bibliothèque du Roi, et Autres Bibliothèques*, X:2 (1818), 3-65. Summaries of scholarship are given by H.L.D. Ward, *Catalogue of Romances in the Department of Manuscripts in the British Museum* (London: Printed by order of the Trustees, 1893), II, 154, 159-61 and Consuelo López Morillas, 'A Broad View of *Calila e Digna* Studies on the Occasion of a New Edition', *RPh*, XXV (1971-72), 85-95, at pp. 87-88.

9. *Notice sur les fables latines d'origine indienne* (Paris: Firmin-Didot, 1898).

10. *Journal des Savants* (Mars 1898), 158-73.

11. Gaston Paris, 'Raimond de Béziers, traducteur et compilateur', in *Histoire littéraire de la France . . .* , XXXIII (Paris: Imprimerie Nationale, 1906), pp. 191-253.

12. *Calila e Dimna*, edited by Juan Manuel Cacho Blecua and María Jesús Lacarra, Clásicos Castalia, CXXXIII (Madrid: Castalia, 1984), pp. 42-44.

13. f. 32v4 = p. 408.4; f. 39r4-5 = p. 441.24-25; f. 44r2-4 = p. 451.20-21; f. 44v7-18 = p. 452.16-24; f. 53r24-25 = p. 466.19-20; f. 58v16-19 = p. 477.25-28; f. 91v4 = p. 564.8; f. 95v9-10 = p. 575.17; f. 103r19-20 = p. 587.23; f. 182r8-9 = p. 734.20. The quotations of Walter are at pp. 408, 441, 451, 466; of *DC*, at p. 452.

14. There is an analogous case in the textual history of the *Disciplina clericalis*, of which ten of the 63 manuscripts known to its editors preserve only the *exempla*: see Petri Alfonsi, *Disciplina Clericalis*, von Alfons Hilka und Werner Söderhjelm, I: *Lateinischer Text*, Acta Societatis Scientiarum Fennicae, XXXVIII:4 (Helsinki: Druckerei der Finnischen Litteraturgesellschaft, 1911); II: *Französischer Prosatext*, ibid., XXXVIII:5 (1912), I, xxvii-xxix.

15. RB 444.11-21 = JC 109.29-110.8; 495.3-15, 22-496.23 = 162.26-163.27; 500.26-501.8 = 167.5-14; 535.13-17 = 193.22-25.

16. *El libro de Calila e Digna*, edited by John E. Keller and Robert White Linker, Clásicos hispánicos, II, xiii (Madrid: CSIC, 1967). The correspondences are RB

662.6-11 = *SpA* 270.4172-271.4178; 740.9-743.2 = 343.5737-346.5794. The
fragmentary Old Spanish translation from Hebrew seems not to enter into the
reckoning here, but see the editions by María Jesús Lacarra, 'Un fragmento
inédito del *Calila e Dimna* (MS. *P*)', *El Crotalón*, I (1984), 679-706, and by Josep
M. Sola-Solé, 'El *Calila e Digna* castellano traducido del hebreo', in *Hispania
Judaica: studies on the history, language, and literature of the Jews in the Hispanic
world*, III: *Language*, edited by Josep M. Sola-Solé, Samuel G. Armistead and
Joseph H. Silverman (Barcelona: Puvill, 1984), pp. 101-31.

17. 'Problemas de texto en *Calila e Dina*', in *Essays on Narrative Fiction in the Iberian
Peninsula in Honour of Frank Pierce*, edited by Robert Brian Tate (Oxford:
Dolphin, 1982), pp. 229-42.

18. Eero K. Neuvonen, *Los arabismos del español en el siglo XIII*, Studia Orientalia,
X:1 (Helsinki: Societas Orientalis Fennica, 1941), pp. 237-38.

19. For example, the pseudo-Augustinian *De vita christiana* has approximately 7500
words, its Old Spanish translation about 21000: see Braulio Justel Calabozo, *El
libro de la vida cristiana (versión castellana medieval de una obra apócrifa de San
Agustín): edición crítica y estudio*, Biblioteca Ciudad de Dios, XXII (Real
Monasterio de El Escorial, 1976), p. 26. The use of doublets in translations from
Latin is discussed by Inna Koskenniemi, *Repetitive Word Pairs in Old and Early
Middle English Prose*, Annales Universitatis Turkuensis, Series B, CVII (Turku:
Turun Yliopisto, 1968). (I owe this last reference to Geoffrey West.)

20. Norman Blake, *The English Language in Medieval Literature*, Everyman's
University Library (London: Dent, 1977), pp. 26-27.

21. See, for example, Dante Alighieri, *De vulgari eloquentia*, edited by Pier Vincenzo
Mengaldo, I: *Introduzione e testo*, Vulgares eloquentes, III (Padua: Antenore,
1968), I, i, § 2 (p. 3): 'vulgarem locutionem . . . quam sine omni regula nutricem
imitantes accipimus'.

22. On biblical glosses, see C.F.R. De Hamel, *Glossed Books of the Bible and the
Origins of the Paris Booktrade* (Woodbridge: D.S. Brewer, 1984). On the glosses of
Cato, see Richard Hazelton, 'The Christianization of "Cato": The *Disticha Catonis*
in the light of late mediaeval commentaries', *Medieval Studies*, XIX (1957), 157-73,
and 'Chaucer and Cato', *Sp*, XXXV (1960), 357-80. The commentaries on Walter
are discussed by Douglas Gray, *Robert Henryson*, Medieval and Renaissance
Authors (Leiden: Brill, 1979), pp. 125-27 and pl. 9.

23. *Auctores octo opusculorum cum commentarijs diligentissime emendati* . . . (Lyon:
s.n., 14 Mar. 1495) (BL: IB 42056), f. aviiᵛ. The prologue to *DC* begins 'Summi
deus largitor'.

24. The *Disticha* are available in *Minor Latin Poets*, with introduction and English
translations by J. Wight Duff and Arnold M. Duff, Loeb Classical Library

(London: Heinemann, 1934), pp. 585-639. The gloss quoted is comparable with, but different from, the *Cato novus* in leonines edited by [Friedrich] Zarnecke, 'Beiträge zur mittellateinischen Spruchpoesie. I. Zwei gereimte Uebertragungen der s.g. *Disticha Catonis*. II. Der s.g. *Facetus* und das *Supplementum Catonis'*, *Berichte über die Verhandlungen der Königlich Sächsischen Gesellschaft der Wissenschaften zu Leipzig, Philologisch-Historisch Classe*, XV (1863), 23-78, at pp. 24-48.

25. Editions used: Albertani, causidici brixiensis, *Tractatus de arte loquendi et tacendi*, in Thor Sundby, *Della vita e delle opere di Brunetto Latini* (Florence: Successori Le Monnier, 1884), pp. 475-506; *Liber consolationis et consilii . . .*, edited by Thor Sundby (London: N. Trübner, Pro Societate Chauceriana, 1883); *De amore et dilectione Dei et proximi*, in Albertani moralissimi *Opus de loquendi et tacendi modo . . .* (Cuneo: V. de Dulcis, 1507), f. 25r-6lr (BL: C.103.i.18; formerly 8407.h.1).

26. Albertanus also yields the following anonymous quotations: RB 415.22-26 = *LCons* 94.8-12; 453.29-30 = 557.17 = 624.23-24 = *ALT* 495.21-22 = *LCons* 15.16-18; 554-5 = *Dil* 35va36-39; 587.23 = 558.20 = *LCons* 60.7.

27. RB 454.2-5 = *LCons* 40.12-17; 549.18-29 = *LCons* 99.21-100.16; 557.17-22 = 15.16-25; 560.20-25 = 120.18-121.8; 567.16-29 = 49.3-50.6; 569.28-570.11 = 93.1-17; 571.6-12 = 108.8-15 etc.; 572.25-573.10 = 106.7-107.8; 578.24-579.3 = 40.8-41.8; f. 84vb-96ra = *LCons* chs II-XXXV, XLVI; 622.3-14 = 18.12-19.12.

28. As noted in Alain de Lille, *Anticlaudianus*, edited by R. Bossuat, Textes philosophiques du Moyen Age, I (Paris: J. Vrin, 1955), p. 46, n. 3. PR need not have known the *Anticlaudianus* in its entirety, as the poem to the Virgin seems to have circulated separately: see Alani de Insulis, *Opera omnia*, *PL*, CCX, 579-80, note.

29. See *The Panchatantra*, translated from the Sanskrit by Franklin Edgerton (London: Allen and Unwin, 1965), p. 11; Esin Atil, *'Kalila wa Dimna': fables from a fourteenth-century Arabic manuscript* (Washington: Smithsonian Institute Press, 1981), p. 61. Also on *Kalila*, see Zelfa Hourani, 'The Cycle of Miniatures in Arabic and Persian Manuscripts of *Kalila wa Dimna* Produced Before 1500 A.D.' (unpublished M. Litt. dissertation, University of Oxford, 1979). (I am grateful to David Wasserstein for this reference.) For illustrated fable-books in general, see *Fabula docet: illustrierte Fabelbücher aus sechs Jahrhunderten*, Ausstellungskataloge der Herzog August Bibliothek, Wolfenbüttel, XLI (Wolfenbüttel, 1983) and Anne Stevenson Hobbs, *Fables* (London: Victoria and Albert Museum, 1986), both with full bibliographies.

30. Omissions: RB 443 cf *SpB* 38.697-705; 445-57 cf *SpA* 54.868-75; 464 cf 68.1022-31; 482 cf 103.1552-56. Plain reproduction: 450.27-45.2 = *SpB* 47.878-82; 452-53 = *SpA*

50.791-96; 453-54 = 51.822-52.830. Slight expansion: 474.2-3 cf *SpA* 83-84; 510.26-27 cf 142; 554.31 cf 187; 663-64 cf 272-73.

31. The Persian and Turkish versions are available in translation as: *The Anwár-i-Suhailí or Lights of Canopus . . . being an adaptation by Mullá Husain bin 'Alí Al Wái'z-al-Káshifí of the Fables of Bídpái*, translated from the Persian by Arthur N. Wollaston (London: W.H. Allen, 1867); *Espejo politico, y moral, para principes, y ministros, y todo genero de personas*, traducido de la lengua turca . . . [from the *Hümayunname* of Ali Çelebi] en la castellana por Vicente Bratuti, Parte primera (Madrid: Domingo Garcia y Morràs, 1654). Martin Sprengling, '*Kalîla* Studies, I', *American Journal of Semitic Languages and Literatures*, XL (1924), 81-97, at pp. 95-96.

32. Francesco Gabrieli, 'L'opera de Ibn al-Muqaffaᶜ', *Rivista degli Studi Orientali*, XIII (1931-32), 197-247, at pp. 198-207.

33. Morris Epstein, *Tales of Sendebar . . . : An edition and translation of the Hebrew version of the 'Seven Sages' based on unpublished manuscripts*, Judaica, Texts and Translations, 1st Series, II (Philadelphia: Jewish Publication Society of America, 1967). See Barry Taylor, 'Wisdom Forms in the *Disciplina clericalis* of Petrus Alfonsi', in *Litterae Judaeorum in Terra Hispanica: proceedings of a Jerusalem colloquium -- June 1984*, edited by I. Benabu and J. Yahalom (Jerusalem: Hebrew University of Jerusalem, forthcoming), bibliography cited in n. 5.

34. *Sendebar (Libro de los engaños de las mujeres)*, modernized edition by José Fradejas Lebrero, Biblioteca de la literatura y el pensamiento universales, XXXVI (Madrid: Editora Nacional, 1981). The Spanish version recommends itself for these comparisons because it conveniently represents a presumed Arabic original.

35. *The Seven Sages of Rome*, edited by Killis Campbell, The Albion Series (Boston: Ginn, 1907), pp. xc-xvi. The tale seems to be absent from the Arabic and Hebrew versions. See also Haim Schwarzbaum, 'International Folklore Motifs in Petrus Alphonsi's *Disciplina clericalis*, [II],' *Sefarad*, XXII (1962), 17-59, at pp. 28-30. I wish to thank Charles Burnett and David Hook for their comments on a draft of this paper.

JIMENA'S 'VERGÜENÇAS MALAS'
(POEMA DE MIO CID, LINE 1596)

Roger M. Walker
Milija N. Pavlović

In the *Poema de mio Cid*, when the Cid and his wife are finally reunited outside Valencia after their long separation, Jimena's first words to her husband are:

> ¡Merçed, Campeador, en buen ora cinxiestes espada!
> Sacada me avedes de muchas vergüenças malas;
> aféme aquí, señor, yo e vuestras fijas amas;
> con Dios e convusco buenas son e criadas. (ll. 1595-98)[1]

Jimena's reference here to her 'vergüenças malas' appears to have puzzled a number of recent commentators on the poem. Ian Michael, for example, writes: 'El poeta no ha revelado antes que Jimena hubiera sufrido ningún tipo de deshonra, sino, al contrario, da a entender que se la había cuidado bien en Cardeña.'[2] In an attempt to explain this apparently illogical statement by Jimena, Michael, somewhat uncharacteristically, has recourse to a rather Pidalian argument:

> Parece ser éste otro caso de inesperada fidelidad histórica, puesto que Alfonso VI, al desterrar al Cid por segunda vez, hizo prisioneros a Jimena y sus hijos en diciembre de 1089 en el castillo de Ordejón, según la *Crónica particular del Cid*, comp. *Historia Roderici*, 34: 'Necnon mandauit intrare suam propriam hereditatem, et, quod deterius est, suam uxorem et liberos in custodia illaqueatos crudeliter retrudi ...'. El Cid mandó un mensaje al rey, quien, a pesar de su enojo, permitió a Jimena y sus hijos que fueran a Alcudia de Valencia para reunirse con el Cid, comp. *Historia Roderici, ibid.*: 'Rex autem, vehementer contra illos iratus, suam excond[i]tionem licet iustissimam non solum ei accipere, uerum etiam benigne audire noluit: verumptamen et uxorem et liberos ad eum redire permisit.' Las *vergüenças malas* del *Poema* corresponden a la expresión *illaqueatos crudeliter* de la *Historia*. (p. 189)[3]

Colin Smith makes no comment on line 1596 in his edition of the poem.[4] However, in his recent book on the *PMC*, Smith twice confesses his own uneasiness and puzzlement at Jimena's reference to the 'vergüenças malas' from which she has been rescued.[5] In his chapter on the poem's sources, he tentatively accepts Michael's argument that the poet had in mind at this point the *Historia Roderici*'s account of the

King's imprisonment of the Cid's family on the occasion of the second banishment of his vassal. He goes on to say that 'the line is otherwise mysterious, since all that the poem has conveyed hitherto was that Jimena and her children were living comfortably in Cardeña' (p. 148). Smith returns to line 1596 when he discusses 'narrative lapses of a minor kind' (p. 208). Although he now appears to accept Michael's explanation of the 'vergüenças malas' more firmly, Smith still regards the unexplained reference to them as a clear fault on the poet's part:

> It is also arguable that Jimena's line 1596 . . . needs justification by some allusion to these 'vergüenças' at an earlier stage. Even if we can now see that the line is there because the *Historia Roderici* tells of the King harshly imprisoning Jimena and her family, this does not justify a textual inadequacy within the poem. (p. 209)[6]

Another recent editor of the poem offers a different explanation of line 1596. Miguel Garci-Gómez writes: 'No debe extrañar que los personajes del *Cantar*, cuya *hondra* es inseparable, si no indistinta, de las *ganancias* y *riqueças*, se refieran a la pobreza en que les hundió el destierro como *muchas vergüenças malas*.'[7] This explanation, however, is rejected by Jules Horrent, who argues that 'cette "vergüença" ne doit pas se borner à la pauvreté, elle a été diversifiée ("muchas"). On aurait tort d'épiloguer historiquement sur ce que le poète veut ne suggérer que d'un mot'.[8] A stronger argument against Garci-Gómez's narrow interpretation of 'vergüenças' as poverty is implied by both Michael and Smith in their comments on line 1596: there is not a shred of evidence in the poem that Jimena and her daughters suffer any penury during the Cid's exile. Indeed, the poet goes to some lengths to suggest quite the opposite. When the Cid makes the initial arrangements for his family's stay at Cardeña, he gives the Abbot 100 marks on account (l. 253). Since his only capital at this time is the 600 marks he has inveigled out of the Jewish moneylenders, a sum with which he will have to support himself and his entire *mesnada* for the foreseeable future, his earmarking of one-sixth of this for his family's upkeep is not a negligible gesture. Furthermore, the Cid promises to repay fourfold any expense in excess of the 100 marks incurred by the Abbot (ll. 258-60).[9] Offered such advantageous interest rates, the Abbot would surely have been eager to make Jimena's stay at the monastery as comfortable as possible. Later, as he is about to leave on his first mission to the King, Minaya Alvar Fáñez is instructed by the Cid to give his wife and daughters 'lo que rromaneçiere' (l. 823) from the bootful of gold and silver destined to pay for the 1000 votive masses promised by the Cid to the cathedral of Burgos. On Minaya's second mission the Cid sends a further 1000 'marcos de plata' for the Abbot (ll. 1285-86), 500 of which Minaya spends on decking out the Cid's family in rich finery for their triumphal journey to Valencia (ll. 1422-28).[10] In short, at no time is there any suggestion that the Cid's family suffers material deprivation as a result of the hero's exile.

It is apparent, then, that those editors and commentators who have felt that line 1596 of the *PMC* calls for some elucidation have all put forward interpretations of 'vergüenças malas' that are at odds in some way or another with the rest of the evidence in the poem. Only Edmund de Chasca, to our knowledge, accepts without question that Jimena shares the Cid's dishonour, although his reasons for doing so are intuitive: 'Jimena siente algo más que el dolor personal de la separación. A su manera típicamente femenina, comparte con su esposo la vergüenza social de la deshonra.'[11] Our purpose in this article is to suggest that the explanation of line 1596, as of so much else in the *PMC*, may lie in contemporary (that is, late twelfth- or early thirteenth-century) legal prescriptions and practices, especially those concerned with an individual's honour.

The essentially Germanic preoccupation with personal honour permeates medieval Castilian society and much of its literature. The concept of honour as the maximum dignity, an individual's most precious possession, more prized than life itself, is not surprisingly the subject of extensive treatment in medieval Castilian legal texts. The supreme importance of honour may be seen, for example, in a recorded *fazaña*, in which the very first request made to the King of Castile by an *hidalgo* banished from Portugal is: 'que mandedes que en vuestra tierra que aya my onrra et mi calonnya commo otro fijodalgo'.[12] The numerous references to *honra* and the extensive legislation on the subject in the Castilian *fueros* leave one in no doubt that, in the words of Rafael Serra Ruiz, 'la honra constituía la vida íntima y social semiplenas del hombre castellano del siglo XIII'.[13] In these circumstances, it is no surprise to find that the loss of honour, *deshonra*, should often be regarded as the supreme evil, subsuming all others: expressions such as 'de facerle desonra nin mal ninguno' are found in several codes.[14] More important for our purposes, however, is the strongly Germanic notion of what Serra Ruiz has called 'el eco social de la deshonra' (p. 125): an individual's dishonour often extended to his relatives, to the members of his clan, even to his neighbours. In fact, in the territorial *fueros* of Castile it is laid down that a man's *deshonra* should be publicly proclaimed so that his family and his neighbours are made to participate in it.[15]

Clearly, the ones most affected by an individual's dishonour would be the closest members of his family. In the *Fuero Viejo* it is plainly stated that in certain circumstances, as a consequence of certain *yerros*, the wife of a banished man would participate in both his dishonour and his exile:

> si algunos [vasallos] facen yerro ... al señor natural, el Rey puedeles entrar todo quanto les fallare en sua tierra, e puedeles derribar las casas, e destruirles las

viñas, e los arboles, e quanto les fallare, *e puedeles echar las mugeres de sua tierra, e aun los fijos*, e develes dar plaço a que salga[n] de la tierra. (I, 4, I; our italics)

The same *título* in the *Fuero Viejo* also indicates that the major *yerro* which could bring about such catastrophic consequences was 'facer guerra . . . al Rey en toda sua tierra'. This legal principle, we believe, throws new light on the Cid's conduct both as he prepares to go into exile and during the early part of the exile proper.

First, it must be remembered that the Cid is banished not for an act of war against the King but for suspected financial irregularities. Even after the pronouncement of banishment, which severed all bonds of fealty between the two men, the Cid still refuses to renege on his loyalty to the King or to commit any act that might be interpreted as an act of war against his lord or his lands during his very orderly withdrawal from Castile. We suggest that one of the reasons why the Cid does not behave in the expected 'rebel-vassal' fashion is to ensure that the King will have no grounds for extending the order of banishment to Jimena and her daughters.

Perhaps even more striking is the Cid's behaviour during and after his first military exploit in exile, the capture of Castejón. The settlement is taken by trickery rather than by military force; the casualties appear to be fairly light; the booty is sold back to the inhabitants for a fraction of its total value;[16] no prisoners are taken, sold, or put to the sword. The whole operation hardly qualifies as an act of war, and the Cid is anxious that it should not seem to be such. He several times publicly proclaims that he is unwilling to wage war against settlements and people who have treaties with Alfonso and are thus under his protection, even though they are not strictly part of 'sua tierra':

> Moros en paz, ca escripta es la carta,
> buscar nos ie el rrey Alfonso con toda su mesnada;
> quitar quiero Casteión . . .
> Cras a la mañana pensemos de cavalgar
> con Alfonso mio señor non querría lidiar.
>> (ll. 527-29, 537-38; cf. ll. 508-09, 531-32)[17]

Protestations such as the above may be taken as an illustration of the Cid's prudence and pragmatism: his small band of soldiers would have little chance if the King were to send a sizeable company against him. They may also be interpreted on a rather more idealistic level as evidence of the Cid's extraordinary loyalty to a King who has banished him unjustly but whose lordship he still recognizes. No doubt there is some justification for both these interpretations of the Cid's anxiety not to anger the King further. We believe, however, that there is a third motive for the Cid's very lenient and chivalrous treatment of the people of Castejón and for his apprehension at the possibility of being involved in military action against Alfonso: he must avoid giving the King the legal justification for banishing his family along with himself. In this he appears to be successful, since the King does not take further action against Jimena and her daughters. This is not, we feel, to be interpreted as leniency on Alfonso's part, as his previous application of the laws of banishment has been very strict indeed: for example, he gave the Cid the absolute minimum amount of time prescribed by the *fueros* to leave the country.[18] In view of this legalistic severity, it is not unreasonable to assume that the King accepts that the Cid's attack on Castejón is not an act of war against 'sua tierra'.

However, although Jimena and her daughters are spared the dishonour of exile through the Cid's circumspection (and knowledge of the law), it is important to recall that Jimena's words to her husband at their reunion are not '*salvada* me avedes de muchas vergüenças malas' but '*sacada* me avedes de muchas vergüenças malas'. In other words, she saw her position in Cardeña, although materially comfortable, as one of actual dishonour with potential for further dishonour: through no fault of her own, she and her children are affected by the 'eco social' of the Cid's *deshonra*. If this is the case, what form do her 'vergüenças malas' take?

First, and most obviously, Jimena is alone and without home or status, the 'abandoned' wife of an outlaw, a 'viuda', as de Chasca calls her, with two daughters who would be 'incasables si su esposo fracasaba' (p. 79). Secondly, she is dependent on the charity of others, in particular 'a la merced de la generosidad del abad' (*ibid.*): despite the Cid's promises, there is no absolute guarantee that he will be able to repay the money expended on Jimena's upkeep by the Abbot. Thirdly, although being in the monastery of Cardeña gives her some protection under the laws of sanctuary, the poet's audience would have been well aware that those who normally sought sanctuary were fugitives from justice: it was not a normal recourse for people of honour. Fourthly, although she was technically safe in Cardeña, Jimena's position was in fact extremely precarious; she was at the mercy of 'los caprichos del desavenido rey' (de Chasca, *ibid.*). Although it is unlikely that the King would actually violate sanctuary, if he were to decide, for example, that some action of the Cid constituted an act of war against the royal person, he could easily make her position and that of the Abbot intolerable by simply cutting off supplies to the monastery. Moreover, although the Abbot may not have been directly subject to secular law, he must have displeased the King mightily by providing the Cid with food and lodging on his way into exile, in flagrant defiance of Alfonso's express orders that no one was to render him any aid under pain of death.[19] There can be little doubt, then, that Jimena's position is one of actual dishonour and stigma with explosive potential for further dishonour.

The details of the negotiations for Jimena's being allowed to leave Cardeña and join the Cid in Valencia are of great significance for the theme of her – and her husband's – dishonour and their rehabilitation. The very fact that the Cid has to ask Alfonso's permission for his family to join him stresses that Jimena is not a free agent but a virtual prisoner sharing the dishonour of her outlawed husband. The Cid's recognition of his wife's dependence on the King's mercy emerges quite clearly from his instructions to Minaya, his ambassador:

> Desí por mí besalde la mano e firme ge lo rrogad
> por mi mugier e mis fijas,. . .
> si fuere su merçed, / quen' las dexe sacar;
> enbiaré por ellas e vós sabed el mensage:
> la mugier de Mio Çid e sus fijas las infantes
> de guisa irán por ellas que a grand ondra vernán
> a estas tierras estrañas que nos pudiemos ganar. (ll. 1275-81)

Minaya relays the message to the King in the same supplicating terms:

> Merçed vos pide el Çid, si vos cayesse en sabor,
> por su mugier doña Ximena e sus fijas amas a dos:
> saldrién del monesterio dó elle las dexó
> e irién pora Valençia al buen Campeador. (ll. 1351-54)

The King's response to Minaya's request is not only favourable but positively enthusiastic:

> Essora dixo el rrey: 'Plazme de coraçón;
> yo les mandaré dar conducho mientra que por mi tierra fueren,
> de fonta e de mal curial*l*as e de desonor;
> quando en cabo de mi tierra aquestas dueñas fueren,
> catad cómmo las sirvades vós e el Campeador.' (ll. 1355-59)

A little later the King makes another significant offer to Minaya:

> Levedes un portero, tengo que vos avrá pro;
> si leváredes las dueñas, sírvanlas a su sabor,
> fata dentro en Medina denles quanto huebos les fuer,
> desí adelant piense d'ellas el Campeador. (ll. 1380-83)

We feel that not enough attention has been paid to the legal implications of the King's offers of *conducho* for the journey and of a *portero* to guarantee the party's safe

conduct through Castile. In the *Fuero Viejo* it is laid down that 'quando ovier el Rico
ome a salir de la tierra, devel' el Rey dar quel' guie por sua tierra, e devel' dar vianda
por suos dineros' (I, 4, I). In the light of this, it would seem that the King went beyond
the law when he exiled the Cid: he certainly did not appoint a *portero* to guarantee his
safe passage, and he expressly forbade the citizens of Burgos to sell provisions to the
Cid. This is in striking contrast to his conduct here: he fulfils his legal obligations by
appointing a *portero* to escort Minaya and the Cid's family, and he goes well beyond his
obligations by defraying the expenses of the journey himself. We would suggest that this
gesture, together with the insistence on saving the women 'de fonta e de mal . . . e de
desonor' (l. 1357), represents a public and ostentatious restoration of Jimena's honour
and a clear step in the restoration of that of her husband, especially as it is linked with
the public pardoning and rehabilitation of the Cid's vassals who went with him into
exile:

> A todas las escuelas que a él dizen señor,
> por que los deseredé, todo ge lo suelto yo:
> sírvanle[s] sus herdades dó fuere el Campeador,
> atrégoles los cuerpos de mal e de ocasión,
> por tal fago aquesto que sirvan a so señor. (ll. 1362-66)

The King has obviously made up his mind to pardon his vassal, and this public – and
unasked for – removal of the stigma of dishonour from those associated with him clears
the way for the great reconciliation. The Cid interprets the signs correctly, and as soon
as he formally asks for pardon for himself he receives it.

A final indication that the King's treatment of Jimena at this point represents the
restoration of her honourable status (and, by implication, much of the Cid's) is that the
Infantes de Carrión immediately, and for the first time, entertain thoughts of marrying
the Cid's daughters, something they would surely not have done had the women been
still dishonoured:

> Mucho creçen las nuevas de Mio Çid el Campeador,
> bien casariemos con sus fijas pora huebos de pro;
> non la osariemos acometer nós esta rrazón,
> Mio Çid es de Bivar e nós de los condes de Carrión. (ll. 1373-76)

Thus, the Infantes are held back not by the fact that the women's father is a
dishonoured exile but because he is of lowly status compared with themselves.

We would suggest, then, that an examination of the Cid's exile and dishonour in the
light of late twelfth-century legislation in the territorial *fueros* shows that Jimena's

participation in the dishonour is real and that her reinstatement is a vital step towards that of her husband. By his exemplary conduct the Cid has indeed rescued her from 'muchas vergüenças malas'.

It might be argued that it is unlikely that the lawyer-poet's audience would have been as versed as he was in the elaborate legal technicalities surrounding banishment and the responsibilities of a lord towards an outlawed vassal. However, several scholars have recently argued that the average medieval person was probably much more familiar with the law than we might suppose.[20] Elsewhere we have attempted to show that when introducing new and unfamiliar romanized legal concepts and institutions into his work the poet describes them in some detail, but that he seems to take for granted some familiarity with concepts and institutions that are Germanic and had formed part of the fibre of Castilian society for centuries.[21] In this respect it is worth noting that the laws surrounding banishment were almost entirely Germanic in origin.[22]

Birkbeck College, London
Imperial College, London

NOTES

1. All references to the *Poema de Mio Cid* are to the edition of Ian Michael (Madrid: Castalia, 1976; 2nd edition, 1978).

2. *Poema de Mio Cid*, p. 189, note to line 1596.

3. Ramón Menéndez Pidal quotes this same passage from the *Historia Roderici*, but for a different purpose, in *En torno al 'Poema del Cid'* (Barcelona: EDHASA, 1963), p. 131. He defines *vergüença* as 'afrenta, deshonra' (quoting line 1596) in *Cantar de Mio Cid*, 4th edition, 3 vols (Madrid: Espasa-Calpe, 1964-69), II, 895. However, he makes no comment on line 1596 in his critical edition of the poem (III, 1085).

4. *Poema de mio Cid* (Oxford: Clarendon, 1972; Spanish edition, Madrid: Cátedra, 1976; rpt 1985).

5. *The Making of the 'Poema de mio Cid'* (Cambridge: Cambridge University Press, 1983).

6. The same explanation based on the passage from the *Historia Roderici* is offered in *The Poem of My Cid*, translated with an introduction and commentary by Peter Such and John Hodgkinson (Warminster: Aris & Phillips, 1987): 'There is no indication in the *Poema* of the nature of this dishonour, but the *Historia Roderici* furnishes a possible explanation, telling how, on the occasion of the Cid's second banishment, the King ordered Jimena to be "cruelly imprisoned"' (p. 138).

7. *Cantar de Mio Cid* (Madrid: CUPSA, 1977), p. 201.

8. *Cantar de Mio Cid/Chanson de Mon Cid*, 2 vols (Ghent: E. Story-Scientia, 1982), II, 292, note (d) to page 59*b*. The other major edition of the *PMC* in recent years, that of María Eugenia Lacarra (Madrid: Taurus, 1983), has no comment on line 1596.

9. David Hook has noted interesting parallels of content and terminology between this deal involving the Cid and the Abbot and other formal agreements concluded with monasteries by knights about to leave for war; see 'The Legal Basis of the Cid's Agreement with Abbot Sancho', *Ro*, CI (1980), 517-26.

10. The manuscript reading of lines 1285-86 is: 'E mando mill marcos de plata   a San Pero leuar / e que los diesse   al abbat don Sancho.' Many editors, including Michael, emend the second hemistich of line 1286 to 'a don Sancho [e]l abbat' to make it conform to the -/*á* assonance pattern of *laisse* 77. It is possible that it is the 'irregularity' of the second hemistich which has prompted some critics to look more closely at the first hemistich and to postulate a further corruption of the line there. As the manuscript stands, it is quite clear that the Cid intended the whole 1000 marks to be given to the Abbot; but later we are told that 'los quinientos marcos   dio Minaya al abbat' (l. 1422). In order to reconcile these seemingly conflicting accounts, Menéndez Pidal, following Bello, assumes a haplography of '[.d.]' (i.e., 500) before 'diesse' in line 1286; see *Cantar de Mio Cid*, III, 1074-75. This emendation is also adopted by Smith in his edition (p. 42). Michael, however, prefers to retain the manuscript reading, suggesting that the apparent contradiction contained in lines 1286 and 1422 may be 'otro descuido del poeta' (p. 342). We also accept the manuscript reading, but we do not think it necessary to attribute the discrepant accounts of the fate of the 1000 marks to a 'descuido del poeta'. We suggest that, in keeping back half the money to deck out the Cid's family, Minaya is acting on his own initiative. This is not the first, or the last, example of independent behaviour on the part of Minaya in the poem, a subject we hope to develop in a later study.

11. *El arte juglaresco en el 'Cantar de Mio Cid'*, 2nd edition (Madrid: Gredos, 1972), p. 79.

12. See Federico Suárez, 'La colección de "fazañas" del ms. 431 de la Biblioteca Nacional', *AHDE*, XIV (1942-43), 579-92, at 588.

13. *Honor, honra e injuria en el derecho medieval español* (Murcia: Universidad de Murcia, 1969), p. 118.

14. See, for example, *El Fuero Viejo de Castilla*, edited by Ignacio Jordán de Asso y del Río and Miguel de Manuel y Rodríguez (Madrid: Joaquín Ibarra, 1771), I, 5, XII. All references to the *Fuero Viejo* are to this edition.

15. See, for example, Serra Ruiz, *Honor, honra,* pp. 256-57. A striking illustration of the use of a *pregonero* to proclaim publicly a matter concerning the honour of a citizen is to be found in Murcia as late as 1460; see Juan Torres Fontes, 'Honor y honra medievales', *Revista de Murcia,* XLV (1967), 4-6.

16. For the mathematics involved, see Michael, *Poema de Mio Cid,* p. 116, note to lines 513-21.

17. Israel G. Burshatin and B. Bussell Thompson, '*Poema de Mio Cid,* line 508: the Cid as a rebellious vassal?', *La Corónica,* V (1976-77), 90-92, argue on the basis of the manuscript reading of line 508 (which most editors emend) that, flushed by his success at Castejón, the Cid momentarily entertains authentic 'rebel-vassal' thoughts and considers taking on the King's might. They concede, however, that this rush of blood is short-lived and that 'in a careful, gradual process the thought of fighting diminishes' (p. 91).

18. For a detailed discussion of the legal background, see María Eugenia Lacarra, *El 'Poema de Mio Cid': realidad histórica e ideología* (Madrid: Porrúa Turanzas, 1980), pp. 8-32, especially p. 26. Lacarra relies heavily in this section on the important study of Hilda Grassotti, 'La ira regia en León y Castilla', *CHE,* XLI-XLII (1965), 5-135.

19. For a very perceptive study of the Abbot's flouting of the royal authority seen in the light of the strict Benedictine obligation to provide hospitality to travellers and of the historical defiance of King Alfonso VII by the Cardeña monastery, see Conrado Guardiola, 'La *hospitalitas* en la salida del Cid hacia el destierro', *La Corónica,* XI (1982-83), 265-72.

20. See, for example, Peter N. Dunn, '*Poema de mio Cid,* vv. 23-48: epic rhetoric, legal formula, and the question of dating', *Ro,* XCVI (1975), 255-64; Brian Dutton, 'The Popularization of Legal Formulae in Medieval Spanish Literature', in *Medieval, Renaissance, and Folklore Studies in Honor of John Esten Keller,* edited by Joseph R. Jones (Newark, Delaware: Juan de la Cuesta, 1980), pp. 13-28; Ivy A. Corfis, 'The Count of Barcelona Episode and French Customary Law in the *Poema de mio Cid*', *La Corónica,* XII (1983-84), 169-77.

21. See our 'Money, Marriage and the Law in the *Poema de mio Cid*', *MAe,* LI (1982), 197-212, at 206-12.

22. We are grateful to the editors of this volume for their helpful comments on an earlier version of this article.

TABULA GRATULATORIA

Samuel G. Armistead
Birkbeck College, London, Department of Spanish
Birmingham University Library
Roger Boase
Charles Burnett
Dwayne E. Carpenter
J.A. Cremona
Trevor J. Dadson
Alan Deyermond
John Edwards
Exeter University Library
Brenda Fish
Ángel M. García Gómez
Eduardo Garrigues
Thomas F. Glick
Anthony Gooch
T.J. Gorton
Nigel Griffin
Joseph J. Gwara
Gerold Hilty
Richard Hitchcock
David Hook
B.W. Ife
Lynn Ingamells
Instituto de España, London
Lloyd Kasten
King's College Library, London
John Derek Latham
Thomas A. Lathrop
H.V. Livermore
Derek W. Lomax
C. Alex Longhurst
Helder Macedo
Angus Mackay
David Mackenzie
Francisco Marcos Marín
John S. Miletich